Foundations of Risk Management and Insurance

Foundations of Risk Management and Insurance

Edited by

Arthur L. Flitner, CPCU, ARM, AIC, AU

3rd Edition • 1st Printing

The Institutes
720 Providence Road, Suite 100
Malvern, Pennsylvania 19355-3433

3rd Edition • 1st Printing • April 2018

Library of Congress Control Number: 2018938168

ISBN: 978-0-89462-224-3

Foreword

The Institutes are the trusted leader in delivering proven knowledge solutions that drive powerful business results for the risk management and property-casualty insurance industry. For more than 100 years, The Institutes have been meeting the industry's changing professional development needs with customer-driven products and services.

In conjunction with industry experts and members of the academic community, our Knowledge Resources Department develops our course and program content, including Institutes study materials. Practical and technical knowledge gained from Institutes courses enhances qualifications, improves performance, and contributes to professional growth—all of which drive results.

The Institutes' proven knowledge helps individuals and organizations achieve powerful results with a variety of flexible, customer-focused options:

Recognized Credentials—The Institutes offer an unmatched range of widely recognized and industry-respected specialty credentials. The Institutes' Chartered Property Casualty Underwriter (CPCU®) professional designation is designed to provide a broad understanding of the property-casualty insurance industry. Depending on professional needs, CPCU students may select either a commercial insurance focus or a personal risk management and insurance focus and may choose from a variety of electives.

In addition, The Institutes offer certificate or designation programs in a variety of disciplines, including these:

- Claims
- Commercial underwriting
- Fidelity and surety bonding
- General insurance
- Insurance accounting and finance
- Insurance information technology
- Insurance production and agency management
- Insurance regulation and compliance

- Management
- Marine insurance
- Personal insurance
- Premium auditing
- Quality insurance services
- Reinsurance
- Risk management
- Surplus lines

Ethics—Ethical behavior is crucial to preserving not only the trust on which insurance transactions are based, but also the public's trust in our industry as a whole. All Institutes designations now have an ethics requirement, which is delivered online and free of charge. The ethics requirement content is designed specifically for insurance practitioners and uses insurance-based case studies to outline an ethical framework. More information is available in the Programs section of our website, TheInstitutes.org.

Flexible Online Learning—The Institutes have an unmatched variety of technical insurance content covering topics from accounting to underwriting, which we now deliver through hundreds of online courses. These cost-effective self-study courses are a convenient way to fill gaps in technical knowledge in a matter of hours without ever leaving the office.

Continuing Education—A majority of The Institutes' courses are filed for CE credit in most states. We also deliver quality, affordable, online CE courses quickly and conveniently through CEU. Visit CEU.com to learn more. CEU is powered by The Institutes.

College Credits—Most Institutes courses carry college credit recommendations from the American Council on Education. A variety of courses also qualify for credits toward certain associate, bachelor's, and master's degrees at several prestigious colleges and universities. More information is available in the Student Services section of our website, TheInstitutes.org.

Custom Applications—The Institutes collaborate with corporate customers to use our trusted course content and flexible delivery options in developing customized solutions that help them achieve their unique organizational goals.

Insightful Analysis—Our Insurance Research Council (IRC) division conducts public policy research on important contemporary issues in property-casualty insurance and risk management. Visit www.Insurance-Research.org to learn more or purchase its most recent studies.

The Institutes look forward to serving the risk management and property-casualty insurance industry for another 100 years. We welcome comments from our students and course leaders; your feedback helps us continue to improve the quality of our study materials.

Peter L. Miller, CPCU
President and CEO
The Institutes

Preface

Foundations of Risk Management and Insurance is the assigned textbook for CPCU 500, designed to serve as the first course in the Chartered Property Casualty Underwriter (CPCU) designation program.

The goals of CPCU 500 are to enable you to understand and apply basic concepts of risk management and insurance, to comprehend insurance within the larger context of risk management, to learn a systematic approach for analyzing property-liability insurance policies, and to understand the role of big data analytics and emerging technology in insurance and risk management. Each assignment in the textbook supports one or more of those goals.

Assignment 1, Overview of Risk Management, discusses risk classifications, enterprise risk management, risk management benefits, risk management objectives and goals, and the risk management process.

Assignment 2, Identifying Loss Exposures, describes the elements of four broad categories of loss exposures—property, liability, personnel, and net income—and explains how to use various methods for identifying loss exposures.

Assignment 3, Analyzing Loss Exposures, examines probability; the construction of probability distributions; and how central tendency, dispersion, and normal distributions can be used to analyze loss exposures.

Assignment 4, Selecting Risk Control Techniques, examines six basic risk control techniques and how to select risk control techniques that are appropriate for meeting an organization's risk control goals. The assignment also examines how smart products are being used in risk assessment and control.

Assignment 5, Selecting Risk Financing Techniques, examines risk financing techniques and how to select risk financing techniques or measures that are appropriate for meeting an organization's risk financing goals.

Assignment 6, Data Analytics, examines the characteristics and sources of big data, the data mining process, and the role of data-driven decision making in risk management and insurance.

Assignment 7, Insurance Policy Fundamentals, considers ideally insurable loss exposures, the characteristics and structure of insurance policies, the different categories of policy provisions, and how to analyze an insurance policy.

Assignment 8, Common Features of Insurance Policies, explains basic concepts affecting property-casualty insurance policies, including insurable interest, insurance to value, valuation methods, deductibles or retentions, and alternative sources of recovery.

The individuals who participated in developing the present and previous editions of the text are acknowledged on the Contributors page.

For more information about The Institutes' programs, please call our Customer Success Department at (800) 644-2101, email us at CustomerSuccess@TheInstitutes.org, or visit our website at TheInstitutes.org.

Arthur L. Flitner

Contributors

The Institutes acknowledge with deep appreciation the contributions made to the content of this text by the following persons:

Richard Berthelsen, JD, MBA, CPCU, AIC, AU, ARe, ARM

Pamela J. Brooks, MBA, CPCU, AAM, AIM, AIS

Doug Froggatt, CPCU, AINS

Kevin Kibelstis, AINS, AIS

Beth Illian, CPCU, AINS, AIS

Jacqueline Lorince, AIM, AIS

Pamela Lyons, BA, FCIP, CRM

Ann E. Myhr, CPCU, ARM, AU, AIM, ASLI

Charles Nyce, PhD, CPCU, ARM

Contents

1

Overview of Risk Management

Educational Objectives

After learning the content of this assignment, you should be able to:

▷ Describe each of the following in the context of risk:

- Uncertainty

- Possibility

- Possibility compared with probability

▷ Explain how classifying and categorizing risk help an organization meet its risk management goals.

▷ Compare the concepts of enterprise risk management and traditional risk management.

▷ Illustrate how big data is changing the risk management environment.

▷ Describe the benefits of risk management and how it reduces the financial consequences of risk for individuals, organizations, and society.

▷ Summarize various objectives and goals for organizations to manage risk.

▷ Describe each of the steps in the risk management process.

Overview of Risk Management

1

UNDERSTANDING AND QUANTIFYING RISK

Although risk may intuitively seem undesirable, it can yield both positive and negative outcomes. Opportunities cannot be pursued, and reward cannot be obtained, without incurring some risk. Because of this risk/reward relationship, individuals and organizations seek to maximize reward while minimizing the associated risk. Risk management helps individuals and organizations to avoid, prevent, reduce, or pay for the negative outcomes of risk so that opportunities for reward can be pursued. Understanding and quantifying risk are the logical starting point for learning how to use risk management.

Risk is a term regularly used by individuals in both their personal and professional lives and is generally understood in context. However, properly defining risk is often difficult because it can have many different meanings. As used in this discussion, risk is defined as the uncertainty about outcomes, with the possibility that some of the outcomes can be negative. Risk can be quantified by knowing the probability of the possible outcomes. See the exhibit "Industry Language—Risk."

Industry Language—Risk

Risk can be used in many contexts in risk management and insurance and can have any of the following meanings:

- The subject matter of an insurance policy, such as a structure, an auto fleet, or the possibility of a liability claim arising from an insured's activities

- The insurance applicant (the insured)

- The possibility of bodily injury or property damage

- A cause of loss (or peril), such as fire, lightning, or explosion

- The variability associated with a future outcome

[DA02845]

Uncertainty and Possibility

The two elements within the definition of risk are these:

* Uncertainty of outcome
* Possibility of a negative outcome

First, risk involves uncertainty about the type of outcome (what will actually occur), the timing of the outcome (when the outcome will occur), or both the type and timing of the outcome. Consider an individual who buys a share of stock in a publicly traded corporation. This individual may experience a positive outcome if the value of the stock increases or a negative outcome if the value of the stock decreases. The timing of either outcome is uncertain because the individual does not know if or when the stock price is going to change or what the new stock price will be. Whether uncertainty involves what will actually happen, when something will happen, or both, it results from the inability to accurately predict the future.

Second, risk involves the possibility of a negative outcome. Possibility means that an outcome or event may or may not occur. The fact that something may occur does not mean that it will occur. For example, it is possible that an individual may be injured while driving to or from work, loading a truck at work, moving some furniture at home, or falling in an icy parking lot at the mall. However, the possibility that these events may occur does not mean that they will occur. Nonetheless, because of the possibility of a negative outcome (injury), risk exists.

Possibility and Probability

The possibility that something may occur does not indicate its likelihood of occurring. Possibility does not quantify risk; it only verifies that risk is present. To quantify risk, one needs to know the **probability** of the outcome or event occurring.

Probability

The likelihood that an outcome or event will occur.

Unlike possibility, probability is measurable and has a value between zero and one. If an event is not possible, it has a probability of zero, whereas if an event is certain, it has a probability of one. If an event is possible, but not certain, its probability is some value between zero and one. Probabilities can be stated as a decimal figure (.4), a percentage (40 percent), or a fraction (four-tenths or two-fifths).

To help understand the difference between possibility and probability, consider the possibility that an individual will be injured in an auto accident while driving to or from work tomorrow. That person will not necessarily be injured in an auto accident tomorrow, and the fact that it is possible does not give any indication of its likelihood. The risk exists and has simply been identified.

Contrast this with there being a 5 percent probability that the same individual will be injured in an auto accident while driving to or from work tomorrow. This statement not only indicates that it is possible the individual will be injured tomorrow, it gives the likelihood. The risk has now been not only identified but also quantified.

Understanding the probability of various outcomes helps focus risk management attention on those risks that can be appropriately managed. Probability can also be used to help decide which activities (and associated risks) to undertake and which risk management techniques to use.

In the previous example:

- If the probability of injury while driving to or from work was 5 percent, and the probability of injury if the individual took the train to work was 1 percent, the individual may decide to take the train.
- However, if the risk of auto injury was reduced to 1 percent by driving a car with airbags and antilock brakes, and if it was more convenient and quicker to drive, then the individual may decide (cost permitting) to buy a new car with airbags and antilock brakes and then drive to work.

RISK CLASSIFICATIONS AND CATEGORIES

Classifying the various types of risk can help an organization understand and manage its risks. The categories should align with an organization's objectives and risk management goals.

Classification can help with assessing risks, because many risks in the same classification have similar attributes. It also can help with managing risk, because many risks in the same classification can be managed with similar techniques. Finally, classification helps with the administrative function of risk management by helping to ensure that risks in the same classification are less likely to be overlooked.

These classifications of risk are some of the most commonly used:

- Pure and speculative risk
- Subjective and objective risk
- Diversifiable and nondiversifiable risk
- Quadrants of risk (hazard, operational, financial, and strategic)

These classifications are not mutually exclusive and can be applied to any given risk.

Pure and Speculative Risk

A **pure risk** is a chance of loss or no loss, but no chance of gain. For example, the owner of a commercial building faces the risk associated with a possible fire loss. The building will either burn or not burn. If the building burns, the owner suffers a financial loss. If the building does not burn, the owner's financial condition is unchanged. Neither of the possible outcomes would produce

Pure risk
A chance of loss or no loss, but no chance of gain.

a gain. Because there is no opportunity for financial gain, pure risks are always undesirable. See the exhibit "Classifications of Risk."

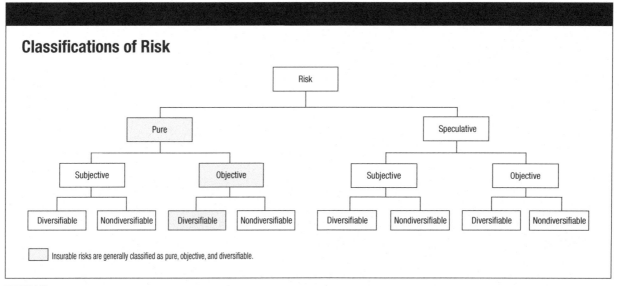

Classifications of Risk

Insurable risks are generally classified as pure, objective, and diversifiable.

[DA02396]

Speculative risk

A chance of loss, no loss, or gain.

In comparison, **speculative risk** involves a chance of gain. As a result, it can be desirable, as evidenced by the fact that every business venture involves speculative risks. For example, an investor who purchases an apartment building to rent to tenants expects to profit from this investment, so it is a desirable speculative risk. However, the venture could be unprofitable if rental price controls limit the amount of rent that can be charged.

Certain businesses involve speculative risks, such as these:

- Price risk—Uncertainty over the size of cash flows resulting from possible changes in the cost of raw materials and other inputs (such as lumber, gas, or electricity), as well as cost-related changes in the market for completed products and other outputs.

Credit risk

The risk that customers or other creditors will fail to make promised payments as they come due.

- **Credit risk**—Although a credit risk is particularly significant for banks and other financial institutions, it can be relevant to any organization with accounts receivable.

Financial investments, such as the purchase of stock shares, involve a distinct set of speculative risks. See the exhibit "Speculative Risks in Investments."

Insurance deals primarily with risks of loss, not risks of gain; that is, with pure risks rather than speculative risks. However, the distinction between these two classifications of risk is not always precise—many risks have both pure and speculative aspects.

Distinguishing between pure and speculative risks is important because those risks must often be managed differently. For example, although a commercial

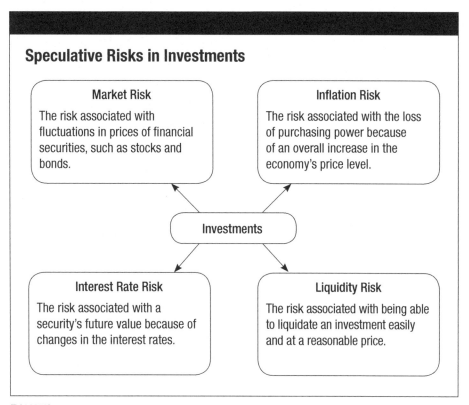

Speculative Risks in Investments

Market Risk

The risk associated with fluctuations in prices of financial securities, such as stocks and bonds.

Inflation Risk

The risk associated with the loss of purchasing power because of an overall increase in the economy's price level.

Investments

Interest Rate Risk

The risk associated with a security's future value because of changes in the interest rates.

Liquidity Risk

The risk associated with being able to liquidate an investment easily and at a reasonable price.

[DA02398]

building owner faces a pure risk from causes of loss such as fire, he or she also faces the speculative risk that the market value of the building will increase or decrease during any one year. Similarly, although an investor who purchases an apartment building to rent to tenants faces speculative risk because rental income may produce a profit or loss, the investor also faces a pure risk from causes of loss such as fire.

To properly manage these investments, the commercial building owner and the apartment owner must consider both the speculative and the pure risks. For example, they may choose to manage the pure risk by buying insurance or taking other measures to address property loss exposures. The speculative risk might be managed by obtaining a favorable mortgage and maintaining the property to enhance its resale value.

Subjective and Objective Risk

When individuals and organizations must make a decision that involves risk, they usually base it on the individual's or organization's assessment of the risk. The assessment can be based on opinions, which are subjective, or facts, which are objective.

Because it is based on opinion rather than fact, **subjective risk** may be quite different from the actual underlying risk that is present. In fact, subjective

Subjective risk

The perceived amount of risk based on an individual's or organization's opinion.

Objective risk

The measurable variation in uncertain outcomes based on facts and data.

risk can exist even where **objective risk** does not. The closer an individual's or organization's subjective interpretation of risk is to the objective risk, the more effective its risk management plan will likely be.

The reasons that subjective and objective risk can differ substantially include these:

- Familiarity and control—For example, although many people consider air travel (over which they have no control) to carry a high degree of risk, they are much more likely to suffer a serious injury when driving their cars, where the perception of control is much greater.

- Consequences over likelihood—People often have two views of low-likelihood, high-consequence events. The first misconception is the "It can't happen to me" view, which assigns a probability of zero to low-likelihood events such as natural disasters, murder, fires, accidents, and so on. The second misconception is overstating the probability of a low-likelihood event, which is common for people who have personally been exposed to the event previously. If the effect of a particular event can be severe, such as the potentially destructive effects of a hurricane or earthquake, the perception of the likelihood of deaths resulting from such an event is heightened. This perception may be enhanced by the increased media coverage given to high-severity events.

- Risk awareness—Organizations differ in terms of their level of risk awareness and, therefore, perceive risks differently. An organization that is not aware of its risks would perceive the likelihood of something happening as very low.

Both risk management and insurance depend on the ability to objectively identify and analyze risks. However, subjectivity is also necessary because facts are often not available to objectively assess risk.

Diversifiable and Nondiversifiable Risk

Diversifiable risk

A risk that affects only some individuals, businesses, or small groups.

Diversifiable risk is not highly correlated and can be managed through diversification, or spread, of risk. An example of a diversifiable risk is a fire, which is likely to affect only one or a small number of businesses. For instance, an insurer can diversify the risks associated with fire insurance by insuring many buildings in several different locations. Similarly, business investors often diversify their holdings, as opposed to investing in only one business, hoping those that succeed will more than offset those that fail.

Nondiversifiable risk

A risk that affects a large segment of society at the same time.

Examples of **nondiversifiable risks** include inflation, unemployment, and natural disasters such as hurricanes. Nondiversifiable risks are correlated—that is, their gains or losses tend to occur simultaneously rather than randomly. For example, under certain monetary conditions, interest rates increase for all firms at the same time. If an insurer were to insure firms against interest rate increases, it would not be able to diversify its portfolio of interest rate risks by underwriting a large number of insureds, because all of them would suffer losses at the same time.

Systemic risks are generally nondiversifiable. For example, if excess leverage by financial institutions causes systemic risk resulting in an event that disrupts the financial system, this risk will have an effect on the entire economy and, therefore, on all organizations. Because of the global interconnections in finance and industry, many risks that were once viewed as nonsystemic (affecting only one organization) are now viewed as systemic. For instance, many economists view the failure of Lehman Brothers in early 2008 as a trigger event: highlighting the systemic risk in the banking sector that resulted in the financial crisis.

Systemic risk

The potential for a major disruption in the function of an entire market or financial system.

Quadrants of Risk: Hazard, Operational, Financial, and Strategic

Although no consensus exists about how an organization should categorize its risks, one approach involves dividing them into risk quadrants:

- Hazard risks arise from property, liability, or personnel loss exposures and are generally the subject of insurance.

- Operational risks fall outside the hazard risk category and arise from people or a failure in processes, systems, or controls, including those involving information technology.

- Financial risks arise from the effect of market forces on financial assets or liabilities and include **market risk**, credit risk, **liquidity risk**, and price risk.

- Strategic risks arise from trends in the economy and society, including changes in the economic, political, and competitive environments, as well as from demographic shifts.

Market risk

Uncertainty about an investment's future value because of potential changes in the market for that type of investment.

Liquidity risk

The risk that an asset cannot be sold on short notice without incurring a loss.

Hazard and operational risks are classified as pure risks, and financial and strategic risks are classified as speculative risks.

The focus of the risk quadrants is different from the risk classifications previously discussed. Whereas the classifications of risk focus on some aspect of the risk itself, the four quadrants of risk focus on the risk source and who traditionally manages it. For example, the chief financial officer traditionally manages financial risk, and the risk manager traditionally manages hazard risk. Just as a particular risk can fall into more than one classification, a risk can also fall into multiple risk quadrants. For example, embezzlement of funds by an employee can be considered both a hazard risk, because it is an insurable pure risk, and an operational risk, because it involves a failure of controls. See the exhibit "Risk Quadrants."

Organizations define types of risk differently. Some organizations consider legal risks as operational risk, and some may characterize certain hazard risks as operational risk. Financial institutions generally use the categories of

Risk Quadrants

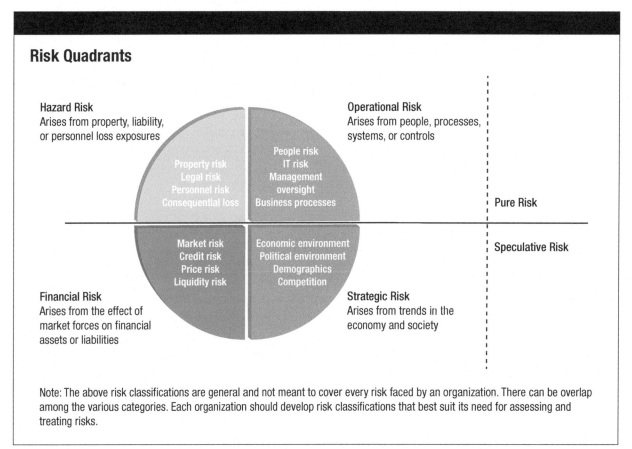

Hazard Risk
Arises from property, liability, or personnel loss exposures

Property risk
Legal risk
Personnel risk
Consequential loss

Operational Risk
Arises from people, processes, systems, or controls

People risk
IT risk
Management oversight
Business processes

Pure Risk

Market risk
Credit risk
Price risk
Liquidity risk

Economic environment
Political environment
Demographics
Competition

Speculative Risk

Financial Risk
Arises from the effect of market forces on financial assets or liabilities

Strategic Risk
Arises from trends in the economy and society

Note: The above risk classifications are general and not meant to cover every risk faced by an organization. There can be overlap among the various categories. Each organization should develop risk classifications that best suit its need for assessing and treating risks.

[DA08677]

market, credit, and operational risk (defined as all other risk, including hazard risk). Each organization should select categories that align with its objectives and processes.

Apply Your Knowledge

The New Company manufactures electronic consumer products. The company's manufacturing plant is highly automated and located in the United States. However, it purchases components from three companies in Asia. The majority of its sales are in the U.S., but European sales represent a growing percentage.

Describe the types of risk New Company would have in each of the four risk quadrants.

Feedback: In the hazard risk quadrant, New Company would have property damage risks to its plant and equipment resulting from fire, storms, or other events. It would also have risk of injury to its employees and liability risks associated with its products.

In the operational risk quadrant, New Company would have risks from employee turnover or the inability to find skilled employees. It would also have business process risk related to how it manages its supply chain and information technology risk related to its automated manufacturing process.

In the financial risk quadrant, New Company would have exchange rate risk related to its European sales. It would also have price risk for raw materials and supplies.

Strategic risks include competition, economic factors that could affect consumer demand, and the political risk arising from countries in which the company's component suppliers are located.

ENTERPRISE RISK MANAGEMENT

The concept of **enterprise risk management** (ERM) was developed as a way to manage all of an organization's risks, including operational, financial, and strategic risk.

Traditional risk management is concerned with an organization's pure risk, primarily hazard risk. In practice, there is no clear dividing line between risk management and ERM, with the terms often used interchangeably.

ERM Definitions

The evolving similarity of the concepts of risk management and ERM is demonstrated in the International Organization for Standardization (ISO) definition of risk management in ERM terms: "coordinated activities to direct and control an organization with regard to risk."[1] The ISO definition of risk as "the effect of uncertainty on objectives" also reflects an ERM approach to risk and risk management.

There are many similar definitions of ERM, including one from the Committee of Sponsoring Organizations of the Treadway Commission: "the culture, capabilities, and practices, integrated with strategy-setting and performance, that organizations rely on to manage risk in creating, preserving, and realizing value."[2]

The various definitions of ERM all include the concept of managing an organization's risks to help that organization meet its objectives. This link between management of an organization's risks and its objectives is a key driver in deciding how to assess and treat risks.

Enterprise risk management

An approach to managing all of an organization's key business risks and opportunities with the intent of maximizing shareholder value. Also known as enterprise-wide risk management.

Theoretical Pillars

Whether the source of a risk is financial, hazardous, operational, or strategic, risks managed separately are not the same as they are when managed together. Three main theoretical concepts explain how ERM works:

- Interdependency
- Correlation
- Portfolio theory

The silo type of management that is typical of traditional risk management ignores any interdependencies and assumes that a financial risk is unrelated to a hazard risk. Events are statistically independent if the probability of one event occurring does not affect the probability of a second event occurring. However, the traditional assumption of independence may not always be valid—and when it is not, the result may be inefficient treatment of an organization's portfolio of risks.

For example, mortgage loans in different geographical regions may seem independent. But the 2008 financial crisis revealed that there was actually a significant interdependency.

Correlation increases risk, while uncorrelated risks can provide a balance or hedge. For example, if all of an organization's suppliers are located in an earthquake-prone region in Asia, there is a significant correlation among suppliers in the organization's supply-chain risk.

The third concept that makes ERM work well is the portfolio theory. In an ERM context, a portfolio is a combination of risks. The portfolio theory assumes that risk includes both individual risks and their interactions. For example, an airline may experience an increased portfolio risk from increased fuel prices. This increase may affect not only the airline's costs but also consumer demand. The effect of rising gas prices on consumers' available disposable income could reduce the demand for air travel and constrict the airline's ability to offset its higher costs with higher prices. An airline that successfully hedged against rising oil prices may be able to take advantage of these circumstances to increase its market share.

Organizational Relationships

Under the traditional risk management organizational model, there is a risk manager and a risk management department to manage hazard risk. This traditional function mainly provides risk transfer, such as insurance, for the organization. Larger organizations typically include a claims management function. Many organizations include safety and loss prevention in the risk management department. See the exhibit "Example of a Traditional Risk Management Department."

Example of a Traditional Risk Management Department

Risk Management Director

- Insurance Manager
  - Insurance Administrator
- Safety and Loss Prevention Manager
  - Safety Engineer
  - Industrial Hygienist
- Claims Manager
  - Claims Administrator

[DA01662]

In ERM, the responsibility of the risk management function is broader and includes all of an organization's risks, not just hazard risk. Additionally, the entire organization at all levels becomes responsible for risk management as the ERM framework encompasses all stakeholders.

The board of a public company has the ultimate responsibility for oversight of the organization's risks. The Dodd-Frank Act requires that certain types of financial companies appoint board risk committees. A board risk committee may consist of the full board, the audit committee, or a dedicated risk committee. In addition, some public companies have formed an executive-level risk committee to assist the board in its risk oversight function. The executive-level committee might be chaired by a chief risk officer (CRO), who reports to both the chief executive officer (CEO) and the board risk committee. See the exhibit "Example of an ERM Governance Model."

As facilitator, the CRO engages the organization's management in a continual conversation that establishes risk strategic goals in relationship to the organization's strengths, weaknesses, opportunities, and threats (SWOT). The stakeholders in the organization include employees, management, the board of directors, and shareholders. External stakeholders include customers, regulators, and the community.

The CRO's responsibility includes helping the enterprise to create a risk culture in which managers of the organization's divisions and units, and eventually individual employees, become risk owners. In the fully integrated ERM organization, identifying and managing risk become part of every job

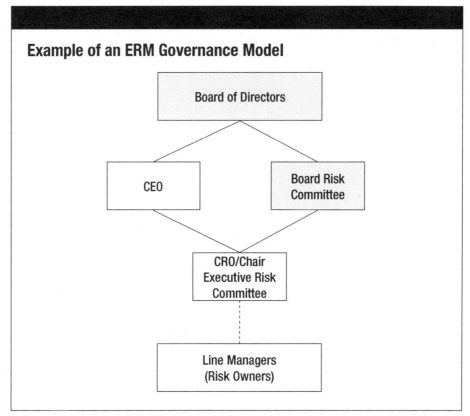

Example of an ERM Governance Model

Board of Directors

CEO

Board Risk Committee

CRO/Chair Executive Risk Committee

Line Managers (Risk Owners)

[DA08658]

description and project. Successful risk management of strategic objectives becomes a measure on all evaluations.

Implementation

It is essential to have senior management's commitment in a midsize to large organization to successfully implement an ERM program. The risk management professionals must have access to data from all organizational areas and levels to identify and assess the organization's risks. The risk management process to manage those risks must be integrated throughout the organization. To accomplish this, risk managers must have authority to make and enforce necessary changes, often against significant resistance.

Effective communication is essential to a successful ERM program. The CEO should meet with the senior managers of each organizational function to discuss the purpose and goals of ERM and the importance of management support. A task force composed of representatives from each function to work with the CRO and/or risk professionals can help achieve buy-in from key stakeholders. It is important for risk professionals to communicate with representatives from the various functions as well as receive communication from them. For example, operations managers may want more information about various types of risks, including hazard risks, such as employee injuries, or opportunity risks, such as communities with high growth rates. It is also essential to find out the type of information the CEO and other senior managers need to understand the organization's risk portfolio.

An organization with a fully integrated ERM program develops a communication matrix that moves information throughout the organization. Communications include dialogue and discussions among the different units and levels within the organization. The establishment of valid metrics and the continuous flow of cogent data are a critical aspect to this communication process. The metrics are carefully woven into reporting structures that engage the entire organization, including both internal and external stakeholders.

Impediments

An impediment to successfully adopting ERM is technological deficiency. For ERM to succeed, people have to receive relevant information. Management needs information on all organizational risks in a timely and concise manner—for example, a dashboard highlighting the critical risks affecting the organization's ability to meet its objectives.

Some risk management functions are able to use existing internet technology systems to produce this information, while others require new systems. The risk management information system (RMIS) of a broker or insurer could provide a starting point for a system to be tailored to the organization's ERM program.

Perhaps the single largest impediment to successful implementation of ERM is the organizational culture of entrenched silos. The risk management function traditionally purchased insurance and had claims oversight. The human resource function typically managed employee benefits and absences. The financial function managed prices; credit; investments, including hedges; and exchange rates. The operations function managed the core business operations, such as manufacturing or distribution. The safety function was separate or part of either risk management or operations. Information technology was a separate function or part of finance. Each of these functions typically had its own management structure.

In the new ERM culture, risk management is integrated throughout the organization. In many organizations, this involves operations managers taking responsibility for risk management within their areas of responsibility. For example, a bank branch manager would assume responsibility for speculative risk involved in growing the business and for financial risk, such as credit risk associated with the loans written by the branch. In large organizations, there may be a risk committee or task force headed by the CRO that includes representatives of each major function within the organization. To achieve accountability, many organizations charge back the gains and costs associated with risk management to the responsible function. For example, an operating division would be charged for the cost of hazard insurance and claims and also receive credit for new business or production improvements.

Apply Your Knowledge

An organization, with locations throughout the U.S., provides oxygen and related supplies to customers who need oxygen for medical reasons. Oxygen is an oxidizer that, although not a flammable gas, makes other substances around it more likely to burn faster and hotter. Therefore, there is a risk of fire and explosion at these locations. Describe a traditional risk management approach to this risk, versus an ERM approach.

Feedback: A traditional risk management approach would be to procure property, liability, and workers compensation insurance for this risk. Additionally, risk management might include the safety function to help prevent the occurrence and to provide an analysis of the cause if the event occurs. An ERM approach, in addition to risk transfer and safety, would assess additional risks such as those associated with the ability to provide a necessary medical product to customers, the organization's reputational risks in communities, the effect of demographics on the future of the business, and the ability to continue operations after a disaster.

THE CHANGING RISK MANAGEMENT ENVIRONMENT

Traditional risk assessment techniques focus on root cause analysis (RCA), which identifies a loss's predominant cause. The inherent weakness of this approach is obvious—RCA can only look backward. Plus, it might not identify all root causes and the related events that contribute to a loss and can only be performed periodically.

Today, however, a universe of data about past events can empower decision making that is further refined through data about previously imperceptible risk factors. Examples may include a worker's dangerous package-lifting technique, the presence of a hazardous chemical in the air at a factory, or the catastrophic intersection of seemingly disconnected financial transactions as they unfold in real time. The ways that technology and risk management intersect to achieve this can seem complex, but the basics are simple: The big data revolution is fueled by the capture, storage, and analysis of data. See the exhibit "How Big Data Has Transformed the Risk Management Environment."

Smart product

An innovative item that uses sensors; wireless sensor networks; and data collection, transmission, and analysis to further enable the item to be faster, more useful, or otherwise improved.

Internet of Things (IoT)

A network of objects that transmit data to computers.

Data Capture

Data capture is enabled primarily by **smart products** that sense their environment, process data, and communicate with other smart products and smart operations through the **Internet of Things (IoT)**. These interactions generate the data to which advanced analytics can be applied. The availability and

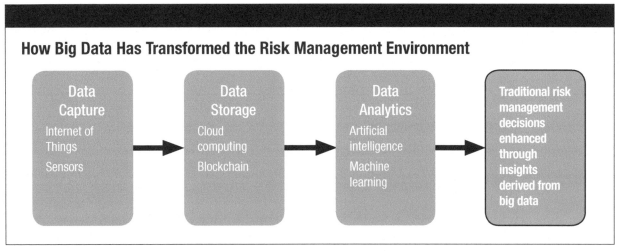

How Big Data Has Transformed the Risk Management Environment

Data Capture
Internet of Things
Sensors

→

Data Storage
Cloud computing
Blockchain

→

Data Analytics
Artificial intelligence
Machine learning

→

Traditional risk management decisions enhanced through insights derived from big data

[DA12739]

sophistication of smart products and the IoT's continued growth have led to an explosion of risk management innovation. Here are just a few examples:

- An accelerometer, a device that measures acceleration, motion, and tilt, can generate data about vehicle fleets, such as operator acceleration and braking, and detect excessive vibration in an industrial machine that is about to explode.

- Wearable exoskeletons, which are essentially wearable robots, can significantly reduce stress on the wearer's body when he or she is exerting force or lifting objects. This is accomplished through sensors that monitor each step or other movement of the user and transmit data that allows the mechanism to provide assistive movement.

- A closed-loop system, which integrates feedback into existing outcome data to establish the continuous input and output of data and information, collects detailed data about supply chain assets. This allows for immediate identification of discrepancies and interruptions as well as timely actions that can prevent or reduce supply chain losses.

Data Storage

The decision-making value of data produced by smart products, the IoT, and other data-capturing technology can be undermined by its volume, velocity, and veracity—more and faster is not necessarily better. **Cloud computing** enables the storage and sharing of vast amounts of data. But what if there was a way to ensure that the data used for risk management analysis was from a trusted source and independently verified? That is the premise underlying the data storage and sharing medium known as the blockchain.

Think of the blockchain as a virtual distributed ledger that maintains a list of dynamically updated data records (blocks). These records are not actually recorded in the ledger, however, until the veracity of data within them is

Cloud computing
Information, technology, and storage services contractually provided from remote locations, through the internet or another network, without a direct server connection.

confirmed and verified through a consensus process called mining. This verification process removes intermediary validation and establishes trust without the use of a centralized authority.

After a block is confirmed and the data within it is verified through mining, the block is timestamped and added to the preexisting blocks in the chain—hence the term "blockchain." The blockchain is encrypted and protected against tampering and revision.

The myriad risk management ramifications of the blockchain are a by-product of the medium's immutability; security; transparency; scalability; and ability to facilitate the sharing of verified, quality data. For example, a supply chain linking disparate entities across a continent could be connected through a blockchain-enabled database. This virtual ledger could record sensor-enhanced data about inventory levels, weather, labor conditions, and other data relevant to the welfare of the supplier's products collected from radio-frequency identification (RFID) sensors and other sources at each link in the chain and shared among all participants. The supplier could use the data not only to monitor conditions in real time—potentially staving off losses—but also to inform ongoing analysis of its products, processes, and employment practices to continually refine its management of supply chain and other risks.

Data Analytics

The collection, storage, and sharing of data empowers real-time risk management for organizations that use data gleaned from sensors to react immediately to hazardous situations. For instance, sensors affixed to the clothing of an assembly line worker might sense the worker's hydration level dropping to a dangerous level.

Collected and stored data can also be used to reveal forward-thinking risk management strategies when that data is organized and analyzed through methods that use artificial intelligence, such as machine learning and data modeling. In short, insurers and risk managers can improve their business results through data-driven decision making in an ever-increasing variety of ways, such as these:

- Automating decision making for improved accuracy and efficiency—Many insurers provide online quotes for personal auto insurance based on a computer algorithm.

- Organizing large volumes of new data—An insurer could organize data according to multiple characteristics, such as the information provided by **telematics**, which can include speed, braking patterns, left turns, and distance traveled.

- Discovering new relationships in data—A risk manager could identify the characteristics of workers who have never had a workplace accident and use that information to identify how to improve safety for all workers.

Telematics

The use of technological devices in vehicles with wireless communication and GPS tracking that transmit data to businesses or government agencies; some return information for the driver.

- Exploring new sources of data—An insurer could use **text mining** to analyze claims adjusters' notes for various purposes, such as developing an automated system to predict a claim's severity, and assign the appropriate resources to those claims predicted to become severe.

- Developing new products—The increasingly accurate predictive modeling of hazards, particularly catastrophe modeling, enabled by sources of shared, comprehensive data about the complex interactions of contributing factors, has led to product innovations. One notable example is parametric insurance, coverage that pays a predetermined amount to the insured if a particular set of parameters occur, such as a hurricane's wind speed.

Text mining
Obtaining information through language recognition.

RISK MANAGEMENT BENEFITS

Risk management involves the efforts of individuals or organizations to efficiently and effectively assess, control, and finance risk in order to minimize the adverse effects of losses or missed opportunities. Properly managing risk reduces its negative financial consequences and thereby benefits individuals, organizations, and society.

An organization with an effective risk management program should experience smaller expected losses (less frequent or less severe) and experience less residual uncertainty than a comparable organization that does not practice good risk management. For example, an organization that installs a state-of-the-art security system would expect to have fewer thefts (and therefore lower expected losses) and a better sense of security (less residual uncertainty).

For individuals and families, risk management is usually an informal series of efforts, not a formalized process. Individual or personal risk management may be viewed as part of the financial planning process that encompasses broader matters such as capital accumulation, retirement planning, and estate planning.

In small organizations, risk management is not usually a dedicated function, but one of many tasks carried out by the owner or senior manager. In many larger organizations, the risk management function is conducted as part of a formalized risk management program. A risk management program is a system for planning, organizing, leading, and controlling the resources and activities that an organization needs to protect itself from the adverse effects of accidental losses. See the exhibit "Risk Management Benefits."

The exhibit summarizes the benefits of risk management for individuals, organizations, and society in terms of its reduction of expected losses and residual uncertainty.

Risk Management Benefits

	Component	
	Lower Expected Losses	Less Residual Uncertainty
Individuals	Preserves financial resources	Reduces anxiety
Organizations	Preserves financial resources Makes an organization more attractive as an investment opportunity	Reduces deterrence effect
Society	Preserves financial resources	Improves allocation of productive resources

[DA02293]

Reducing the Financial Consequences of Risk

The overall financial consequence of risk for a given asset or activity is the sum of three costs: (1) the cost of the value lost because of actual events that cause a loss, (2) the cost of the resources devoted to risk management for that asset or activity, and (3) the cost of residual uncertainty. However, because it is difficult to assign a specific value to the cost of residual uncertainty, it is also difficult to establish a benchmark against which the performance of the risk management program can be assessed. As a result, organizations typically evaluate a subset of costs that form part of the financial consequences of hazard risk and refer to this subset of costs as the **cost of risk**.

Cost of risk

The total cost incurred by an organization because of the possibility of accidental loss.

For a particular asset or activity, the cost of risk can be broken down in this way:

- Cost of losses not reimbursed by insurance or other external sources
- Cost of insurance premiums
- Cost of external sources of funds—for example, the interest payments to lenders or the transaction costs associated with noninsurance indemnity
- Cost of measures to prevent or reduce the size of potential losses
- Cost of implementing and administering risk management

By reducing the long-term, overall cost of risk and devoting a minimum of resources to the actual process of managing risk without interfering with normal activities, risk management helps an individual or an organization to be more productive, promotes safety, and enhances profitability.

Benefits to Individuals

Risk management can preserve an individual's financial resources by reducing his or her expected losses. Most individuals have limited financial resources and are therefore not able—or willing—to bear the financial consequences of substantial risks.

For example, most people cannot afford to pay thousands (or millions) of dollars in damages if they seriously injure or kill someone in an auto accident. For some, avoiding loss is a viable alternative, and they choose not to drive. Purchasing auto liability insurance enables drivers to transfer their auto liability loss exposures to insurers.

The second benefit of risk management for individuals is that it reduces the residual uncertainty associated with risk. Most individuals are at least somewhat risk averse. Risk aversion means that, all else being equal, individuals prefer certainty to uncertainty, or less risk to more risk.

For example, if given a choice between the 100 percent certainty of paying $100 or a 20 percent chance of paying $500 (and, therefore, an 80 percent chance of paying nothing), a risk-averse individual would choose the 100 percent certainty of paying $100. Risk management allows an individual to invest time and money into managing risks in order to reduce uncertainty and its associated anxiety.

Benefits to Organizations

Organizations tend to have more resources than individuals and therefore are better equipped to bear risk. Consequently, organizations do not exhibit the same degree of risk aversion as individuals. Nonetheless, organizations usually choose to manage their risks, because they, too, benefit from preserving their financial resources.

Preservation of financial resources adds value to the organization and makes it a safer and more attractive investment, because shareholders or other investors want to know that their equity is safe and will generate future income and creditors seek assurance that the money they have loaned the organization will be repaid on time with interest. Risk management can protect the financial resources necessary to satisfy these parties and other stakeholders.

The protection that risk management affords an organization's financial resources can, in turn, provide confidence that capital is protected against future costs such as property loss, interruption of future income, liability judgments, or loss of key personnel. This sense of confidence is attractive both to suppliers and customers. As a result, suppliers may be more willing to allow the organization to buy on credit, and customers may purchase more products or services the organization offers.

Risk management also can reduce the deterrence effect of risk; that is, it can improve an organization's capacity to engage in business activities by minimizing the adverse effects of risk. Consequently, the organization can plan for its future with less uncertainty about potential outcomes. The fear of possible future losses tends to make senior management reluctant to undertake activities or investments it considers too risky, thereby depriving the organization of their associated benefits.

By making losses less frequent, less severe, or more predictable, risk management can alleviate management's fears about potential losses. This increases the feasibility of activities such as research and development, joint ventures, or investment in other organizations, which previously appeared too risky.

Benefits to Society

Society also faces a cost of risk, as well as uncertainty about future losses. Its cost of risk is slightly different from that of an individual or organization. Nonetheless, risk management benefits society in the same ways that it does individuals and organizations, by lowering expected losses and reducing residual uncertainty.

A nation's economy has limited resources with which to produce goods and services. When, for example, a fire or an earthquake demolishes a factory or destroys a highway, that economy's overall productive resources are reduced. Beyond the resources directly consumed in a loss, a significant portion of a nation's productive resources is devoted to preventing, repairing, or compensating for the results of losses.

When losses are possible, some portion of the economy's resources must be devoted to risk management for the benefit of society as a whole. Minimizing the resources consumed in running an economy's risk management program is analogous to an organization minimizing the administrative costs of its risk management department.

By reducing residual uncertainty, risk management also improves the allocation of productive resources. Risk management makes those who own or run an organization more willing to undertake risky activities, because they are better protected against losses that those activities might have produced. This makes executives, workers, and suppliers of financial capital more able to pursue activities that maximize profits; returns on investments; and, ultimately, wages. Such shifts increase productivity within an economy and improve the overall standard of living.

RISK MANAGEMENT OBJECTIVES AND GOALS

A structured, logical, and appropriate program is the foundation on which an organization's entire risk management effort rests.

The support of an organization's senior management is essential to an effective risk management program. To gain that support, a risk management professional should design a program with objectives and goals that align with the organization's overall objectives. In some circumstances, a trade-off will be necessary between organizational objectives and risk management goals.

Risk Management Objectives

Each organization should align its risk management objectives with its overall objectives. Common objectives for risk management are balancing risk and reward and supporting decision-making. These objectives should reflect the organization's risk appetite and the organization's internal and external context. Objectives can emphasize certain goals, such as business continuity, protection of reputation, or growth. See the exhibit "Example of an Organization's Risk Management Objectives: Zurich's Enterprise Risk Management."

Example of an Organization's Risk Management Objectives: Zurich's Enterprise Risk Management

Mission and Objectives of Risk Management

The mission of Zurich's Enterprise Risk Management is to promptly identify, measure, manage, report and monitor risks that affect the achievement of our strategic, operational and financial objectives. This includes adjusting the risk profile in line with the Group's stated risk tolerance to respond to new threats and opportunities in order to optimize returns.

Our major Enterprise Risk Management objectives are to:

- Protect the capital base by monitoring that risks are not taken beyond the Group's risk tolerance

- Enhance value creation and contribute to an optimal risk-return profile by providing the basis for an efficient capital deployment

- Support the Group's decision-making processes by providing consistent, reliable and timely risk information

- Protect our reputation and brand by promoting a sound culture of risk awareness and disciplined and informed risk taking

---

Risk management objectives can emphasize certain goals in order to align the risk management program with the organization's risk philosophy and to help the organization meet its overall objectives.

Risk Management Goals

The risk management program should have goals to manage the risks that an organization will face. These goals should be incorporated into the risk management framework and the process designed to meet a particular organization's objectives. These are typical risk management goals:

- Tolerable uncertainty
- Legal and regulatory compliance
- Survival
- Business continuity
- Earnings stability
- Profitability and growth
- Social responsibility
- Economy of risk management operations

Tolerable Uncertainty

A typical risk management goal is tolerable uncertainty, which means aligning risks with the organization's risk appetite ("the total exposed amount that an organization wishes to undertake on the basis of risk-return trade-offs for one or more desired and expected outcomes").[3] Managers want to be assured that whatever might happen will be within the bounds of what was anticipated and will be effectively addressed by the risk management program.

Risk management programs should use measurements that align with the organization's overall objectives and take into account the risk appetite of senior management. For example, **value at risk (VaR)** can be used to analyze various financial portfolios with different assets and risk factors. VaR can be calculated quickly and easily to determine risk factor returns on a portfolio.

Value at risk

A threshold value such that the probability of loss on the portfolio over the given time horizon exceeds this value, assuming normal markets and no trading in the portfolio.

Legal and Regulatory Compliance

An important goal for risk management programs is to ensure that the organization's legal obligations are satisfied. Such legal obligations are typically based on these items:

- Standard of care that is owed to others
- Contracts entered into by the organization
- Federal, state, provincial, territorial, and local laws and regulations

A risk management professional has an essential role in helping the organization manage regulatory risk and the potential for liability.

Survival

For risk management purposes, an organization can be viewed as a structured system of resources such as financial assets, machinery and raw materials, employees, and managerial leadership. The organization generates income for its employees and owners by producing goods or services that meet others' needs. Many risks can threaten the survival of an organization. Traditionally, hazard risk, which could destroy an organization's facilities or cause injury to employees or customers, was viewed as the major threat to an organization's survival. Risk management professionals use techniques such as loss control and risk transfer to manage hazard risks.

However, the risks that organizations face are much broader than hazard risk. These risks include financial risks such as the value of assets (for example, the organization's stock value), competition, supply-chain risks, and technology (vulnerability to computer attacks and ability to keep pace with technological developments). Survival of an organization depends on identifying as many risks as possible that could threaten the organization's ability to survive and managing those risks appropriately. It also depends on anticipating and recognizing emerging risks, such as those related to climate change.

Business Continuity

Continuity of operations is a key goal for many private organizations and an essential goal for all public entities. Although survival requires that no risk occurrence (no matter how severe) permanently shut down an organization, the goal of continuity of operations is more demanding. To be resilient, an organization cannot interrupt its operations for any appreciable time. When an organization's senior management sets business continuity as a goal, its risk management professionals must have a clear, detailed understanding of the specific operations for which continuity is essential and the maximum tolerable interruption interval for each operation.

These are the steps an organization should take to provide business continuity and, therefore, resiliency:

- Identify activities whose interruptions cannot be tolerated
- Identify the types of accidents that could interrupt such activities
- Determine the standby resources that must be immediately available to counter the effects of those accidents
- Ensure the availability of the standby resources at even the most unlikely and difficult times

Earnings Stability

Earnings stability is a goal of some organizations. Rather than strive for the highest possible level of current profits (or, for not-for-profit organizations, surpluses) in a given period, some organizations emphasize earnings stability over time. Striving for earnings stability requires precision in forecasting fluctuations in asset values; liability values; and risk management costs, such as costs for insurance.

Profitability and Growth

An organization's senior management might have established a minimum amount of profit (or surplus) that no event should reduce. To achieve that minimum amount, risk management professionals must identify the risks that could prevent this goal from being reached, as well as the risks that could help achieve this goal within the context of the organization's overall objectives. For example, an organization concerned that a disaster preventing a key supplier from delivering parts will cause a supply-chain risk could develop a backup plan that might not only avoid this risk but also provide an opportunity to sell the backup parts to other companies.

An organization might measure profitability for its various units on a risk-adjusted basis. For example, high-risk investments require higher expected profits to account for the risk involved. By measuring profit on a risk-adjusted basis, the organization can efficiently deploy its capital.

Most organizations set goals for growth. Emphasizing growth—for example, enlarging an organization's market share, the size and scope of its activities or products, or its assets—might have two distinctly opposing effects on its risk management program: the reduction of the potentially negative consequences of risk versus supporting the organization's entrepreneurial risk-taking. Those effects depend on managers' and owners' tolerance for uncertainty. It is essential that risk managers understand growth goals in the context of senior management's risk appetite. Risk managers should also advise senior management of the potential risk in different growth strategies that the organization considers. For example, before the financial crisis, many financial organizations became highly leveraged in order to achieve growth. Although this strategy provided significant short-term growth, it ultimately caused the failure of several prominent firms.

Social Responsibility

Social responsibility is a goal for many organizations. It includes the organization's ethical conduct as well as the philanthropic commitments that the owners of the organization have made to the community and society as a whole. Beyond the altruistic interests of the organization's owners, many organizations justify pursuing the objective of social responsibility because such activities enhance the organization's reputation. Risk management professionals should consider an organization's societal commitments when developing its risk management program.

Economy of Risk Management Operations

Risk management should operate economically and efficiently; that is, an organization generally should not incur substantial costs for slight benefits gained. Risk management programs should be operated economically and efficiently.

One way to measure the economy of a risk management program is through benchmarking, in which an organization's risk management costs are compared with those of similar organizations. The Risk and Insurance Management Society (RIMS), a global organization of risk management professionals, conducts an annual benchmarking survey, in partnership with

Advisen, that organizations can use to compare their cost of hazard risk with other organizations in their industry. The benchmark survey combines expenditures for risk assessment, risk control, and risk financing, as well as the administrative costs of risk management programs. These costs are then related to revenue so that comparisons can be made between organizations and industry sectors.

Trade-Offs Among Goals

Although an organization's risk management objectives and goals are inter-related, sometimes they are not consistent with one another. For example, to obtain tolerable uncertainty, the risk management professional may have to advise senior management that a growth goal may not be achievable with-out adjusting either the risk appetite or the growth strategy. Legality and social responsibility goals may conflict with the economy of operations goal. Some externally imposed legal obligations, such as safety standards dictated by building codes, are nonnegotiable. Therefore, costs associated with these obligations are unavoidable. Other nonlegal obligations, such as charitable contributions, may be negotiable. However, while meeting social responsi-bility may raise costs in the short term, it can have worthwhile long-term benefits that make the costs acceptable.

In working with others regarding the trade-offs among organizational goals, a risk management professional must consider the likely effects of alternative risk treatment techniques and the costs and benefits of each. The interests and concerns of the various groups affected by an organization's risk manage-ment program should also be considered.

The way in which a risk management department is structured, how it cooperates with other departments, and how it handles communication of information are all relevant in enabling risk management professionals to respond to the goals and concerns of the organization and of affected parties.

THE RISK MANAGEMENT PROCESS

An organization's success depends largely on how well it manages risk, and not just when it's confronted with major events such as an insurance renewal, a serious claim, or passage of a new law or regulation. Prudent organizations don't wait for such external factors to implement the risk management pro-cess, because its six steps are designed to be executed continuously.

The risk management process can be applied to any set of loss exposures:

1. Identifying loss exposures
2. Analyzing loss exposures
3. Examining the feasibility of risk management techniques
4. Selecting the appropriate risk management techniques
5. Implementing the selected risk management techniques
6. Monitoring results and revising the risk management program

Step 1: Identifying Loss Exposures

A wide variety of methods can be used to identify the loss exposures that threaten an organization's goals. Using different methods allows organizations to avoid overlooking important loss exposures. For example, loss history documents may not reveal the possibility of loss exposures related to flood, but a flood insurance rate map or cause-of-loss checklist does.

Step 2: Analyzing Loss Exposures

Analyzing loss exposures involves estimating the likely significance of the possible losses identified in Step One along four dimensions:

- Loss frequency—the number of losses (such as fires, auto accidents, or liability claims) within a specific time period
- Loss severity—the amount, in dollars, of a loss for a specific occurrence
- Total dollar losses—the total dollar amount of losses for all occurrences during a specific time period
- Timing—when losses occur and loss payments are made

Analyzing loss exposures is expensive. The cost of risk includes the cost of acquiring risk-related information used in loss forecasts, estimates of future cash flows, and other planning activities. In some cases, this information can actually reduce losses. Reviewing these dimensions enables the development of loss projections and the prioritization of loss exposures so resources can be properly allocated.

Together, the first and second steps constitute the process of assessing loss exposures and are therefore the most important steps in the risk management process. Once a loss exposure has been assessed, the best ways to manage it often become immediately apparent.

Step 3: Examining the Feasibility of Risk Management Techniques

Loss exposures can be addressed through risk management techniques that entail **risk control** and **risk financing**:

- Broadly speaking, risk control techniques minimize the frequency or severity of losses or make losses more predictable.
- Risk financing techniques generate funds to finance losses that risk control techniques cannot prevent.

Risk management techniques are not usually used in isolation. Unless the loss exposure is avoided, organizations typically apply at least one risk control technique and one risk financing technique to each of their significant loss exposures. The risk control technique alters the estimated frequency and severity of loss, and the financing technique pays for losses that occur despite the controls.

Step 4: Selecting the Appropriate Risk Management Techniques

Most organizations choose risk management techniques by using financial criteria. However, an organization's value may also stem from ethical and other nonfinancial considerations:

- Financial considerations—Organizations compare the potential costs of loss exposures left completely untreated with the costs of possible risk management techniques when considering whether a technique is economical. A risk management technique's cost can be determined through a cost-benefit analysis that considers the technique's effect on the frequency, severity, and timing of expected losses relative to an estimate of the after-tax costs involved in applying the various risk management techniques.
- Nonfinancial considerations—Data based on objective risk factors usually is not the only criterion considered in determining appropriate risk management techniques. An organization might also place a great deal of value on maintaining operations or peace of mind.

Risk control

A conscious act or decision not to act that reduces the frequency and/or severity of losses or makes losses more predictable.

Risk financing

A conscious act or decision not to act that generates the funds to pay for losses and risk control measures or to offset variability in cash flows.

Step 5: Implementing the Selected Risk Management Techniques

The next step is to implement the techniques selected in the previous step. Implementing risk management techniques may involve any of these measures:

- Purchasing loss reduction devices
- Contracting for loss prevention services
- Funding retention programs
- Implementing and continually reinforcing risk control programs
- Selecting agents or brokers, insurers, third-party administrators, and other providers for insurance programs
- Requesting insurance policies and paying premiums

Implementing risk management techniques does not necessarily end with the initial implementation of the selected technique. For example, if an organization purchases a building, it almost certainly will also decide to purchase property insurance. However, additional details, such as the exact placement of fire extinguishers, the terms and cost of insurance and noninsurance contract revisions, which insurer to use, the timing of insurance premium payments, or the actual deposit of funds for a retention program or to cover deductibles, must be addressed as the program is implemented.

Step 6: Monitoring Results and Revising the Risk Management Program

Once implemented, a risk management program must be monitored and revised to ensure that it is achieving expected results and to accommodate changes in loss exposures and the availability or cost-effectiveness of alternative risk management techniques. Monitoring and revising the risk management program requires four steps:

1. Establishing standards of acceptable performance—Standards should consider the organization's results and activities. A results standard focuses on actual achievement of goals, regardless of the effort required to achieve them (for example, a decline in the frequency or severity of employee injuries), while an activity standard focuses on efforts made to achieve a goal regardless of actual results.

2. Comparing actual results with these standards—A proper standard includes specifications for how results or performance will be measured, such as target activity levels or results, or at least desired directions of change (for example, a decrease in the number of worker accidents from one year to the next).

3. Correcting substandard performance or revising standards that prove to be unrealistic—Substandard performance does not necessarily indicate

that the performance itself is the problem. The standard may, in fact, be inappropriate. A risk management program should change when loss exposures change. Similarly, the standards by which that program is evaluated must be reexamined and possibly altered if the environment within which the risk management program operates also changes.

4. Evaluating standards that have been substantially exceeded—Performance should ideally meet or exceed a standard. However, if performance substantially exceeds a standard, then determining why is crucial. One reason may be the superior skills of the employee or employees involved in implementing the standard. Another alternative is that the standard is not sufficiently demanding. Standards that have been substantially exceeded should be revised to more accurately reflect the performance potential of the employees and the organization.

SUMMARY

The word risk can have many different meanings. In this section, risk is defined as the uncertainty about outcomes, some of which can be negative. The two elements within this definition of risk are uncertainty of outcome (uncertainty about what will actually occur, when the outcome will occur, or a combination of the two) and the possibility of a negative outcome.

Possibility means that an outcome or event may or may not occur. This is not the same as probability, which is the likelihood that an outcome or event will occur. Unlike possibility, probability is measurable and has a value between zero and one.

Classifying the various types of risk can help organizations manage risk. Some of the most commonly used classifications are pure and speculative risk, subjective and objective risk, and diversifiable and nondiversifiable risk. An organization's risks can also be categorized into quadrants as hazard risk, operational risk, financial risk, and strategic risk.

Traditional risk management took responsibility for hazard risk, typically arranging for risk transfer. ERM identifies operational, financial, and strategic risks in addition to hazard risks; develops an understanding of their relationships; and evaluates the potential effect of the risk portfolio on an organization's ability to achieve its objectives. ERM seeks to optimize a risk management strategy that is integrated into the entire organization.

Grounded in traditional risk management techniques, today's risk management environment is animated by increasingly potent combinations of inexpensive data-gathering technology and predictive analytics techniques that can transform data into more certainty about risk management decisions than ever before. Simply put, the big data revolution is fueled by the capture, storage, and analysis of data.

For an individual, the specific benefits of risk management are preservation of financial resources and reduction of anxiety. For an organization, the benefits are preservation of financial resources, increased attractiveness to investors, and reduction of the deterrence effect of risk. For society as a whole, the benefits are preservation of financial resources and an improved allocation of productive resources.

A risk management program provides a framework for planning, organizing, leading, and controlling the resources and activities of an organization to achieve the organization's objectives. The risk management program's goals should be aligned with those objectives. Because there may be inconsistency at times between an organization's objectives and risk management goals, trade-offs may be necessary to achieve the desired results.

The risk management process consists of six steps that can be applied to any set of loss exposures:

1. Identifying loss exposures
2. Analyzing loss exposures
3. Examining the feasibility of risk management techniques
4. Selecting the appropriate risk management techniques
5. Implementing the selected risk management techniques
6. Monitoring results and revising the risk management program

ASSIGNMENT NOTES

1. International Organization for Standardization, ISO 31000: 2018 (Geneva, Switzerland: International Organization for Standardization, 2018), p. 2.
2. ©Risk and Insurance Management Society, Inc.—used with permission.
3. "Exploring Risk Appetite and Risk Tolerance," RIMS Executive Report, Risk and Insurance Management Society, 2012, www.rims.org/resources/ERM/Documents/RIMS_Exploring_Risk_Appetite_Risk_Tolerance_0412.pdf (accessed June 1, 2012).

2

Identifying Loss Exposures

Educational Objectives

After learning the content of this assignment, you should be able to:

▷ Describe property loss exposures in terms of assets exposed to loss, causes of loss, financial consequences of loss, and parties affected by loss.

▷ Describe liability loss exposures in terms of assets exposed to loss, causes of loss, and financial consequences of loss.

▷ Describe personnel loss exposures in terms of assets exposed to loss, causes of loss, and financial consequences of loss.

▷ Describe net income loss exposures in terms of assets exposed to loss, causes of loss, and financial consequences of loss.

▷ Describe the following methods of loss exposure identification:

- Document analysis
- Compliance review
- Inspections
- Consultation

Identifying Loss Exposures

2

PROPERTY LOSS EXPOSURES

The elements of a property loss exposure are important to an insurance professional because they provide a framework for analyzing loss exposures that may be handled through appropriate risk management techniques.

There are three important elements of property loss exposures:

- Assets exposed to property loss—The types of property that may be exposed to loss, damage, or destruction.
- Causes of loss—Those that may result in property being lost, damaged, or destroyed.
- Financial consequences—Those consequences that may result from a property loss. A property loss can be the cause of a net income loss; however, that is considered a separate loss exposure.

In addition to describing these elements of property loss exposures, this section discusses the parties who may be affected when property is lost, damaged, or destroyed.

Assets Exposed to Property Loss

An asset is property, which is any item with value. Individuals, families, and businesses own and use property, depend on it as a source of income or services, and rely on its value. Property can decline in value—or even become worthless—if it is lost, damaged, or destroyed. Different kinds of property have different qualities that affect the owner's or user's exposure to loss.

Two basic types of property are real property and personal property. Insurance practitioners further divide these kinds of property into several categories:

- Buildings
- Personal property contained in buildings
- Money and securities
- Vehicles and watercraft
- Property in transit

These categories overlap to some extent. For example, vehicles, when carried on trucks, can be property in transit. These categories are listed separately here because they represent types of property for which specific forms of insurance have been developed.

Buildings

Buildings are more than bricks and mortar. Most buildings also contain plumbing, wiring, and heating and air conditioning equipment, which can lead to leaks, electrical fires, and explosions. Most buildings also contain basic portable equipment, such as fire extinguishers and lawn mowers, that is required to service the building and surrounding land. Under most insurance policies, such equipment is considered part of the building. Property that is permanently attached to the structure, such as wall-to-wall carpeting, built-in appliances, or boilers and machinery, is generally considered part of the building as well.

Fixture

Any personal property affixed to real property in such a way as to become part of the real property.

Boilers and machinery constitute a special class of property. They are often affixed to a building in such a manner that they become a permanent part of the building and are considered to be **fixtures**. This class of property includes any of these types of equipment:

- Steam boilers (large water tanks heated by burning gas, oil, or coal to produce steam for heating or to produce power)
- Unfired pressure vessels, such as air tanks
- Refrigerating and air conditioning systems
- Mechanical equipment, such as compressors and turbines
- Production equipment
- Electrical equipment

Boilers and machinery share these two characteristics:

- They are susceptible to explosion or breakdown that can result in serious losses to the unit and to persons and property nearby.
- They are less likely to have explosions or breakdowns if they are periodically inspected and properly maintained.

Personal Property Contained in Buildings

The contents of a typical home include personal property such as furniture, clothing, electronic equipment, jewelry, paintings, and other personal possessions. The contents of a commercial building may include these items:

- Furniture, such as desks or file cabinets in an office
- Machinery and equipment, such as cash registers in a supermarket
- Stock, such as groceries in a store

Although most policies use the term "personal property" (which is all property other than land and property attached to the land, such as buildings) to refer to the contents of a building, many insurance practitioners and policyholders use the term "contents" as a matter of convenience and common practice. Property insurance policies refer to personal property, rather than contents, because the property is often covered even when it is not literally contained in the building. When the contents of a commercial building are involved, policies generally use the term "business personal property."

Money and Securities

For insurance purposes, money and securities are separate from other types of contents because their characteristics present special problems. **Money** and **securities** are highly susceptible to loss by theft. Cash is particularly difficult to trace because it can be readily spent. In contrast, other types of property must be sold for cash before the thief can make a profit. Money and securities are also lightweight, easily concealed, and easy to transport.

In addition to being susceptible to theft, money and securities can be quickly destroyed in the event of a fire. For example, unless a store owner makes a bank deposit every night after the store closes, the store owner could lose a considerable amount of currency and checks in a fire.

Vehicles and Watercraft

The primary purpose of most vehicles and watercraft is to move people or property, and this movement exposes vehicles and watercraft to several causes of loss. Vehicles may be grouped by vehicle type, by operator type, by typical usage, or by a combination of these characteristics. No matter which classifications are used, some vehicles (such as snowmobiles or utility vehicles) fit into more than one category, depending on the purpose for which they are owned and used. However, these categories are useful in identifying property loss exposures:

- Autos and other highway vehicles
- Mobile equipment
- Recreational vehicles

In insurance terminology, the word " **auto**" can also include such diverse vehicles as fire engines, ambulances, motorcycles, and camping trailers. **Mobile equipment** may be damaged in a highway collision, but the most frequent exposures to loss involve off-road situations. In some cases, the owners of **recreational vehicles** face exposures to loss both on and off the road.

Watercraft are exposed to special perils not encountered in other means of transit. Those perils include extreme weather conditions that can create rougher seas than the craft can handle; poor navigation, resulting in striking the ground or another obstacle; and, depending on the shipping route, piracy.

Property in Transit

A great deal of property is transported by truck, but property is also moved in cars, buses, trains, airplanes, and watercraft. When a conveyance containing cargo overturns or is involved in a collision, the cargo can also be damaged. In addition, cargo can be destroyed without damage to the transporting vehicle

Money

Currency, coins, bank notes, and sometimes traveler's checks, credit card slips, and money orders held for sale to the public.

Securities

Written instruments representing either money or other property, such as stocks and bonds.

Auto

As defined in commercial general liability and auto forms, a land motor vehicle, trailer, or semitrailer designed for travel on public roads, including attached machinery or equipment; or any other land vehicle that is subject to a compulsory or financial responsibility law or other motor vehicle insurance law in the state where it is licensed or principally garaged.

Mobile equipment

Various types of vehicles designed for use principally off public roads, such as bulldozers and cranes.

Recreational vehicle

A vehicle used for sports and recreational activities, such as a dune buggy, all-terrain vehicle, or dirt bike.

or watercraft. Liquids can leak out, fragile articles can be jostled during transit, and perishables can melt or spoil.

When property is damaged or lost in transit, it must be replaced. Delays often result, because replacement property may have to be shipped from the location of the original shipment. The property owner may also incur expense to move damaged property.

Property being transported by watercraft could be lost entirely if the watercraft were to sink. Even more so than other property, ocean cargoes fluctuate in value according to their location. If the watercraft cannot reach its intended destination and the cargo must be sold in a different port, the price received for the cargo might be less than the price expected at the original destination.

Causes of Property Loss

Peril

The cause of a loss.

Causes of loss (or **perils**) include fire, lightning, windstorm, hail, and theft. Most causes of loss adversely affect property and leave it in an altered state. A fire can reduce a building to a heap of rubble. A collision can change a car into twisted scrap. Some causes of loss do not alter the property itself, but they affect a person's ability to possess or use the property. For example, property lost or stolen can still be usable, but not by its rightful owner.

The terms "peril" and "hazard" are often confused. As stated, a peril is a cause of loss. Fire, theft, collision, and flood are examples of perils that cause property losses. (Many property insurance policies use the term "cause of loss" instead of peril.)

A hazard is anything that increases the frequency or the severity of a loss. These are two examples:

- Careless smoking practices are a fire hazard because they increase the frequency of fires.
- Keeping large amounts of money in a cash register overnight is a theft hazard affecting both the frequency and the severity of loss.

Financial Consequences of Property Losses

When a property loss occurs, the property is reduced in value. The reduction in value can be measured in different ways, sometimes with differing results. If the property can be repaired or restored, the reduction in value can be measured by the cost of the repair or the restoration. Property that must be replaced has no remaining worth, unless some salvageable items can be sold. Consider these examples:

- A fence worth $7,000 was damaged by a car, and the fence owner has to pay $2,000 to have the damage repaired. The fence owner has incurred a partial loss that reduced the fence's value by $2,000.
- A camera worth $400 is run over by a truck. The camera owner has incurred a total loss that reduced the camera's value by $400.

If property is lost, is stolen, or otherwise disappears, its value to the owner is reduced just as though it had been destroyed and retained no salvage value. A further reduction in value might occur if repaired property is worth less than it would have been if it had never been damaged. This is true for items such as fine paintings and other art objects. Many collectibles are valuable largely because they are in mint or original condition. An object that has been repaired after damage from a tear, a scratch, or fire is no longer in that unspoiled condition, and its value will decline. The owner faces loss in the form of the cost to repair the object, as well as a reduction in value because of the altered condition.

Property may have different values, depending on the method by which the value is determined. The most common valuation measures used in insurance policies are replacement cost and actual cash value (ACV). In certain situations, however, other valuation measures are used, such as agreed value.

Parties Affected by Property Losses

Parties that may be affected by a property loss include these:

- Property owners
- Secured lenders of money to the property owner
- Property holders

Property Owners

The party that is affected most when property is lost, damaged, or destroyed is usually the owner of the property. If the property has some value, the owner of the property incurs a financial loss to repair or replace it. In a supermarket fire, for example, the store's owner could incur a considerable financial loss because it had to rebuild the store and restock the shelves.

Secured Lenders

When money is borrowed to finance the purchase of a car, the lender usually acquires some conditional rights to the car, such as the right to repossess the car if the car's owner (the borrower) fails to make loan payments. This right gives the lender security. Such a lender is therefore called a secured lender or a secured creditor. When a person or business borrows money to buy a home or a building and the property serves as security for the loan, the secured

Mortgagee

A lender in a mortgage arrangement, such as a bank or another financing institution.

Mortgagor

The person or organization that borrows money from a mortgagee to finance the purchase of real property.

lender is called a **mortgagee** (or mortgageholder), and the borrower is called a **mortgagor**.

When property is used to secure a loan, the lender is exposed to loss. Returning to the supermarket fire example, if the store owner had a mortgage on its supermarket building, the mortgagee would lose the security for the mortgage loan if the building burned. Similarly, if a financed car is destroyed in an accident, no vehicle would be available for the lender to repossess in the event that the owner defaulted on the loan. Property insurance policies generally protect the secured lender's interest in the financed property by naming the lender on the insurance policy and by giving the lender certain rights under the policy.

Property Holders

Bailee

The party temporarily possessing the personal property in a bailment.

Bailees are responsible for safekeeping property they do not own. Dry cleaners, repair shops, common carriers, and many other businesses temporarily hold property belonging to others. To estimate its property loss exposures, such a business has to consider not only its own property, but also the property held for others.

Apply Your Knowledge

Sam rents retail space in a strip mall, in which he operates a florist shop. His employees make deliveries with two vans owned by the shop. How should an insurance professional analyze each of the three elements of the florist shop's property loss exposures?

Feedback:

- Assets exposed to property loss—Sam has exposure in each of the property types, except for a building. Because he rents the retail space from which his store operates, he does not have the exposure of a building being damaged. However, he does have personal property contained in the rented space of the building. Specifically, he is likely to have equipment to run his business, such as refrigerated display cabinets, telephones, file cabinets, computer equipment, a cash register, and an inventory of flowers and the tools and supplies to arrange and display them. Sam also has exposure with money and securities, as he collects payments from customers. He has exposure related to the vehicles used to deliver flowers as well. The vehicles have a high value and could be expensive to repair or replace. Finally, he has exposure connected to property in transit. The flowers are valuable inventory, and if they are damaged in transit to a customer, Sam will probably have to replace them at his expense.

- Causes of loss—Some of the perils include fire, theft, and collision. Fire could damage or destroy all the types of property at the store or in a van. Theft could also involve all of the individual types of property, including money and securities in particular, personal property in the building, vehicles, and property in transit. Another peril is collision of a van with another object, which could damage both the vehicle and the property in transit in the same accident.

- Financial consequences—Each type of property, if damaged or destroyed, could incur a reduction in value. If property is damaged, the cost to repair or restore it is often the amount of reduction in value. For example, if Sam's van were involved in a collision while making a delivery, it may be possible to have it repaired for a cost that is less than the value of the van; therefore, it would not be a total loss. The value of the van after the collision would be reduced until repairs were completed. The flower arrangements in the van at the time of the collision may be difficult to repair. Consequently, it may be more cost effective to consider them destroyed and replace them. The damaged flowers would have lost all value.

LIABILITY LOSS EXPOSURES

Understanding the elements of liability loss exposures provides an essential foundation for managing them.

These are the three elements of liability loss exposures:

- Assets exposed to liability loss
- Causes of liability loss
- Financial consequences of liability loss

Assets Exposed to Liability Loss

The first element of liability loss exposures consists of assets exposed to liability losses. The asset can be anything of value an individual or organization owns. However, the asset that plaintiffs claim most frequently is money. Money can be used, for example, to make a payment of damages to a plaintiff or to pay attorneys' fees and other costs of defending against claims. Assets owned by an individual or organization, such as property (including buildings, automobiles, and furniture) and investments, can be sold and converted to money that can be used to make a payment to a plaintiff. Furthermore, a plaintiff can claim income that a defendant will receive in the future.

Causes of Liability Loss

The second element of liability loss exposures consists of the causes of liability losses. The cause of a liability loss is the initiation of a claim or lawsuit against an individual or organization by another party seeking damages or some other legal remedy. Even the threat of another party's initiating such a claim or suit can cause a liability loss in the form of costs an individual or organization incurs to investigate and, if necessary, settle the threatened liability claim or suit. Liability claims can arise from various activities. Common examples of such activities include these:

- Autos, watercraft, and other vehicles
- Premises
- Personal activities
- Business operations
- Completed operations
- Products
- Advertising
- Pollution
- Liquor
- Professional activities

Autos, Watercraft, and Other Vehicles

A significant liability loss exposure for almost all persons and businesses comes from the ownership, maintenance, and use of automobiles. In the United States, auto accidents produce the greatest number of liability claims. Even people or businesses that do not own an auto can be held vicariously liable for the operation of an auto by others. For example, an employer could be held liable for an auto accident caused by its employee making a sales call on a customer, whether the employee was driving his own vehicle or one owned by the employer.

Liability loss exposures are also created by owning and operating other conveyances, such as watercraft, aircraft, and recreational vehicles.

Premises

Anyone who owns or occupies real property has a premises liability loss exposure. If a visitor slips on an icy front porch and is injured, the homeowner may be held liable for the injury. A business has a similar loss exposure arising from its premises. For example, a grocery store will probably be held liable if a customer is injured after slipping and falling on a wet floor in the store.

Personal Activities

Individuals can become liable to others when engaged in a personal activity not business related and away from the defendant's premises. For example, a person could hit a golf ball off a tee at a golf course and strike and injure another golfer with the ball. The activity need not be recreational; it could involve, for instance, owning a dog that escapes from the owner's premises and bites a neighbor.

Business Operations

In terms of liability loss exposures, businesses must be concerned not only about the condition of their premises but also about their business operations. Whatever activity the business performs has the potential to cause harm to someone else. Many business operations occur away from the organization's premises. A plumbing contractor, for example, may start a fire in a customer's house while soldering a copper pipe. Similarly, a roofing contractor may drop debris from a ladder and injure a member of the customer's family. In both cases, the customer could make a liability claim against the contractor.

Completed Operations

Even after a plumber, an electrician, a painter, or another contractor completes a job and leaves the work site, a liability loss exposure remains. If faulty wiring or toxic paint leads to an injury, the person or business that performed the work may be liable. Considerable time could pass in the interim, but the person or business may still be held liable if faulty work created the condition that eventually caused the injury. If, for example, a homeowner could prove that a natural-gas explosion in her house was caused by the negligence of the contractor who installed her new furnace, the contractor may be liable for the resulting damage to the house.

Products

Liability resulting from products that cause bodily injury or property damage is a significant exposure for manufacturers. This exposure begins with the design of the product and might not end until the consumer properly disposes of the product. Millions of customers use or consume mass-produced products, foods, and pharmaceuticals. A prescription drug may be dangerous, but the danger might not be known for several years, after which it is too late to help those who have taken the drug.

Advertising

Businesses often include photographs of people using their products in their advertisements. If a local retailer cannot afford professional models, it might use pictures of people using its products or shopping in its store. Unless the retailer obtains proper permission, publishing the pictures could lead to a lawsuit alleging invasion of privacy. Using another company's trademarked slogan or advertisement can also generate a liability claim.

Pollution

Many types of products pollute the environment when they are discarded. In addition, the manufacture of some products creates contaminants that, if not disposed of properly, can cause environmental impairment, or pollution. If an explosion at an oil refinery polluted a nearby body of water, the refinery owner might have a liability loss. The Love Canal case in New York State remains a good example of how industrial products or wastes can have serious detrimental effects on the environment. Toxic wastes in the Love Canal area polluted the ground water and made the surrounding community a dangerous place to live. Cleanup costs and expenses to relocate persons living in the contaminated area can be enormous in such cases.

Liquor

The consumption, serving, and sale of alcohol can present liability loss exposures. Intoxicated persons can pose a threat to themselves as well as to others. Providers of alcohol can be held responsible for customers or guests who become intoxicated and injure someone while driving drunk. Both the drunk driver and the person who served the alcohol can be held legally liable. A business that sells or serves alcoholic beverages, therefore, has a significant liability loss exposure.

Professional Activities

Negligence involves a failure to exercise the degree of care that is reasonable under given circumstances. It is reasonable to expect that professionals with special competence in a particular field or occupation will exercise a higher standard of care in performing their duties than someone without special competence. Attorneys, physicians, architects, engineers, and other professionals are considered experts in their field and are expected to perform accordingly. Professional liability arises if injury or damage can be attributed to a professional's failure to exercise the appropriate standard of care. For insurance professionals and others, this failure is sometimes called errors and omissions (E&O). For medical professionals, it is often called malpractice. For example, a physician who prescribes a drug but ignores the possible side effects may be held liable for any resulting harm to the patient, because accepted medical practice requires the doctor to consider possible side effects. When professionals make errors, the injured party usually expects to be compensated.

Financial Consequences of Liability Loss

The third element of liability loss exposures consists of the financial consequences of such losses. In theory, the financial consequences of a liability loss exposure are limitless. In practice, financial consequences are limited to the total wealth of the person or organization. Although some jurisdictions limit the amounts that can be taken in a claim, liability claims can result in the loss of most or all of a person's or organization's assets. For a person or an organization that has been held legally liable for injury or damage, the financial consequences can be the payment of damages, the payment of defense costs, and damage to the person's or organization's reputation.

Damages

The damages of a liability loss can be more difficult to determine than those involved with other types of losses. For example, the ultimate value of liability claims resulting from a hotel fire injuring hundreds of guests may be hard to predict because each claim is different and it may take years for all of them to reach settlement or be tried in court to a final judgment.

Defense Costs

In addition to damages, the financial consequences of a liability loss may include costs to defend the alleged wrongdoer in court. These defense costs include not only the fees paid to lawyers but also all the other expenses associated with defending a liability claim. Such expenses can include investigation expenses, expert witness fees, premiums for necessary bonds, and other expenses incurred to prepare for and conduct a trial. Even in the unlikely event that all the possible lawsuits against a defendant are ultimately found groundless, defendants and their liability insurers will probably incur substantial defense costs.

Damage to Reputation

A third financial consequence of liability loss may be the defendant's loss of reputation. Such consequences are often difficult to quantify, but they do exist. For example, in 2000, a tire manufacturer recalled more than six million tires after they were alleged to be a factor in rollover crashes. In addition to damages paid and defense costs for the lawsuits that followed, the manufacturer suffered a damaged reputation and resultant loss of sales.

Apply Your Knowledge

Robert and Lillian are married and own a home with a pool in the backyard. Robert frequently goes hunting for sport. Joey, their son, plays Little League baseball. Their daughter, Sally, plays soccer on a team in an organized league. Lillian frequently drives Sally and several of her teammates to and from games. Lillian also serves on the local YMCA board. Describe the family's liability loss exposures in terms of these three elements:

- Assets exposed to a liability loss
- Causes of liability loss
- Financial consequences of liability loss

Feedback:

- Assets exposed to liability loss—Robert and Lillian's cash accounts, home, furniture, autos, future income, and other personal property are exposed to the risk of being liquidated to pay damages to a plaintiff.
- Causes of liability loss—Claims and suits by plaintiffs could result from any of the activities described. The swimming pool in the backyard is

a premises loss exposure that could attract neighborhood children. If a child were to drown while swimming in the pool, his or her parents could accuse Robert and Lillian of negligence. Robert's hunting is a personal activity that could result in a claim for accidently shooting a person. Joey's playing baseball is a personal activity that could result in a claim that Joey hit someone with a ball or bat. Sally's playing soccer is a personal activity that probably has the least significant liability exposure, but other players could claim she injured them by running into or tripping them. Lillian's driving Sally and her teammates to and from games is an auto-related activity that could result in an auto accident and claims that she negligently injured the teammates. Lillian's board service could be considered a professional activity, which could in turn result in a claim alleging that she failed to exercise the standard of care expected of a board member.

• Financial consequences of liability loss—Each of these activities could result in a claim or suit whose value is limited only by the wealth of the family. Even if the claim or suit is without merit, the defense costs and damage to the family members' reputation may be substantial.

PERSONNEL LOSS EXPOSURES

For many organizations, their most valuable assets are their employees because they add to the value of the organization through their physical and mental labor. Understanding the elements of personnel loss exposures provides an essential foundation for managing these exposures and protecting these assets.

A **personnel loss exposure** is composed of these elements:

• Assets exposed to a personnel loss

• Causes of a personnel loss

• Financial consequences of a personnel loss

Assets Exposed to Personnel Loss

While everyone in an organization has value, some people are more easily replaced than others. Valuable employees (**key employees**) present a critical loss exposure to an organization. Similarly, groups of employees who perform crucial functions, if they are all lost simultaneously, can cause a crisis for an organization.

Personnel loss exposures can include several categories of key personnel:

• Individual employees

• Owners, officers, and managers

• Groups of employees

Personnel loss exposure

A condition that presents the possibility of loss caused by a person's death, disability, retirement, or resignation that deprives an organization of the person's special skill or knowledge that the organization cannot readily replace.

Key employee

An employee whose loss to a firm through death or disability before retirement would have economic effects on the company.

Individual Employees

The category of individual employees includes employees with unique talents, creativity, or special skills vital to the organization's ability to meet its goals. These employees do not own, manage, or oversee the organization, but they add value to it. They could be high-performing sales representatives or systems engineers who help focus a firm's efforts on customer needs during a complex engineering project.

Owners, Officers, and Managers

Owners, officers, and managers are responsible for making decisions essential to the organization, as well as managing and motivating others. In organizations in which the owner is a key person, that person's activities, health, and managerial competence all influence the organization's value. A sole proprietorship literally ceases to exist as a legal entity when its owner dies or retires. Similarly, partnerships may legally terminate when a partner dies or retires. The same is true in close corporations, in which ownership is typically concentrated in just a few major shareholders, most of whom are also managers.

 Reality Check

Example of Losing a Key Person

Steve Jobs of Apple, Inc., is an example of how one visionary key person can have a major influence on the success of even a large corporation. The company, which relied on Jobs for its run of successes, was shaken by his health concerns that started when he was diagnosed with pancreatic cancer in 2003. As part of Apple's succession plan to replace Jobs' contributions, the company has hired high-profile academics to provide training for its executives.

[DA07696]

Groups of Employees

Sometimes a group of employees is critically important to an organization, even if an individual employee in that group is not. An organization may be unable to function without the contributions of an important group. With the exception of layoffs, group departure is rare, and when an entire group is laid off, it is usually because it is considered expendable. However, over a short time period, an entire group may leave because of common dissatisfaction (such as poor management), may follow a manager to a new organization, or may be lost because of a catastrophic event.

Causes of Personnel Loss

The causes of personnel losses are the actual means by which an employee is removed from the service of an employer. Each cause of loss varies considerably in frequency and severity. These are some of the major causes of loss:

- Death
- Disability
- Resignation, layoffs, and firing
- Retirement
- Kidnapping

Causes of loss could occur inside or outside the workplace; however, the personnel loss remains the same in both instances.

Death

The death of an employee results in the complete, permanent loss of the employee's services. Unless a disaster occurs, most losses from death are low frequency, and the severity of impact on the employer depends on the employee's value to the organization. The risk of death varies widely according to the nature of the organization's business (for example, financial services versus oil exploration and extraction). Numerous events, accidental or natural, can cause death of key employees. Risk control efforts can focus on events that can result in the death of large numbers of employees at once, such as fire, explosion, severe windstorm, and terrorist attacks.

Disability

Disability

The inability (because of impairment) of a person to meet his or her personal, social, or occupational demands; other activities of daily living; or statutory or other legal requirements.

Although death as a cause of loss often attracts more media attention than disability, overall disability occurs far more frequently than death. The severity of personnel losses resulting from **disability** can be equal to those resulting from death if the disability is permanent and total. However, temporary disability is more common than permanent disability, and partial disability is more common than total disability.

As with death, numerous accidental or natural events can cause disability of key employees. Risk control efforts can focus on events that can disable large numbers of employees at once and on events that disable many employees over time, such as workplace injuries.

Workplace injuries are often related to companies' failing to take adequate safety measures. Examples include these:

- Failing to apply ergonomics to prevent injuries, such as carpal tunnel syndrome, from repetitive motions
- Not allowing workers performing physical labor to take periodic breaks
- Operating an assembly process too quickly, thereby encouraging workers to take chances assembling products and increasing their exposure to potential injury

Resignation, Layoffs, and Firing

Employees may leave an employer voluntarily (for example, by resignation) or involuntarily (for example, by a layoff or firing). Resignation (voluntary separation) is an expected part of doing business. The frequency of resignations depends, in part, on the type of industry. Some organizations, such as fast-food restaurants or construction companies, could expect very high turnover rates, while others, such as accounting firms or governments, could expect a low turnover rate. The severity of a resignation depends on who is resigning. If a key person leaves or if a group of employees sharing a similar function departs simultaneously, the severity of the personnel losses may be high.

Involuntary employee separations generally are not considered a personnel loss because the organization has determined that it is better off without the employees. If, for example, a layoff is the result of a change in the organization's goals—meaning that the laid-off employees are no longer needed for the organization to operate efficiently—their departure will have a minimal effect on the organization's success. Employees are typically fired for cause—that is, for not performing their jobs effectively or behaving in an unacceptable manner. Usually, organizations rationally consider all the costs and benefits of retaining an employee before firing him or her.

Retirement

While death and voluntary resignation often occur suddenly, retirement is usually planned. With plenty of notice, an organization can usually prepare for the retirement of even key personnel by locating and training replacements. However, as with resignation or death, when a key person decides to retire suddenly, the losses can be severe.

Kidnapping

Kidnapping of a key employee can be a significant cause of loss for employers, especially for those with operations outside the United States. Some kidnappings result from political unrest, but employers are more likely to face financially motivated kidnappings, such as kidnapping for ransom.

Kidnapping is a fairly low-frequency event that tends to occur mostly in high-risk locations. The most obvious loss to an employer is the absence of a key employee. In this sense, kidnapping losses are similar to death and disability losses; the severity depends on the importance of the employee and the cost of temporarily or permanently replacing him or her.

Financial Consequences of Personnel Losses

Because employees are assets of an organization, the financial effect of the loss of these assets (personnel losses) on an organization is similar to the effect of property and liability losses in that they reduce the value of the organization. The major difference is that personnel losses typically manifest themselves as net income losses. These are some of the financial consequences of personnel losses:

- Loss of the value the employee contributed to the organization. (In cases in which a key person is lost, this may be severe, with the organization's value lowered at least for the short term.)
- Replacement costs (recruitment, interviewing, and training of replacement personnel).
- Losses to the organization's value caused by negative publicity.
- Losses caused by low morale, such as reduced productivity and increased illness.

Apply Your Knowledge

Roger and Susan are realtors and employees of the same real estate agency. Roger has been with the agency for thirty years and plans to retire next month. He has an excellent reputation and almost more referral business than he can service. Susan has been with the agency for a year and is considering a job offer from another agency. She is a hard worker but is still learning how to best serve her clients and has few referrals. Roger and Susan were traveling to a sales convention in Susan's car when they were broadsided by a driver who failed to stop at a red light. Both Roger and Susan were injured and taken to a hospital. The doctors estimate both Roger and Susan will be totally disabled for four months. Describe the real estate agency's personnel loss exposures in terms of the three elements of personnel loss exposures:

Feedback:

- Assets exposed to personnel loss—Roger and Susan are valuable assets of the agency because they add to the value of the organization through their physical and mental labor. While both Roger and Susan have value, Susan can be replaced more easily than Roger. Roger is a key employee of the agency because of his referral business, which provides substantial income to the agency.
- Causes of personnel loss—The four-month disability resulting from the auto accident is an immediate cause of loss for the agency. Roger's planned retirement is another cause of loss. By the time Roger recovers from the accident, it will be past his retirement date. So, in effect, the

agency might as well consider Roger's disability to be permanent. Susan's potential resignation to go work for another agency once she recovers from her disability is another possible cause of loss.

- Financial consequences of personnel loss—The referral business may not continue if Roger is not working at the agency. However, Roger's employer probably knows about his planned retirement date. Therefore, his replacement has likely been hired and trained and may have met with Roger's clients to assure them that the same excellent level of service will continue after Roger's departure. The costs to replace Roger were probably incurred before the auto accident, and Roger's loss of value to the agency minimized. Furthermore, the accident may generate sympathy in the market that may result in more business for the agency. Susan has few referrals, and her absence will not be as much of a loss to the agency economically whether she comes back in four months or decides to work for another agency.

NET INCOME LOSS EXPOSURES

Understanding the elements of net income loss exposures and how they result from other causes of loss provides an essential foundation for managing such exposures.

A net income loss exposure is a condition that presents the possibility of loss caused by a reduction in net income. These are the three elements of net income loss exposures:

- Assets exposed to net income loss
- Causes of net income loss
- Financial consequences of net income loss

Assets Exposed to Net Income Loss

The asset exposed to loss in a net income loss exposure is the future stream of net income of the individual or organization. The future stream of net income includes revenues minus expenses and income taxes in a given time period. If income taxes are considered to be part of an organization's expenses, a net income loss is a reduction in revenue, an increase in expenses, or a combination of the two.

For example, a fire at an organization's production facilities could not only destroy the facilities (a property loss exposure), but also force the organization to stop operations for a few weeks, resulting in a loss of sales revenue (a net income loss exposure). Similarly, if a tornado damaged the retail store of a self-employed business owner, the inability to earn income while the store is being repaired represents a net income loss exposure.

Net income losses are often the result of a property, liability, or personnel loss (all of which are direct losses). Therefore, net income losses are considered to be indirect losses. A direct loss is a loss that occurs immediately as the result of a particular cause of loss, such as the reduction in the value of a building that has been damaged by fire.

An indirect loss is a loss that results from, but is not directly caused by, a particular cause of loss. For example, the reduction in revenue that an organization suffers as a result of fire damage to one of its buildings is an indirect loss. Estimating indirect losses is often challenging because of the difficulty in projecting the effects that a direct loss will have on revenues and expenses. For instance, a litigation manager working for a restaurant chain may be able to project with some certainty the amount needed to settle a lawsuit brought by a customer accusing the restaurant of food poisoning (a direct liability loss). However, projecting the effect on future restaurant sales (an indirect loss) of any negative publicity relating to the lawsuit would be more difficult.

In the insurance industry, the term "net income losses" is usually associated with property losses, and some insurance policies provide coverage for net income losses related to property losses. However, there are many other causes of net income losses.

Causes of Net Income Loss

Various circumstances can lead to a net income loss. For many of these causes of loss, it can often be difficult to discern when the direct property loss, liability loss, personnel loss, or business risk loss ends and when the indirect net income loss begins.

Property Loss

A property loss is a loss sustained by a person or an organization resulting from damage to property in which that person or organization has a financial interest. Damage to property can cause a reduction in that property's value, sometimes to zero. For example, when a car is stolen, the owner suffers a total loss of that property because the owner no longer has use of it. As a result of the theft, the owner could incur a net income loss by renting a replacement vehicle. The owner's expenses will increase, but the added expense may be necessary in order to allow the owner to continue commuting to and from work.

Similarly, a nuclear power plant that just endured an earthquake may incur a net income loss when it pays the extra expense of immediately shipping in a replacement water pump. By incurring the additional shipping costs to receive the pump more quickly, the plant may be able to prevent a larger direct loss of radiation contamination and resume operations sooner. This action would also avoid a larger loss of income and, consequently, a larger net income loss.

Liability Loss

Liability losses are caused by a claim of legal liability from someone who is usually seeking monetary damages against a person or an organization. The direct costs that a person or an organization can incur as a result of a liability claim include damages and defense costs. In addition, a liability loss can result in a net income loss. For example, if a driver of a car develops a history of poor driving and injures multiple parties in a series of accidents who claim liability against the driver, the costs of renewing the driver's personal auto policy, if available, will likely be substantially higher. Many doctors also incur an increase in net income losses when their professional liability insurance coverage renews at a higher rate as a consequence of successful claims of professional malpractice made against them.

Another example of increased net income losses can occur when two organizations merge or one organization acquires another. Part of the negotiations associated with drafting the agreement joining the organizations involves whether either of them is facing pending or expected litigation. If so, the organization being sued will often have to sacrifice some form of net income.

Personnel Loss

A personnel loss is often caused by a key person's death, disability, retirement, or resignation. Such a loss deprives those dependent on that person of a special skill or knowledge that cannot be readily replaced. As an example, a family incurs a net income loss as a result of a personnel loss when a homemaker is temporarily disabled because of an auto accident and the family must pay someone else to perform many of the essential services needed to maintain the household while the homemaker is recovering. The wages paid to the worker to perform these services constitute a net income loss. If the homemaker were also a wage earner outside the home, the loss of income while he or she recovers from the disability would also be a net income loss.

An example of personnel losses that cause organizations to incur net income losses involves contractors recruiting employees to work in areas of the world where hostile military conflicts are ongoing. The frequent personnel losses caused by death or disability of the contractors' current employees force the contractors to pay higher salaries to attract new employees and retain existing ones.

Business Risks

Business risk refers to risk that is inherent in the operation of a particular organization. These are examples of potential net income losses from business risk that may affect individuals or organizations:

- Loss of goodwill—Organizations are concerned with maintaining goodwill among customers and other stakeholders. Goodwill can be lost in many ways, including providing poor service, offering obsolete products, or mismanaging operations. For a not-for-profit organization, goodwill is equivalent to reputation. Goodwill has broader implications than just reputation in for-profit organizations, because goodwill may have a monetary value. To maintain goodwill, many organizations choose to pay for certain accidents for which they are not legally responsible. For example, if a guest sustains an injury on an organization's premises and the organization did not cause or contribute to the injury, that organization might still choose to pay any medical bills in order to maintain goodwill and avoid adverse publicity.

- Failure to perform—Net income losses may occur as a result of some type of failure to perform, including a product's failure to perform as promised, a contractor's failure to complete a construction project as scheduled, or a debtor's failure to make scheduled payments.
- Missed opportunities—An organization may suffer a net income loss as a result of a missed opportunity for profit. For example, an organization that delays a decision to modify its product in response to market demand might lose market share and profit that it could have made on that updated product.

Financial Consequences of Net Income Losses

The financial consequences of a net income loss are a reduction in revenues, an increase in expenses, or a combination of the two. To determine the severity of a net income loss, it is sometimes necessary to project what revenue and expenses would have been had no loss occurred. Once a loss occurs, the difference between the projected net income and the actual net income earned after the accident is the net income loss. The worst-case scenario for a net income loss is a decrease in revenues to zero and a significant increase in expenses for a prolonged period.

Apply Your Knowledge

Sally is a single parent of two boys. She owns the house they live in and rents an apartment above their garage to a young married couple. The rent pays half of Sally's monthly mortgage payment. The rest of Sally's income comes from her job as a reporter for a newspaper whose advertising income has been declining for years. Describe a significant net income loss exposure, based on the facts presented, that could result from each of the following: a property loss, a liability loss, and a personnel loss.

Feedback:

- Property loss—The house that Sally and her boys live in could become uninhabitable because of fire, flood, or another disaster. If that happened, the value of their home would decrease sharply—a direct property loss. Furthermore, the family would incur the indirect, consequential loss of paying for another place to live. Costs to rent a hotel room or an apartment would be incurred until the house was repaired, which could take months. If the apartment over the garage also became uninhabitable, the young couple would move out, and the monthly rent they paid would stop. Without the rental income, Sally may not be able to pay the full amount of the mortgage herself, which could result in the bank declaring her mortgage in default and foreclosing on the property. Sally and her boys would then lose their home.

- Liability loss—If the husband of the young couple slipped on the outdoor stairs going down to his car and injured his knee, he may decide to sue Sally. He could claim the stairs were not properly maintained and presented a hazardous condition that she should have prevented. Sally would incur the direct costs of her defense but may also incur the indirect costs of repairing the steps and losing income for being off work on the days she must attend trial of the lawsuit. The indirect costs would increase Sally's expenses and thereby lower her net income.

- Personnel loss—The newspaper for which Sally works has been losing advertising income for years. If its management decides it must cut expenses, it may decide to do so by laying off workers, including Sally. She will probably be able to find other employment eventually, but until she does, her family will lose the income she would have earned.

LOSS EXPOSURE IDENTIFICATION METHODS

For individuals, common property and liability exposures can be identified by a property-casualty insurance producer as part of an assessment of insurance needs. Similarly, individuals' net income loss exposures can be identified by life insurance producers as part of a needs assessment for life and health insurance products. For organizations, loss exposure identification is more complex, using a variety of methods and sources of information.

The methods that organizations use to identify their loss exposures include document analysis, compliance review, inspections, and consultations.

Document Analysis

The documents used and produced by an organization can be a key source of information regarding loss exposures. Some of these documents are standardized and originate from outside the organization, such as questionnaires, checklists, and surveys. Other documents are organization-specific, such as financial statements and accounting records, contracts, insurance policies, policy and procedure manuals, flowcharts and organizational charts, and loss histories.

Checklists and Questionnaires

Standardized documents published outside an organization, such as insurance coverage checklists and risk assessment questionnaires, broadly categorize the loss exposures that most organizations typically face. Although commercial publishers and trade associations have developed checklists and question-naires, most are created by insurers.

A questionnaire captures more descriptive information than a checklist. For example, as well as identifying a loss exposure, a questionnaire may capture information about the values exposed to loss. The questionnaire can be designed to include questions that address key property, liability, net income, and personnel loss exposures.

Questionnaires produced by insurers are known as insurance surveys because most of the questions on these surveys relate to loss exposures for which insurance is generally available. In contrast with insurance surveys, risk man-agement or risk assessment questionnaires have a broader focus and address both insurable and uninsurable loss exposures. However, a disadvantage of risk assessment questionnaires is that they typically can be completed only with considerable expense, time, and effort and still may not identify all possible loss exposures.

Financial Statements

Risk professionals with accounting or finance expertise sometimes begin the loss exposure identification process by reviewing an organization's financial statements, including the balance sheet, income statement, statement of cash flows, and supporting statements. As well as identifying current loss exposures, financial statements and accounting records can be used to identify any future plans that could lead to new loss exposures.

An organization's **balance sheet** is the financial statement that reports the assets, liabilities, and owners' equity of the organization as of a specific date. Owners' equity, or net worth, is the amount by which assets exceed liabilities. Asset entries indicate property values that could be reduced by loss. Liability entries show what the organization owes and enable the risk professional to identify obligations (such as mortgage payments) that the organization must fulfill, even if it were to close temporarily as a result of a business interruption.

The **income statement** shows an organization's revenues, expenses, and net income (profit or loss) for the particular accounting period.

The **statement of cash flows** (also called the statement of sources and uses of funds) is the financial statement that summarizes the cash effects of an organi-zation's operating, investing, and financing activities during a specific period.

Funds-flow analysis on the statement of cash flows can identify the amounts of cash either subject to loss or available to meet continuing obligations. For example, the statement of cash flows would indicate the amount of cash that

Balance sheet

The financial statement that reports the assets, liabilities, and owners' equity of an organization as of a specific date.

Income statement

The financial statement that reports an organization's profit or loss for a specific period by comparing the revenues generated with the expenses incurred to produce those revenues.

Statement of cash flows

The financial statement that summarizes the cash effects of an organization's operating, investing, and financing activities during a specific period.

is typically on hand to pay for any losses resulting from loss exposures that have been retained by the organization.

The primary advantage of financial statements from a risk professional's perspective is that they help to identify major categories of loss exposures. For example, property loss exposures can be seen in the asset section of the balance sheet, and the income statement discloses the amount of net income that could be lost during a suspension of operations.

A major disadvantage of using financial statements for identifying loss exposures is that although they identify major categories of loss exposures, they do not identify or quantify the individual loss exposures. For example, the balance sheet may show that there is $5 million in property exposed to loss, but it does not specify how many properties make up that $5 million, where those properties are located, or how much each individual property is worth. Moreover, the real and personal property values recorded in financial statements are based on accounting conventions and are not accurate for purposes of insurance or risk management.

Another disadvantage is that financial statements depict past activities—for example, revenue that has already been earned, expenses that have already been incurred, prior valuations of assets and liabilities, and business operations that have already taken place. They are of limited help in identifying projected values or future events. Therefore, even after using financial statements for loss exposure identification, risk professionals still need to project what events might occur in the future, determine how these future events could change loss exposures, and analyze and quantify potential losses accordingly.

Contracts

A contract is an agreement entered into by two or more parties that specifies the parties' responsibilities to one another. Analyzing an organization's contracts may help identify its property and liability loss exposures and help determine who has assumed responsibility for which loss exposures. It is often necessary to consult with legal experts when interpreting contracts.

Contract analysis can both identify the loss exposures generated or reduced by an organization's contracts and ensure that the organization is not assuming liability that is disproportionate to its stake in the contract. Ongoing contract analysis is part of monitoring and maintaining a risk management program.

A contract can generate liability loss exposures in two ways. First, the organization can accept financial responsibility for another party's losses through a contract, such as a **hold-harmless agreement** (also referred to as an indemnity agreement). For example, a manufacturer may enter into a hold-harmless agreement with its distributor under which the manufacturer agrees to indemnify the distributor (pay the losses for which the distributor is liable) if the distributor is found liable for injuries caused by a defect in the manufacturer's product.

Hold-harmless agreement (or indemnity agreement)
A contractual provision that obligates one of the parties to assume the legal liability of another party.

The second way a contract may generate a liability loss exposure is if the organization breaches a valid contract. For example, if a manufacturer agrees to deliver goods to a distributor and then fails to deliver those goods, the manufacturer has breached the contract and the distributor is entitled to bring a claim against the manufacturer.

Alternatively, an organization can reduce or eliminate the financial consequences of its liability loss exposures by entering into a contract that transfers its liability to another organization. For example, an organization can enter into a hold-harmless agreement under which the other party agrees to indemnify the organization in the event of a liability claim.

Insurance Policies

Analyzing insurance policies reveals many of the insurable loss exposures that an organization faces. However, an organization does not necessarily face every loss exposure covered by its policies. Furthermore, the organization may face many other loss exposures that either cannot be covered by insurance policies or are covered by policies the organization has chosen not to purchase.

To identify insurance coverage that an organization has not purchased, and therefore potentially identify insurable loss exposures that have not been insured, a risk professional can compare his or her organization's coverage against an industry checklist of insurance policies currently in effect.

Organizational Policies and Records

Loss exposures can be identified using organizational policies and records, such as corporate by-laws, board minutes, employee manuals, procedure manuals, mission statements, and risk management policies. For example, policy and procedure manuals may identify some of the organization's property loss exposures by referencing equipment, or pinpoint liability loss exposures by referencing hazardous materials with which employees come into contact.

As well as identifying existing loss exposures, some documents may indicate impending changes in loss exposures. For example, board minutes may indicate management's plans to sell or purchase property, thereby either reducing or increasing its property loss exposures.

One drawback to using policies and records to identify loss exposures is the sheer volume of documents that some organizations generate internally. It may be virtually impossible to have one employee or a group of employees examine every internal document. In these instances, insurance and risk management professionals would need to examine a representative sample of documents. This makes the task manageable but increases the likelihood that some loss exposures will be overlooked.

Flowcharts and Organizational Charts

A flowchart is a diagram that depicts the sequence of activities performed by a particular organization or process. An organization can use flowcharts to show the nature and use of the resources involved in its operations as well as the sequence of and relationships between those operations.

A manufacturer's flowchart might start with raw material acquisition and end with the finished product's delivery to the ultimate consumer. Individual entries on the flowchart, including the processes involved and the means by which products move from one process to the next, can help identify loss exposures—particularly critical loss exposures.

For example, the flowchart might illustrate that every item produced must be spray-painted during the production process. This activity presents a critical property loss exposure, because an explosion at the spray-painting location might disable the entire production line. The simplified flowchart in the exhibit reveals that difficulties with getting the furniture through customs at the Los Angeles/Long Beach Seaport could disrupt the entire furniture supply chain. See the exhibit "Manufacturer Flowchart."

Information can also be obtained from organizational charts. An organizational chart depicts the hierarchy of an organization's personnel and can help to identify key personnel for whom the organization may have a personnel loss exposure. This chart can also help track the flow of information through an organization and identify any bottlenecks that may exist. Although organizational charts can be fundamental in properly identifying personnel loss exposures, an individual's place on an organizational chart does not guarantee that he or she is a key employee. The organizational chart does not necessarily reflect the importance of the individual to the continued operation or profitability of the organization.

Loss Histories

Loss history analysis, that is, reviewing an organization's own losses or those suffered by comparable organizations, can help a risk professional to identify and analyze loss exposures. Loss histories of comparable organizations are particularly helpful if the organization is too small or too new to have a sizeable record of its own past losses, or if the organization's own historical loss records are incomplete.

Any past loss can recur unless the organization has had a fundamental change in operations or property owned. Accordingly, loss histories are often an important indicator of an organization's current or future loss exposures. However, loss histories will not identify any loss exposures that have not resulted in past losses.

Manufacturer Flowchart

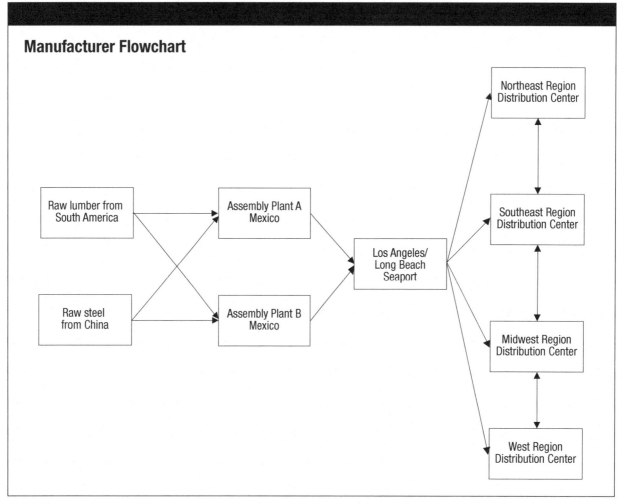

[DA02556]

Compliance Review

In addition to document analysis, risk professionals may also conduct compliance reviews to identify loss exposures. A compliance review determines an organization's compliance with local, state, and federal statutes and regulations. The organization can conduct most of the compliance review itself if it has adequate in-house legal and accounting resources. Otherwise, it may have to use outside expertise.

Compliance reviews can be expensive and time consuming. Furthermore, because regulations are often changing, remaining in compliance requires ongoing monitoring. As a result, conducting a compliance review simply to identify loss exposures is often impractical. However, the cost of compliance reviews can be justified by the possibility that monitoring and maintaining compliance can prevent significant losses that the organization would otherwise incur.

Inspections

Some loss exposures are best identified by inspections, that is, information-gathering visits to critical sites both within and outside an organization. Such visits often reveal loss exposures that would not appear in written descriptions of the organization's operations and therefore should lead to a more complete list of loss exposures.

Inspections should ideally be conducted by individuals whose background and skills equip them to identify unexpected loss exposures. Additionally, the inspector should take the opportunity to discuss the particular operations with front-line personnel, who are often best placed to identify nonobvious loss exposures. Therefore, an inspection can overlap the method discussed next.

Consultation

Thorough loss exposure identification includes consultations with employees inside the organization and expert practitioners outside the organization, to render a more complete and objective picture of the organization's loss exposures.

While an inspection can only reveal what is happening during the inspection, a consultation or an interview can elicit information about what occurred before the inspection, what might be planned for the future, or what could go or has gone wrong that has not been properly addressed.

Interviews with employees can be conducted to gather information about their jobs and departments. These interviews should include a range of employees from every level of the organization. Questionnaires can be designed for use in conjunction with these interviews to ensure that they are comprehensive and are eliciting as much information as possible.

To obtain an external perspective, practitioners in fields such as law, finance, statistics, accounting, auditing, information technology, and risk management can be consulted. The special knowledge of experts in identifying particular loss exposures is an invaluable resource.

One area of specialization that often requires such expert services is **hazard analysis**. For example, concerns about environmental hazards might require a specialist to take air or water samples and a specialized laboratory to analyze them. Although hazard analysis is focused on loss exposures that have already been identified, the results of the analysis often identify previously overlooked loss exposures.

Hazard analysis
A method of analysis that identifies conditions that increase the frequency or severity of loss.

SUMMARY

Property loss exposures are analyzed in these terms:

- Assets exposed to property loss
- Causes of loss to property
- Financial consequences of property losses
- Parties affected by property losses

These are the three elements of liability loss exposures:

- Assets exposed to a liability loss, which include a defendant's property and future income
- Causes of liability loss, which could arise from various activities
- Financial consequences of liability loss, which include damages, defense costs, and damage to reputation

These are the three elements of personnel loss exposures:

- Assets exposed to a personnel loss, which include individual employees; owners, officers, and managers; and groups of employees
- Causes of a personnel loss, which include death, disability, resignation, layoffs, firing, retirement, and kidnapping
- Financial consequences of a personnel loss, which include loss of the value of an employee's contribution, replacement costs, loss due to negative publicity, and reduced productivity and increased illness caused by low morale

Net income loss exposures are characterized by these three elements:

- Assets exposed to a net income loss exposure—The future stream of net income of the individual or organization.
- Causes of net income loss—Direct property, liability, and personnel losses or business risks.
- Financial consequences of net income loss—These include a reduction in revenues, an increase in expenses, or a combination of the two.

Because identifying loss exposures is the beginning of the risk management process, it should be done thoroughly and systematically. Various methods can be used to identify loss exposures, including document analysis, compliance review, inspections, and consultation.

3

Analyzing Loss Exposures

Educational Objectives

After learning the content of this assignment, you should be able to:

▷ Explain why data used in analyzing loss exposures should be relevant, complete, consistent, and organized.

▷ Describe the nature of probability with respect to theoretical and empirical probability and the law of large numbers.

▷ Describe the two requirements of any properly constructed probability distribution and the characteristics of discrete and continuous probability distributions.

▷ Describe the measures of central tendency and how they can be used in analyzing loss exposures.

▷ Explain how the standard deviation and the coefficient of variation measure dispersion in a probability distribution.

▷ Describe the characteristics of normal distributions and how they can be used in risk management and insurance.

▷ Explain how to analyze loss exposures considering the four dimensions of loss and data credibility.

Analyzing Loss Exposures

DATA REQUIREMENTS FOR EXPOSURE ANALYSIS

Loss exposure analysis is often based on probability and the statistical analysis of data. The statistical analysis of loss exposures starts with gathering sufficient data in a suitable form. Once the data has been collected, it can be subjected to a variety of probability and statistical techniques that are frequently used by risk professionals.

The most common basis of an analysis of current or future loss exposures is information about past losses arising from similar loss exposures. To accurately analyze loss exposures using data on past losses, the data should be relevant, complete, consistent, and organized.

Relevant Data

To analyze current loss exposures based on historical data, the past loss data for the loss exposures in question must be relevant to the current or future loss exposures. For example, if an organization is trying to assess its auto physical damage loss exposures for the next twelve months, it may examine its auto physical damage losses for the last four or five years and then take into account any changes in the makeup of its auto fleet and the rate of increase for repair costs to determine potential losses for the next twelve months.

Although the organization may have auto physical damage records for the last twenty or thirty years, much of that data may no longer be relevant because of advances in auto engineering. Modern cars use different designs, materials, and systems that increase passenger safety at the expense of increased physical damage to the auto in the event of an accident. Therefore, data from past years may not be relevant to today's auto physical damage loss exposures.

Similarly, relevant data for property losses includes the property's repair or replacement cost at the time it is to be restored, not the property's historical value (its original cost) or book value (its historical value minus accumulated depreciation). For liability losses, the data should relate to past claims that are substantially the same as the potential future claims being assessed. Even relatively minor differences in the factual and legal bases of liability claims can produce substantially different outcomes and costs.

Complete Data

Obtaining complete data about past losses for particular loss exposures often requires relying on others, both inside and outside the organization. What constitutes complete data depends largely on the nature of the loss exposure being considered.

Having complete information helps to isolate the cause of each loss. Furthermore, having complete data enables the risk professional to make reasonably reliable estimates of the dollar amounts of the future losses.

For example, considering loss exposures related to employee injuries would require historical loss data to include information regarding loss amounts, the employee's experience and training, the time of day of the loss, the task being performed, and the supervisor on duty at the time. Similarly, complete data on a property loss to a piece of machinery would include the cost of repairing or replacing any damaged or inoperative machinery, the resulting loss of revenue, any extra expenses, or any overtime wages paid to maintain production.

Consistent Data

To be valid for making risk management decisions about future losses, loss data must also be consistent in at least two respects. If data is inconsistent in either respect, the future loss exposures could be significantly underestimated or overestimated.

First, the loss data must be collected on a consistent basis for all recorded losses. Loss data is often collected from a variety of sources, each of which may use different accounting methods. Consequently, data collected in this manner is likely to be inconsistent.

For example, one common source of inconsistency results when some of the loss amounts being analyzed are reported as estimates and others are reported as actual paid amounts. Similarly, data will be inconsistent if some amounts are reported at their original cost and others are reported at their current replacement cost.

Second, data must be expressed in constant dollars, to adjust for differences in price levels. Differences in price levels will also lead to inconsistency. Two physically identical losses occurring in different years will probably have different values. Inflation distorts the later loss, making it appear more severe because it is measured in less valuable dollars.

To prevent this distortion, historical losses should be adjusted (indexed) so that loss data is expressed in constant dollars. To express data in constant dollars means that the amounts reported are comparable in terms of the value of goods and services that could be purchased in a particular benchmark year. Price indices are used to adjust data so that they are in constant dollars.

For example, suppose losses were reported over the four-year period 20X1 through 20X4. To convert the 20X1 losses to 20X4 (constant) values for comparison, multiply the 20X1 losses by 1.08 (assuming an 8 percent increase in prices from 20X1 through 20X4). Similarly, the 20X2 losses and 20X3 losses would be multiplied by the appropriate price indices (for example, 1.06 and 1.03, respectively) to convert them to constant values for comparison.

Organized Data

Even if relevant, complete, and consistent, data that is not appropriately organized will be difficult to use to identify patterns and trends that will help to reveal and quantify potential future loss exposures. Data can be organized in a variety of different ways, depending on which is most useful for the analysis being performed.

For example, listing losses for particular loss exposures by calendar dates may be useful for detecting seasonal patterns but may not disclose patterns that could be revealed by listing such losses by size. An array of losses—amounts of losses listed in increasing or decreasing value—could reveal clusters of losses by severity and could also focus attention on large losses, which are often most important for insurance and risk management decisions. Organizing losses by size is also the foundation for developing loss severity distributions or loss trends over time.

NATURE OF PROBABILITY

The probability of an event is the relative frequency with which the event can be expected to occur in the long run in a stable environment. Determining the probability that a certain event will occur can be an important part of exposure analysis in the risk management process.

Concepts affecting the basic nature of probability include theoretical probability, empirical probability, and the law of large numbers.

Theoretical Probability and Empirical Probability

Any probability can be expressed as a fraction, percentage, or decimal. For example, the probability of a head on a coin toss can be expressed as 1/2, 50 percent, or .50. The probability of an event that is totally impossible is 0 and the probability of an absolutely certain event is 1.0. Therefore, the probabilities of all events that are neither totally impossible nor absolutely certain are greater than 0 but less than 1.0.

Probabilities can be developed either from theoretical considerations or from historical data. **Theoretical probability** is probability that is based on theoretical principles rather than on actual experience. Probabilities associated with events such as coin tosses or dice throws can be developed from theoretical considerations and are unchanging. For example, from a description of a fair

Theoretical probability
Probability that is based on theoretical principles rather than on actual experience.

coin or die, a person who has never seen either a coin or a die can calculate the probability of flipping a head or rolling a four.

Empirical probability is probability that is based on actual experience. For example, the probability that a sixty-two-year-old male will die in a particular year cannot be theoretically determined, but must be estimated by studying the loss experience of a sample of men aged sixty-two. The empirical probabilities deduced solely from historical data may change as new data are discovered or as the environment that produces those events changes.

Empirical probabilities are only estimates whose accuracy depends on the size and representative nature of the samples being studied. In contrast, theoretical probabilities are constant as long as the physical conditions that generate them remain unchanged.

Although it may be preferable to use theoretical probabilities because of their unchanging nature, they are not applicable or available in most of the situations that insurance and risk management professionals are likely to analyze, such as automobile accidents or workers compensation claims. As a result, empirical probabilities must be used.

Law of Large Numbers

Probability analysis is particularly effective for projecting losses in organizations that have (1) a substantial volume of data on past losses and (2) fairly stable operations so that (except for price level changes) patterns of past losses presumably will continue in the future. In organizations with this type of unchanging environment, past losses can be viewed as a sample of all possible losses that the organization might suffer.

The larger the number of past losses an organization has experienced, the larger the sample of losses that can be used in the analysis. Consequently, the forecasts of future losses are more reliable (consistent over time) because the forecast is based on a larger sample of the environment that produced the losses. This is an application of the **law of large numbers**.

As an example, suppose an urn holds four marbles. One of the marbles is red and three are black. Assume that the number of red or black marbles is not known. The task is to estimate the theoretical probability of choosing a red marble on one draw (sample) from the urn by repeatedly sampling the marbles and replacing each in the urn after the sampling.

After twenty samples a red marble has been chosen eight times, which yields an empirical frequency of 40 percent (8/20). However, this estimate is inaccurate because the theoretical probability is 25 percent (1/4), given that only one of the four marbles is red.

According to the law of large numbers, the relative inaccuracy between the empirical frequency (40 percent in this case) and the theoretical probability (25 percent) will decline, on average, as the sample size increases. That is,

Empirical probability (a posteriori probability)
A probability measure that is based on actual experience through historical data or from the observation of facts.

Probability analysis
A technique for forecasting events, such as accidental and business losses, on the assumption that they are governed by an unchanging probability distribution.

Law of large numbers
A mathematical principle stating that as the number of similar but independent exposure units increases, the relative accuracy of predictions about future outcomes (losses) also increases.

as the number of samples increases from 20 to 200 or 2,000, the empirical frequency of choosing a red marble gets closer and closer to 25 percent.

The law of large numbers has some limitations. It can be used to more accurately forecast future events only when the events being forecast meet all three of these criteria:

- The events have occurred in the past under substantially identical conditions and have resulted from unchanging, basic causal forces.

- The events can be expected to occur in the future under the same, unchanging conditions.

- The events have been, and will continue to be, both independent of one another and sufficiently numerous.

CHARACTERISTICS OF PROBABILITY DISTRIBUTIONS

After probabilities have been determined, probability distributions can be constructed. The information provided by probability distributions can be instrumental in analyzing loss exposures and making risk management decisions.

A properly constructed **probability distribution** always contains outcomes that are both mutually exclusive and collectively exhaustive, and it must also show the probabilities associated with each of the possible outcomes. There are two forms of probability distributions: discrete and continuous. A discrete probability distribution has a finite number of possible outcomes, and a continuous probability distribution has an infinite number of possible outcomes.

Probability distribution
A presentation (table, chart, or graph) of probability estimates of a particular set of circumstances and of the probability of each possible outcome.

Requirements of a Properly Constructed Probability Distribution

The first requirement of any properly constructed probability distribution is that it must contain a list of outcomes that are mutually exclusive and collectively exhaustive. For example, on one flip of a coin, only one outcome is possible: heads or tails. Therefore, those two outcomes are mutually exclusive. In addition, these two outcomes are the only outcomes possible and, therefore, are collectively exhaustive.

To illustrate further, the exhibit shows a probability distribution of the number of hurricanes making landfall in a fictitious state (State X) during any given hurricane season. The six outcomes (either no hurricanes or more than four hurricanes making landfall) are mutually exclusive because only one of these outcomes is possible for any given hurricane season. Moreover, these outcomes are collectively exhaustive because they are the only possible outcomes. See the exhibit "Number of Hurricanes Making Landfall in State X During One Hurricane Season."

Number of Hurricanes Making Landfall in State X During One Hurricane Season

Number of Hurricanes Making Landfall	Probability
0	.300
1	.350
2	.200
3	.147
4	.002
5+	.001
Total Probability	1.000

[DA02572]

The second requirement of any properly constructed probability distribution is that it must show the probabilities associated with each of the possible outcomes. The "Number of Hurricanes Making Landfall in State X During One Hurricane Season" exhibit meets this requirement in its Probability column, which shows the probabilities for each of the six possible outcomes. These probabilities total 1.0 (or 100 percent), which confirms that the outcomes are collectively exhaustive.

Theoretical Probability Distribution Example

Theoretical probability distributions (based on theoretical principles rather than on actual experience) are seldom used in risk management, but they are helpful in understanding probability distributions. For an example of a theoretical probability distribution, consider the probability distribution of the total number of points on one throw of two dice, one red and one green. There are thirty-six equally likely outcomes (green 1, red 1; green 1, red 2; … green 6, red 6). The dice-rolling exhibit shows three alternate presentations of this probability distribution—a table, a chart, and a graph. See the exhibit "Probability Distribution of Total Points on One Roll of Two Dice."

Probability Distribution of Total Points on One Roll of Two Dice

A. Table of Outcomes

Red Die

Green Die		1	2	3	4	5	6
	1	2	3	4	5	6	7
	2	3	4	5	6	7	8
	3	4	5	6	7	8	9
	4	5	6	7	8	9	10
	5	6	7	8	9	10	11
	6	7	8	9	10	11	12

B. Chart Format

Total Points Both Dice	Probability				
2	1/36	or	.028	or	2.8%
3	2/36	or	.056	or	5.6
4	3/36	or	.083	or	8.3
5	4/36	or	.111	or	11.1
6	5/36	or	.139	or	13.9
7	6/36	or	.167	or	16.7
8	5/36	or	.139	or	13.9
9	4/36	or	.111	or	11.1
10	3/36	or	.083	or	8.3
11	2/36	or	.056	or	5.6
12	1/36	or	.028	or	2.8
Total	36/36	or	1.000	or	100.0%

Note: Total may not sum to 1 or 100% because of rounding.

C. Graph Format

Probability Diagram

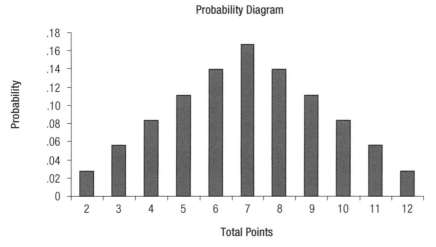

[DA02574]

The probability distribution has these characteristics:

- All possible outcomes are mutually exclusive and collectively exhaustive.

- Eleven point values are possible (ranging from a total of two points to a total of twelve points).

- As the chart in the exhibit indicates, the probability of a total of two points is 1/36 because only one of the thirty-six possible outcomes (green 1, red 1) produces a total of two points. Similarly, 1/36 is the probability of a total of twelve points.

- The most likely total point value, seven points, has a probability of 6/36, represented in the table of outcomes by the diagonal southwest-northeast row of sevens. When the outcomes are presented as a graph, the height of the vertical line above each outcome indicates the probability of that outcome.

Empirical Probability Distribution Example

The auto-damage exhibit shows an empirical probability distribution estimated from historical data. See the exhibit "Estimated Probability Distribution of Auto Physical Damage Losses."

Estimated Probability Distribution of Auto Physical Damage Losses

(1)	(2)	(3)	(4)	(5)
Size Category of Losses (bins)	Number of Losses	Percentage of Number of Losses	Dollar Amount of Losses	Percentage of Dollar Amount
$0–$5,000	7	36.84%	$18,007	10.64%
$5,001–$10,000	7	36.84	51,448	30.39
$10,001–$15,000	2	10.53	27,298	16.13
$15,001–$20,000	1	5.26	15,589	9.21
$20,001–$25,000	1	5.26	21,425	12.66
$25,001+	1	5.26	35,508	20.98
Total	19	100.00%	$169,275	100.00%

Mean dollar amount = $8,909

[DA02575]

This probability distribution has a vast number of possible outcomes, consisting of dollar amounts of loss ranging from $0 to $25,000 or more. Because it would be impossible to calculate a separate probability for each of the possible amounts of loss, the outcomes are divided into the six size categories, or bins, shown in Column 1. To determine the empirical probabilities shown in Column 3, the number of losses shown in Column 2 for each size category is divided by the total number of losses (the sum of Column 2). The probability distribution satisfies the requirements of a properly constructed probability distribution in these ways:

- The outcomes are mutually exclusive, as any given loss falls into only one category, and the outcomes are collectively exhaustive, as the sum of the probabilities shown in Column 3 is 100 percent, or 1.

- Column 3 shows probabilities for all the outcomes as categorized in Column 1.

The empirical probability distribution for auto physical damage losses differs in two ways from the theoretical probability distribution of the dice rolls:

- The outcomes shown in Column 1 of the auto physical damage exhibit (size categories of losses) are arbitrarily defined boundaries, whereas the outcomes of a roll of dice are specific and observable.

- While the maximum possible dice total is twelve, the largest size of auto physical damage losses ($25,000+) has no evident upper limit.

Discrete and Continuous Probability Distributions

Probability distributions come in two forms: discrete and continuous. Discrete probability distributions have a finite number of possible outcomes, while continuous probability distributions have an infinite number of possible outcomes.

Discrete probability distributions are usually displayed in a table that lists all possible outcomes and the probability of each. These distributions are commonly used to analyze how often something will occur; that is, they are frequency distributions. The probability distribution shown in the "Number of Hurricanes Making Landfall in State X During One Hurricane Season" exhibit is an example of a frequency distribution.

Discrete probability distributions have a finite number of outcomes. For example, the hurricane-landfall exhibit has six possible outcomes. In contrast, continuous probability distributions have an infinite number of possible outcome values and are generally represented in one of two ways: either as a graph or by dividing the distribution into a countable number of bins.

The "Continuous Probability Distributions" exhibit shows two graphs of continuous probability distributions. In each graph, the possible outcomes are presented on the horizontal axis, and the probabilities of those outcomes are shown on the vertical axis, labeled "Probability Density." The height of the line or curve above an outcome indicates the probability of that outcome. See the exhibit "Continuous Probability Distributions."

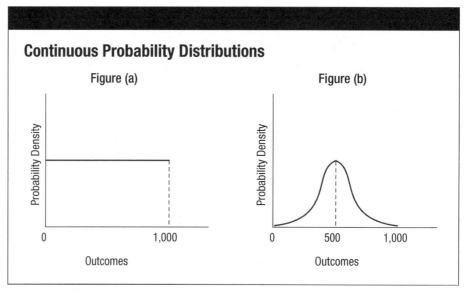

[DA02576]

Figure (a) in the exhibit, which has a flat line above the interval 0 to 1,000, illustrates that all the outcomes between 0 and 1,000 are equally likely. The number on the horizontal axis could represent units of time, distance, weight, money, or other variables. Figure (b), which has a curve that starts at a very low probability on the vertical axis and increases until it reaches a peak at 500 and then declines to a very low probability again at 1,000, illustrates that the very low and very high outcomes are unlikely and that the outcomes around 500 are much more likely.

The other way of presenting a continuous probability distribution is to divide the distribution into a countable number of bins. The "Estimated Probability Distribution of Auto Physical Damage Losses" exhibit displays auto physical damage losses in a continuous probability distribution that has been divided into six bins described by various ranges of losses. Although the auto physical damage distribution is a continuous probability distribution, dividing the losses into bins makes the continuous distribution resemble a discrete probability distribution with several outcomes. This method enables the analyst to calculate the probability that an outcome will fall within a certain range of outcomes.

USING CENTRAL TENDENCY

In analyzing a probability distribution, the measures of central tendency represent the best guess as to what the outcome will be. For example, if a manager asked an underwriter what the expected losses from fire would be for a store that the underwriter had insured, the underwriter's best guess would be one of the measures of central tendency of the frequency distribution multiplied by one of the measures of central tendency of the severity distribution. So, if the expected number of fires was two, and each fire had an expected severity of $5,000, the underwriter would expect $10,000 in losses.

After determining empirical probabilities and constructing probability distributions, a risk professional can use **central tendency** to compare the probability distributions, analyze loss exposures, and make risk management decisions. Many probability distributions cluster around a particular value, which may or may not be in the exact center of the distribution's range of values. The three most widely accepted measures of central tendency are the expected value or mean, the median, and the mode.

Central tendency
The single outcome that is the most representative of all possible outcomes included within a probability distribution.

Expected Value

The **expected value** is the weighted average of all of the possible outcomes of a theoretical probability distribution. The weights are the probabilities of the outcomes. The outcomes of a probability distribution are symbolized as $x1$, $x2$, $x3$, … xn (xn represents the last outcome in the series), having respective probabilities of $p1$, $p2$, $p3$, … pn. The distribution's expected value is the sum of ($p1 \times x1$) + ($p2 \times x2$) + ($p3 \times x3$) + … ($pn \times xn$). See the exhibit "Calculating the Expected Value of a Probability Distribution—The Two-Dice Example."

Expected value
The weighted average of all of the possible outcomes of a probability distribution, or its mean.

In the example of a probability distribution of total points on one roll of a pair of dice, the distribution's expected value of 7.0 is shown in the exhibit as the sum of the values in Column 3.

The procedure for calculating the expected value applies to all theoretical discrete probability distributions. For continuous distributions, the expected value is also a weighted average of the possible outcomes. However, calculating the expected value for a continuous distribution is much more complex and therefore is not discussed here.

Mean

Probabilities are needed to calculate a theoretical distribution's expected value. However, when considering an empirical distribution constructed from historical data, the measure of central tendency is not called the expected value, it is called the **mean**. It is calculated by summing the values in a data set and dividing by the number of values. In other words, the mean is the numeric average. Just as the expected value is calculated by weighting each possible outcome by its probability, the mean is calculated by weighting each observed outcome by the relative frequency with which it occurs.

Mean
The sum of the values in a dataset divided by the number of values.

For example, if the observed outcome values are 2, 3, 4, 4, 5, 5, 5, 6, 6, and 8, then the mean equals 4.8, which is the sum of the values, 48, divided by the number of values, 10. The mean is only a good estimate of the expected outcome if the underlying conditions determining those outcomes remain constant over time.

Calculating the Expected Value of a Probability Distribution— The Two-Dice Example

(1) Total Points— Both Dice (x)	(2) Probability (p)	(3) p × x	(4) Cumulative Probability (sum of p's)
2	1/36	2/36	1/36
3	2/36	6/36	3/36
4	3/36	12/36	6/36
5	4/36	20/36	10/36
6	5/36	30/36	15/36
7	6/36	42/36	21/36
8	5/36	40/36	26/36
9	4/36	36/36	30/36
10	3/36	30/36	33/36
11	2/36	22/36	35/36
12	1/36	12/36	36/36, or 100%
Total	36/36 = 1	252/36 = 7.0	

Expected Value = 252/36 = 7.0
Median = 7 (There is an equal number of outcomes [15] above and below 7.)
Mode = 7 (The most frequent outcome.)

[DA02577]

Unlike the expected value, which is derived from theory, the mean is derived from experience. If the conditions that generated that experience have changed, the mean that was calculated may no longer be an accurate estimate of central tendency. Nonetheless, risk professionals often use the mean as the single best guess for forecasting future events.

For example, the best guess as to the number of workers compensation claims that an organization will suffer in the next year is often the mean of the frequency distribution of workers compensation claims from previous years.

Median
The value at the midpoint of a sequential data set with an odd number of values, or the mean of the two middle values of a sequential data set with an even number of values.

Median and Cumulative Probabilities

Another measure of central tendency is the **median**. To determine a data set's median, its values must be arranged by size, from highest to lowest or lowest to highest. In the array of nineteen auto physical damage losses in the exhibit, the median loss has an adjusted value of $6,782. This tenth loss is the median because nine losses are greater than $6,782 and nine losses are less than $6,782. See the exhibit "Array of Historical and Adjusted Auto Physical Damage Losses."

Array of Historical and Adjusted Auto Physical Damage Losses

(1) Date	(2) Historical Loss Amount	(3) Adjusted Loss Amount*	(4) Rank
09/29/X3	$ 155	$ 200	19
04/21/X3	1,008	1,300	18
03/18/X4	1,271	1,500	17
12/04/X3	1,783	2,300	16
07/27/X5	3,774	4,000	15
06/14/X6	4,224	4,224	14
04/22/X6	4,483	4,483	13
02/08/X5**	5,189	5,500	12
05/03/X3	4,651	5,999	11
01/02/X6**	6,782	6,782	10
07/12/X4	6,271	7,402	9
05/17/X5**	7,834	8,303	8
08/15/X4	7,119	8,403	7
06/10/X6	9,059	9,059	6
12/19/X5	12,830	13,599	5
08/04/X5	12,925	13,699	4
11/01/X4	13,208	15,589	3
01/09/X6	21,425	21,425	2
10/23/X6	35,508	35,508	1

*   Adjusted amount column is the historical loss amount adjusted to current year dollars using a price index.

** Loss for which adjustment of historical amount to current year dollars changes ranking in array.

[DA02578]

A probability distribution's median has a cumulative probability of 50 percent. For example, seven is the median of the probability distribution of points in rolling two dice because seven is the only number of points for which the probability of higher outcomes (15/36) is equal to the probability of lower outcomes (15/36). That is, there are fifteen equally probable ways of obtaining an outcome higher than seven and fifteen equally probable ways of obtaining an outcome lower than seven.

The median can also be determined by summing the probabilities of outcomes equal to or less than a given number of points in rolling two dice, as in the "Calculating the Expected Value of a Probability Distribution—The Two Dice Example" exhibit. The cumulative 50 percent probability (18/36) is reached in the seven-points category (actually, in the middle of the seven-point class of results). Therefore, seven is the median of this distribution.

The cumulative probabilities in Column 4 of the exhibit indicate the probability of a die roll yielding a certain number of points or less. For example, the cumulative probability of rolling a three or less is 3/36 (or the sum of 1/36 for rolling a two and 2/36 for rolling a three). Similarly, the cumulative probability of rolling a ten or less is 33/36, calculated by summing the individual Column 2 probabilities of outcomes of ten points or less.

With probability distributions of losses, calculating probabilities of losses equal to or less than a given number of losses or dollar amounts of losses, individually and cumulatively, can be helpful in selecting retention levels. Similarly, calculating individual and cumulative probabilities of losses equal to or greater than a given number of losses or dollar amounts can help in selecting upper limits of insurance coverage.

The "Cumulative Probabilities" exhibit shows how to derive a cumulative probability distribution of loss sizes from the individual probabilities of loss size in the exhibit. See the exhibit "Cumulative Probabilities That Auto Physical Damage Losses Will Not Exceed Specified Amounts."

Column 3 of the "Cumulative Probabilities" exhibit indicates that, on the basis of the available data, 36.84 percent of all losses are less than or equal to $5,000 and that another 36.84 percent are greater than $5,000 but less than or equal to $10,000. Therefore, the probability of a loss being $10,000 or less is calculated as the sum of these two probabilities, or 73.68 percent, as shown in Column 4 of the "Cumulative Probabilities" exhibit. Similarly, as shown in Column 7 of the same exhibit, individual losses of $10,000 or less can be expected to account for 41.03 percent of the total dollar amount of all losses.

Understanding the cumulative probability distribution will enable an analyst to evaluate the effect of various deductibles and policy limits on insured loss exposures. For example, if an insurance policy has a $5,000 deductible, the analyst would know that 36.84 percent of losses covered by that policy would be below the deductible level and therefore would not be paid by the insurer.

The summed probabilities in Column 4 of the "Cumulative Probabilities" exhibit indicate that the median individual loss is between $5,001 and $10,000, the category in which the 50 percent cumulative probability is reached. This result is consistent with the $6,782 median loss found by examining the "Array of Historical and Adjusted Auto Physical Damage Losses" exhibit.

Cumulative Probabilities That Auto Physical Damage Losses Will Not Exceed Specified Amounts

(1) Loss Size Category	(2) Number of Losses	(3) Percentage of Number of Losses	(4) Cumulative Percentage of Number of Losses Not Exceeding Category	(5) Dollar Amount of Losses	(6) Percentage of Dollar Amount	(7) Cumulative Percentage of Dollar Amount of Losses Not Exceeding Category
$0–$5,000	7	36.84%	36.84%	$18,007	10.64%	10.64%
$5,001–$10,000	7	36.84	73.68	51,448	30.39	41.03
$10,001–$15,000	2	10.53	84.21	27,298	16.13	57.16
$15,001–$20,000	1	5.26	89.47	15,589	9.21	66.37
$20,001–$25,000	1	5.26	94.74	21,425	12.66	79.02
$25,001+	1	5.26	100.00	35,508	20.98	100.00
Total		100.00%			100.00%	

[DA02579]

Mode

Mode

The most frequently occurring value in a distribution.

A further measure of central tendency is the **mode**. In a continuous probability distribution graph, the mode is the value of the outcome directly beneath the peak of the curve. In the distribution of total points of two dice throws, the mode is seven points. In the empirical distribution of auto physical damage losses shown in the "Cumulative Probabilities" exhibit, the mode is the $0–$5,000 range or the $5,001–$10,000 range, because those ranges each have the highest frequency of losses (seven).

Knowing the mode of a distribution allows the analyst to focus on the outcomes that are the most common. For example, knowing that the most common auto physical damage losses are in the $0–$10,000 range may influence decisions regarding deductible levels for insurance coverage.

The relationships among the mean (average), median, and mode for any data set are illustrated by the distribution's shape. The shape of a particular frequency or severity probability distribution can be seen by graphing the data as shown in the "Typical Shapes" exhibit and can be either symmetrical or asymmetrical. See the exhibit "Typical Shapes of Symmetrical and Skewed Distributions."

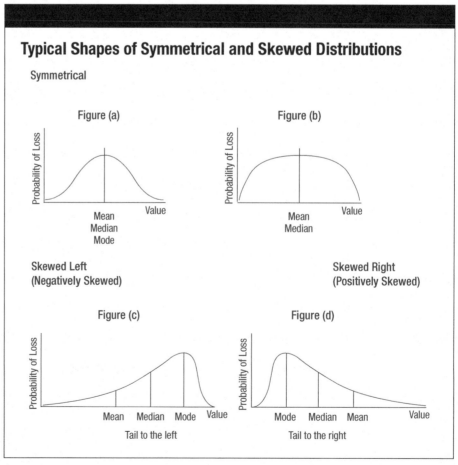

Typical Shapes of Symmetrical and Skewed Distributions

[DA02581]

In a symmetrical distribution, one side of the curve is a mirror image of the other. The distribution in Figure (a) of the exhibit is the standard (normal) distribution commonly called a bell-shaped curve, but the distributions in both Figure (a) and Figure (b) are symmetrical. In a symmetrical distribution, the mean and median have the same value. In a standard bell-shaped distribution, the mode also has the same value as that of the mean and the median.

If a distribution is asymmetrical, it is skewed. Skewed distributions are shown in both Figure (c) and Figure (d) of the exhibit. Many loss distributions are skewed because the probability of small losses is large whereas the probability of large losses is small. Asymmetrical distributions are common for severity distributions where most losses are small losses but there is a small probability of a large loss occurring. If the distribution is skewed, the mean and median values will differ, and the median value of the distribution is often a better guess than the mean as to what is most likely to occur.

For example, if a distribution of workers compensation claims was skewed by two years in which an organization experienced an unusually high level of claims, the mean would be higher than the median. In that situation, the median is more likely a better estimate of next year's claims than the mean.

USING DISPERSION

When analyzing probability distributions, risk professionals can use measures of dispersion to assess the credibility of the measures of central tendency used in analyzing loss exposures.

Measures of central tendency for a distribution of outcomes include the expected value or the mean, which can help risk professionals make best guesses as to which outcome in a probability distribution will occur. Another important characteristic of a distribution is its **dispersion**. Dispersion describes the extent to which the distribution is spread out rather than concentrated around the expected value or the mean. The less dispersion around the distribution's expected value or mean, the greater the likelihood that actual results will fall within a given range of that expected value or mean.

Dispersion
The variation among values in a distribution.

Therefore, less dispersion means less uncertainty about the expected outcomes. An underwriter, for example, may be able to use measures of dispersion around estimated losses to determine whether to offer insurance coverage to an applicant for insurance. Dispersion also affects the shape of a distribution when it is graphed. A more dispersed distribution forms a flatter curve, whereas a less dispersed distribution forms a more peaked curve. Two symmetrical distributions with the same mean but different standard deviations are shown in the exhibit. See the exhibit "Dispersion."

There are two widely used statistical measures of dispersion: the standard deviation and the coefficient of variation.

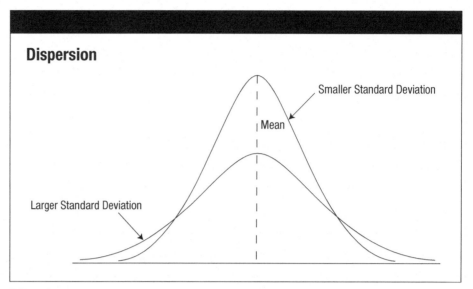

[DA02582]

Standard Deviation

The **standard deviation** is the average of the differences (deviations) between the values in a distribution and the expected value (or mean) of that distribution. The standard deviation therefore indicates how widely dispersed the values in a distribution are.

To calculate the standard deviation of a probability distribution, one must perform these steps:

1. Calculate the distribution's expected value or mean
2. Subtract this expected value from each distribution value to find the differences
3. Square each of the resulting differences
4. Multiply each square by the probability associated with the value
5. Sum the resulting products
6. Find the square root of the sum

The "Calculation of Standard Deviation of the Probability Distribution of Two Dice" exhibit illustrates how to calculate a standard deviation for the distribution of values in rolling two dice. The distribution's expected value is seven. See the exhibit "Calculation of Standard Deviation of the Probability Distribution of Two Dice."

The standard deviation of auto physical damage losses can be estimated using the individual loss amounts shown in Column (1) of the "Calculation of Standard Deviation of Individual Outcomes" exhibit. Calculating a standard deviation using a sample of actual outcomes is done in much the same way as for a probability distribution. To calculate the standard deviation using the actual sample of outcomes, it is not necessary to know the probability of each

Calculation of Standard Deviation of the Probability Distribution of Two Dice

(1) Points (x_i)	(2) Probability (p)	(3) Step 1 EV	(4) Step 2 $x_i - EV$	(5) Step 3 $(x_i - EV)^2$	(6) Step 4 $(x_i - EV)^2 \times p$
2	1/36	7	−5	25	25/36
3	2/36	7	−4	16	32/36
4	3/36	7	−3	9	27/36
5	4/36	7	−2	4	16/36
6	5/36	7	−1	1	5/36
7	6/36	7	0	0	0
8	5/36	7	1	1	5/36
9	4/36	7	2	4	16/36
10	3/36	7	3	9	27/36
11	2/36	7	4	16	32/36
12	1/36	7	5	25	25/36
			Step 5	Total	210/36
			Step 6	$\sqrt{(210/36)} =$	2.42*

*Rounded

[DA02583]

outcome, just how often each outcome occurred. See the exhibit "Calculation of Standard Deviation of Individual Outcomes."

The steps for calculating the standard deviation of a set of individual outcomes not involving probabilities are these:

1. Calculate the mean of the outcomes (the sum of the outcomes divided by the number of outcomes).
2. Subtract the mean from each of the outcomes.
3. Square each of the resulting differences.
4. Sum these squares.
5. Divide this sum by the number of outcomes minus one. (This value is called the variance.)
6. Calculate the square root of the variance.

The "Calculation of Standard Deviation of Individual Outcomes" exhibit illustrates how to calculate a standard deviation using actual loss data rather than a theoretical probability distribution. Risk professionals use

Calculation of Standard Deviation of Individual Outcomes

(1) Adjusted Loss Amount (ALA)	(2) Step 1 Mean Loss (ML)	(3) Step 2 ALA-ML	(4) Step 3 (ALA-ML)^2
$ 200	$8,909	$–8,709	$ 75,846,681
1,300	8,909	–7,609	57,896,881
1,500	8,909	–7,409	54,893,281
2,300	8,909	–6,609	43,678,881
4,000	8,909	–4,909	24,098,281
4,224	8,909	–4,685	21,949,225
4,483	8,909	–4,426	19,589,476
5,500	8,909	–3,409	11,621,281
5,999	8,909	–2,910	8,468,100
6,782	8,909	–2,127	4,524,129
7,402	8,909	–1,507	2,271,049
8,303	8,909	–606	367,236
8,403	8,909	–506	256,036
9,059	8,909	150	22,500
13,599	8,909	4,690	21,996,100
13,699	8,909	4,790	22,944,100
15,589	8,909	6,680	44,622,400
21,425	8,909	12,516	156,650,256
35,508	8,909	26,599	707,506,801

Step 4	Sum		$1,279,202,694
Step 5	Variance [sum ÷ (n − 1)]		71,066,816
Step 6	Standard deviation (sqrt variance)		$8,430

[DA02584]

measurements of dispersion of the distributions of potential outcomes to gain a better understanding of the loss exposures being analyzed.

For example, knowing the expected number of workers compensation claims in a given year is important, but it is only one element of the information that can be gleaned from a distribution. The standard deviation can be calculated to provide a measure of how confident a risk professional can be in his or her estimate of the expected number of workers compensation claims.

Coefficient of Variation

The **coefficient of variation** is a further measure of the dispersion of a distribution. For example, the coefficient of variation for the distribution of total points in rolling two dice equals 2.4 points (the standard deviation of the distribution) divided by 7.0 points (the mean or expected value), which is 0.34. Similarly the coefficient of variation of the sample of outcomes in the "Calculation of Standard Deviation of Individual Outcomes" exhibit is $8,430 divided by $8,909, or approximately 0.95.

In comparing two distributions, if both distributions have the same mean (or expected value), then the distribution with the larger standard deviation has the greater variability. If the two distributions have different means (or expected values), the coefficient of variation is often used to compare the two distributions to determine which has the greater variability relative to its mean (or expected value).

For a simplified example, consider an underwriter who can accept only one of two submissions for insurance. Each submission includes a severity distribution of the applicant's losses incurred over the past five years. In the unlikely event that both distributions have the same mean, the underwriter should, all other things being equal, accept the submission with the lower standard deviation. If, as is more likely, the two distributions have different means and standard deviations, the underwriter should, all other things being equal, accept the submission with the lower coefficient of variation.

Coefficient of variation
A measure of dispersion calculated by dividing a distribution's standard deviation by its mean.

USING NORMAL DISTRIBUTIONS

A **normal distribution** is a probability distribution that can help risk professionals evaluate the variability around the mean and has therefore proven useful in risk management and insurance.

Normal distribution
A probability distribution that, when graphed, generates a bell-shaped curve.

Characteristics of Normal Distributions

The exhibit illustrates the typical bell-shaped curve of a normal distribution. Note that the normal curve never touches the horizontal line at the base of the diagram. In theory, the normal distribution assigns some probability greater than zero for every outcome, regardless of its distance from the mean. The exhibit also shows the percentage of outcomes that fall within a given number of standard deviations above or below the mean of a distribution. See the exhibit "The Normal Distribution—Percentages of Outcomes Within Specified Standard Deviations of the Mean."

For example, for all normal distributions, 34.13 percent of all outcomes are within one standard deviation above the mean and, because every normal distribution is symmetrical, another 34.13 percent of all outcomes fall within one standard deviation below the mean. By addition, 68.26 percent of all outcomes are within one standard deviation above or below the mean. The

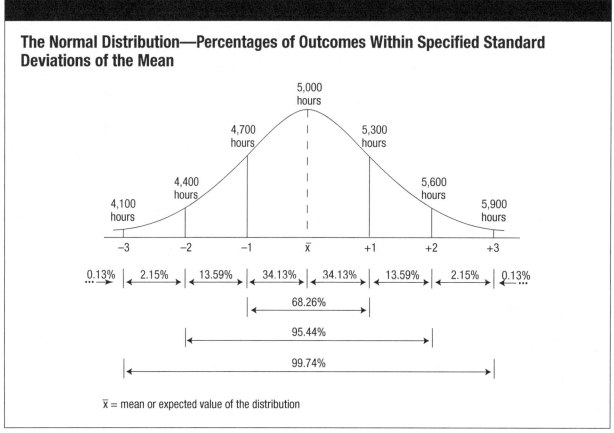

The Normal Distribution—Percentages of Outcomes Within Specified Standard Deviations of the Mean

x̄ = mean or expected value of the distribution

[DA02585]

portion of a normal distribution that is between one and two standard deviations above the mean contains 13.59 percent of all outcomes, as does the portion between one and two standard deviations below the mean. Hence, the area between the mean and two standard deviations above the mean contains 47.72 percent (34.13 percent + 13.59 percent) of the outcomes, and another 47.72 percent are two standard deviations or less below the mean.

Consequently, 95.44 percent of all outcomes are within two standard deviations above or below the mean, and fewer than 5 percent of outcomes are outside two standard deviations above or below the mean. Taking this a step further, 2.15 percent of all outcomes are between two and three standard deviations above the mean, and another 2.15 percent are between two and three standard deviations below the mean. Therefore, 49.87 percent (34.13 percent + 13.59 percent + 2.15 percent) of all outcomes are three standard deviations or less above the mean, and an equal percentage are three standard deviations or less below the mean.

Consequently, the portion of the distribution between three standard deviations above the mean and three standard deviations below it contains 99.74 percent (49.87 percent × 2) of all outcomes. Therefore, only 0.26 percent (100 percent – 99.74 percent) of all outcomes lie beyond three standard deviations from the mean. Half of these outcomes (0.13 percent) are more than three standard deviations below the mean, and the other half (0.13 percent) are more than three standard deviations above the mean.

Practical Application

The relationship between the expected value and the standard deviation of a normal distribution can have useful practical application. For example, suppose that a manufacturer uses 600 electrical elements to heat rubber. The useful life of each element is limited, and an element that is used for too long poses a substantial danger of exploding and starting an electrical fire. An insurance professional underwriting the manufacturer's commercial property insurance would look for evidence that proper maintenance is performed and the elements are replaced periodically to ensure proper fire safety.

The issue is determining when to replace the elements. Replacing them too soon can be costly, whereas replacing them too late increases the chance of fire. The characteristics of the normal probability distribution provide a way of scheduling maintenance so that the likelihood of an element becoming dangerous before it is replaced can be kept below a particular margin of safety that is specified by the organization based on its willingness to assume risk.

Assume that the expected safe life of each element conforms to a normal distribution having a mean of 5,000 hours and a standard deviation of 300 hours. Even if the maintenance schedule requires replacing each element after it has been in service only 5,000 hours (the mean, or expected, safe life), a 50 percent chance exists that it will become unsafe before being changed, because 50 percent of the normal distribution is below this 5,000-hour mean.

If each element is changed after having been used only 4,700 hours [one standard deviation below the mean (5,000 – 300)], a 15.87 percent (50 percent – 34.13 percent) chance still exists that an element will become unsafe before being changed. If this probability of high hazard is still too high, changing each element after 4,400 hours [two standard deviations below the mean (5,000 – (2 × 300))] reduces the probability of high hazard to only 2.28 percent, the portion of a normal distribution that is more than two standard deviations below the mean.

A still more cautious practice would be to change elements routinely after only 4,100 hours [three standard deviations below the mean (5,000 – (3 × 300))], so that the probability of an element becoming highly hazardous before replacement would be only 0.13 percent, slightly more than one chance in 1,000.

Using this analysis, management can select an acceptable probability that an element will become unsafe before being replaced and can schedule maintenance accordingly. See the exhibit "Practice Exercise."

> ### Practice Exercise
>
> An insurer is beginning to write policies in a new state. The insurer's claim manager wants to know how many new claim representatives to hire. The insurer's marketing department has provided an estimate of additional premium volume from the new state. Based on that estimate and industry data, the manager has determined the mean number of new claims to be 8,000, with a standard deviation of 2,000 in a normal distribution. If a claim representative can adjust 600 claims per year and the manager wants to be approximately 98 percent certain that she has enough representatives, how many will she need to hire?
>
> ### Answer
>
> As shown in the exhibit titled "The Normal Distribution—Percentages of Outcomes Within Specified Standard Deviations of the Mean," 2.28 percent of all outcomes (2.15 percent + 0.13 percent) are more than two standard deviations above the mean, and 97.72 percent (100 percent − 2.28 percent) of all outcomes fall under the normal distribution below two standard deviations above the mean. Therefore, by rounding up the 97.72 percent, the claim manager can be approximately 98 percent certain that the actual number of claims will fall at or below two standard deviations above the mean. In the claim manager's distribution, two standard deviations above the mean is 12,000 claims (calculated as 8,000 + 2,000 + 2,000). Because each claim representative can adjust 600 claims per year, the manager will need to hire 12,000/600 or 20 new representatives.

[DA05841]

ANALYZING LOSS EXPOSURES

Analyzing loss exposures enables the risk analyst to develop loss projections that will guide the analyst in prioritizing loss exposures and selecting appropriate risk management techniques to manage the loss exposures most effectively.

The analysis step of the risk management process, also known as risk assessment, involves considering the four dimensions of a loss exposure: loss frequency, loss severity, total dollar losses, and timing. In addition, the credibility of the data used to project these dimensions must be determined. Data credibility is the level of confidence that available data is an accurate indicator of future losses.

Loss Frequency

Loss frequency is the number of losses that occur during a specific period. Relative loss frequency is the number of losses that occur within a given period relative to the number of exposure units (such as the number of buildings or cars exposed to loss).

For example, if an organization experiences, on average, five theft losses per year, five is the mean of an empirical frequency distribution. If the organization has only one building, then both the loss frequency and the relative frequency of losses from theft is five per year. However, if the organization has five buildings, then the organization still has a loss frequency of five theft losses per year, but the relative frequency is one loss per year per building. Two of the most common applications of relative frequency measures in risk management are injuries per employee per hour worked and auto accidents per mile driven.

Frequency distributions are usually discrete probability distributions based on past data regarding how often similar events have happened. For example, the exhibit contains a frequency distribution of the number of hurricanes that make landfall in a fictitious state during a single hurricane season. One way of describing the frequency of hurricanes is to report a mean frequency of occurrence, such as approximately 1.2 hurricanes making landfall per year. See the exhibit "Skewness of Number of Hurricanes Making Landfall in State X During One Hurricane Season."

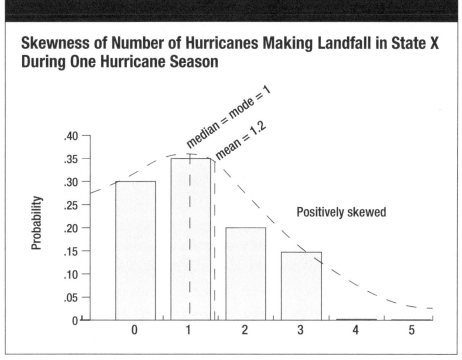

Skewness of Number of Hurricanes Making Landfall in State X During One Hurricane Season

[DA02586]

However, the exhibit does not incorporate some of the other information available from the entire frequency distribution. For example, the most likely outcome may be one hurricane per year (35.0 percent of the time). However, having zero hurricanes per year is also reasonably likely (30.0 percent of the time), but having five or more hurricanes make landfall in State X is reasonably unlikely (0.1 percent of the time). Therefore, an insurance or risk management professional should supplement the mean of 1.2 with other information from the frequency distribution, such as the standard deviation (which is approximately 1.04) and skewness measures.

Loss frequency can be projected with a fairly high degree of confidence for some loss exposures in large organizations. For example, a company that ships thousands of parcels each day probably can more accurately project the number of transit losses it will sustain in a year, based on past experience and adjusted for any expected changes in future conditions, than can a company that ships only hundreds of parcels each month.

Most organizations do not have enough exposure units to accurately project low-frequency, high-severity events (such as employee deaths). However, an estimate with a margin for error is better than no estimate at all, as long as its limitations are recognized.

Loss Severity

The purpose of analyzing loss severity is to determine how serious a loss might be. For example, how much of a building could be damaged in a single fire, and how long might it take the business occupying this building to resume operations after such a fire loss?

Maximum Possible Loss

Effectively managing risk requires identifying the worst possible outcome of a loss. The maximum possible loss (MPL) is the total value exposed to loss at any one location or from any one event. For example, in the case of fire damage to a building and its contents, the maximum possible loss is typically the value of the building plus the total value of the building's contents.

To determine MPL for multiple exposure units, such as a fleet of cars, one should consider factors such as whether multiple vehicles travel together (a circumstance that could cause one event, such as a collision, to damage several vehicles) or whether multiple vehicles are stored in the same location (a circumstance that could cause one event, such as a flood, to affect several vehicles). This helps determine the maximum number of vehicles that could be involved in any one loss and therefore the event's MPL.

Although maximum possible property losses can be estimated based on the values exposed to loss, this estimation is not necessarily appropriate or possible for assessing maximum possible liability losses. In theory, liability losses are limited only by the defendant's total wealth. Therefore, some practical assumptions must be made about the MPL in liability cases to properly assess that loss exposure. Instead of focusing on the defendant's total wealth, a common assumption is that the maximum amount that would be exposed to liability loss 95 percent (or 98 percent) of the time in similar cases is the MPL.

Frequency and Severity Considered Jointly

To fully analyze the significance of a particular loss exposure, the analyst must consider both severity and frequency and how they interact. One method of jointly considering frequency and severity is the Prouty Approach. Another method involves combining frequency and severity distributions to create a single total claims distribution. See the exhibit "The Prouty Approach."

The Prouty Approach

LOSS FREQUENCY

LOSS SEVERITY		Almost Nil	Slight	Moderate	Definite
	Severe	Reduce or prevent / Transfer	Reduce or prevent / Transfer	Reduce or prevent / Retain	Avoid
	Significant	Reduce or prevent / Transfer	Reduce / Transfer	Reduce or prevent / Retain	Avoid
	Slight	Reduce or prevent / Retain	Reduce / Retain	Reduce or prevent / Retain	Prevent / Retain

[DA02588]

As shown in the exhibit, the Prouty Approach entails four categories of loss frequency:

- Almost nil—Extremely unlikely to happen; virtually no possibility
- Slight—Could happen but has not happened
- Moderate—Happens occasionally
- Definite—Happens regularly

There are three categories of loss severity:

- Slight—Organization can readily retain each loss exposure.
- Significant—Organization cannot retain the loss exposure, some part of which must be financed.
- Severe—Organization must finance virtually all of the loss exposure or endanger its survival.

These broad categories of loss frequency and loss severity are subjective. One organization may view losses that occur once a month as moderate, while another would consider such frequency as definite. Similarly, one organization may view a $1 million loss as slight, while another might view it as severe. However, these categories can help insurance and risk management professionals prioritize loss exposures.

A loss exposure's frequency and severity tend to be inversely related. That is, the more severe a loss tends to be, the less frequently it tends to occur.

Conversely, the more frequently a loss occurs because of a particular exposure, the less severe the loss tends to be.

Loss exposures that generate minor but definite losses are typically retained and incorporated into an organization's budget. At the other extreme, loss exposures that generate intolerably large losses are typically avoided. Therefore, most risk management decisions about adopting risk control and risk financing techniques concern loss exposures for which individual losses, although tolerable, tend to be either significant or severe and have a moderate, slight, or almost nil chance of occurring.

A given loss exposure might generate financially significant losses because of either high individual loss severity or high-frequency, low-severity losses that aggregate to a substantial total. Organizations may be tempted to focus on high-profile "shock events," such as a major fire, a hurricane, or a huge liability claim. However, smaller losses, which happen so frequently that they become routine, can eventually produce much larger total losses than a single dramatic event. For example, many retail firms suffer greater total losses from shoplifting, which happens regularly, than they do from large fires that might happen once every fifty years. Minor, cumulatively significant losses usually deserve as much risk management attention as large individual losses.

Another way of jointly considering frequency and severity is to combine both frequency and severity distributions into a total claims distribution, which can provide additional information about potential losses that may occur in a given period. Combining distributions can be difficult because as the number of possible outcomes increases, the possible combinations of frequency and severity grow exponentially. See the exhibit "Total Claims Distribution for Hardware Store Shoplifting Losses."

The exhibit presents a simple example of three possible frequencies (0, 1, and 2) and three possible severities ($100, $250, and $500) that represent shoplifting losses from a hardware store. The frequency and severity distributions for a given year are shown in the exhibit, along with the total claims distribution created by considering all the possible combinations of the frequency and severity distributions.

For example, a 33 percent chance exists of a loss not occurring during the year (frequency = 0). Therefore, in the total claims distribution, a 33 percent chance exists of the total losses being $0. There is only one possible way for a $100 loss to occur: a frequency of 1 and a severity of $100. Therefore, that probability is .11 [.33 (frequency 1) × .33 (severity $100) = .11]. There are two ways that the total claims for the year could equal $500. Either the organization could have one loss of $500, or it could have two losses of $250. Therefore, the probability of a $500 loss is the probability of one $500 loss plus the probability of two $250 losses.

A total claims distribution can be used to calculate the measures of central tendency and dispersion and evaluate the effect that various risk control and risk financing techniques would have on this loss exposure.

Total Claims Distribution for Hardware Store Shoplifting Losses

Frequency	Number of Losses	Probability
F0	0	.33
F1	1	.33
F2	2	.34

Severity	Dollar Loss	Probability
S1	$100	.33
S2	$250	.33
S3	$500	.34

Total Claims Distribution

Dollar Loss	Probability*	Probability Calculation		
$ 0	.33	p(F0)	←	There is only one possible way to have $0 losses: the frequency = 0.
100	.11	p(F1) × p(S1)	←	There is only one possible way to have $100 in losses: one $100 loss.
200	.04	p(F2) × p(S1) × p(S1)	←	There is only one possible way to have $200 in losses: two $100 losses.
250	.11	p(F1) × p(S2)	←	There is only one possible way to have $250 in losses: one $250 loss.
350	.07	[p(F2) × p(S1) × p(S2)] + [p(F2) × p(S2) × p(S1)]	←	There are two possible ways to have $350 in losses: one $100 loss and one $250 loss, or one $250 loss and one $100 loss.
500	.15	[p(F2) × p(S2) × p(S2)] + [p(F1) × p(S3)]	←	There are two possible ways to have $500 in losses: two $250 losses or one $500 loss.
600	.08	[p(F2) × p(S1) × p(S3)] + [p(F2) × p(S3) × p(S1)]	←	There are two possible ways to have $600 in losses: one $100 loss and one $500 loss, or one $500 loss and one $100 loss.
750	.08	[p(F2) × p(S2) × p(S3)] + [p(F2) × p(S3) × p(S2)]	←	There are two possible ways to have $750 in losses: one $250 loss and one $500 loss, or one $500 loss and one $250 loss.
1,000	.04	p(F2) × p(S3) × p(S3)	←	There is only one possible way to have $1,000 in losses: two $500 losses.

*Rounded

[DA02589]

Total Dollar Losses

The third dimension to consider in analyzing loss exposures is total dollar losses for all occurrences during a specific period, calculated by multiplying loss frequency by loss severity. Total dollar losses are a simplified way to combine frequency and severity distributions that have multiple possible outcomes. Expected total dollar losses can be projected by multiplying expected loss frequency by expected loss severity, and worst-case scenarios can be calculated by assuming both high frequency and the worst possible severity. See the exhibit "Total Dollar Losses."

Total Dollar Losses

Frequency

	Number of Losses	Probability
F0	0	.03
F1	1	.05
F2	2	.08
F3	3	.10
F4	4	.15
F5	5	.20
F6	6	.15
F7	7	.10
F8	8	.08
F9	9	.05
F10	10	.01

Severity

	Dollar Loss	Probability
S1	$100	.30
S2	$250	.25
S3	$500	.20
S4	$683	.15
S5	$883	.10

Expected value = $383.25.

Expected value = 4.9.

Expected total dollar losses = 4.9 × $383.25 = $1,877.93

Worst case total dollar losses = 9 × $883.00 = $7,947.00

[DA02590]

Combining the frequency and severity distributions in the exhibit would be difficult given the total number of possible combinations. The risk analyst could make some simpler calculations to determine what the potential total dollar losses may be. In this example, expected total dollar losses would be $1,877.93, and the worst-case scenario could be calculated as $7,947.00, using F9 in the exhibit. (F10 was not used, given its low probability.) These estimates could then be used in managing these loss exposures, such as evaluating whether to insure the loss exposures for the premium an insurer is quoting.

Timing

The fourth dimension to consider in analyzing loss exposures is timing of losses. This analysis requires considering when losses are likely to occur and when payment for those losses will likely be made. The timing dimension is significant because money held in reserve to pay for a loss can earn interest until the actual payment is made. Whether a loss is counted when it is incurred or when it is paid is also significant for various accounting and tax reasons that are beyond the scope of this discussion.

Funds to pay for property losses are generally disbursed relatively soon after the event occurs. In contrast, liability losses often involve long delays between the occurrence of the adverse event, when an occurrence is recognized, the period of possible litigation, and the time when payment is actually made. Damages for disability claims, for example, might be paid over a long period. In some cases, especially those involving environmental loss exposures or health risks, the delay can span several decades. Although this delay increases the uncertainty associated with the loss amount, it allows reserves to earn interest or investment income over a longer period of time.

Data Credibility

After analyzing the four dimensions of a loss exposure, the analyst then evaluates the credibility of the projections of loss frequency, loss severity, total dollar losses, and timing. The term "data credibility" refers to the level of confidence that available data can accurately indicate future losses.

Several factors may influence data credibility. Internally, changes in the way an organization operates, such as alterations to manufacturing processes or changes in data collection methods, may significantly reduce the credibility of previously collected data. Externally, events such as natural catastrophes, large liability awards, or technological change not only alter the data that is collected in that time frame but also may cause shifts in the operating environment that render previously collected data less credible.

This leaves risk professionals with a dilemma: Is it better to use older data, which is accurate but may have been generated in an environment that was substantially different from that of the period for which they are trying to predict, or to use more recent data and sacrifice some accuracy to maintain the integrity of the environment?

SUMMARY

To accurately analyze loss exposures using data on past losses, the data should be relevant, complete, consistent, and organized.

Concepts affecting the use of probability in risk analysis include theoretical probability, empirical probability, and the law of large numbers. Although it may be preferable to use theoretical probabilities because of their unchanging nature, theoretical probabilities are not applicable or available in most situations that insurance and risk management professionals are likely to analyze. Applying the law of large numbers to probability reveals that a forecast of future losses will be more reliable if the forecast is based on a larger sample of the losses used in the analysis.

A properly constructed probability distribution contains outcomes that are both mutually exclusive and collectively exhaustive, and it lists the probabilities associated with each of the possible outcomes. All probability distributions can be classified as either discrete or continuous. A discrete probability distribution has a finite number of possible outcomes, while a continuous probability distribution has an infinite number of possible outcomes.

Central tendency is the single outcome that is the most representative of all possible outcomes included within a probability distribution. The three most widely accepted measures of central tendency are the expected value or mean, the median, and the mode. Like the median, cumulative probabilities can be useful in selecting retention levels and upper limits of insurance coverage.

Dispersion, which is the variation between values in a distribution, can be used with central tendency to compare the characteristics of probability distributions. The less dispersion around a distribution's expected value, the greater the likelihood that actual results will fall within a given range of that expected value. Two widely used statistical measures of dispersion are the standard deviation and the coefficient of variation.

A normal distribution is a probability distribution that, when graphed, generates a bell-shaped curve. It can help risk professionals evaluate the variability around the mean and has therefore proven useful in risk management and insurance.

The analysis step of the risk management process involves considering the four dimensions of a loss exposure: loss frequency, loss severity, total dollar losses, and timing. The analyst also considers the credibility of the data used to project these dimensions.

Selecting Risk Control Techniques

Educational Objectives

After learning the content of this assignment, you should be able to:

▷ Explain how each of these risk control techniques can be used to reduce loss frequency and/or severity:

- Avoidance
- Loss prevention
- Loss reduction

▷ Explain how each of these risk control techniques can be used to reduce loss severity and make losses more predictable:

- Separation
- Duplication
- Diversification

▷ Explain how each of these risk control goals benefits an organization:

- Implement effective and efficient risk control measures
- Comply with legal requirements
- Promote life safety
- Ensure business continuity

▷ Explain how risk control techniques can be selected for property, liability, personnel, and net income loss exposures.

▷ Demonstrate how smart products can be applied to risk management.

▷ Explain how risk mitigation is achieved through business continuity planning.

Selecting Risk Control Techniques

4

USING AVOIDANCE, LOSS PREVENTION, AND LOSS REDUCTION

To select the most appropriate risk management techniques, risk professionals should consider the various techniques available so that they can determine which of them most effectively address an organization's or individual's loss exposures.

Risk management techniques fall into one of two categories: risk control or risk financing. The focus of this section is on these three risk control techniques:

- Avoidance
- Loss prevention
- Loss reduction

Avoidance

The aim of **avoidance** is not just to reduce loss frequency, but also to eliminate any possibility of loss. Avoidance should be considered when the expected value of the losses from an activity outweighs the expected benefits of that activity. For example, a toy manufacturer might decide not to produce a particular toy because the potential cost of products liability claims would outweigh the expected revenue from sales, no matter how cautious the manufacturer might be in producing and marketing the toy.

Because loss exposures do not exist in a vacuum, avoiding one loss exposure could create or enhance another. For example, an individual who is concerned about dying in an airplane crash can choose not to travel by air. However, by avoiding air travel, the individual increases the loss exposure to injury or death from the method of transportation chosen in its place.

Complete avoidance is not the most common risk control technique and is typically neither feasible nor desirable. Loss exposures arise from activities that are essential to individuals and organizations. Therefore, it is not possible to avoid these core activities. For instance, if a manufacturer's principal product is motorcycle safety helmets, it could not stop selling them to avoid liability loss exposures.

Avoidance
A risk control technique that involves ceasing or never undertaking an activity so that the possibility of a future loss occurring from that activity is eliminated.

Loss Prevention

Loss prevention

A risk control technique that reduces the frequency of a particular loss.

Loss prevention reduces the frequency of a particular loss without avoiding it. For instance, pressure relief valves on a boiler are intended to prevent explosions by keeping the pressure in the boiler from reaching an unsafe level. The valve is a type of loss prevention, not avoidance, because a boiler explosion is still possible but not as likely.

To illustrate a loss prevention measure, consider a hypothetical manufacturing company, Etchley Manufacturing (Etchley). Etchley has 500 employees working at a single plant. The workers compensation loss history for this plant shows a significant number of back injuries. Etchley is considering hiring a back injury consultant to host a series of educational seminars for its employees. The consultant estimates that, based on the results of his past seminar series, Etchley will see a 20 percent reduction in the frequency of back injuries. See the exhibit "Example of a Loss Prevention Measure: Etchley Manufacturing."

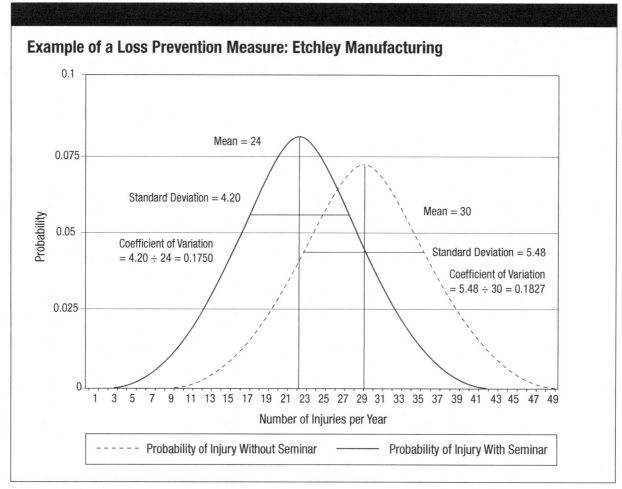

Example of a Loss Prevention Measure: Etchley Manufacturing

Mean = 24

Standard Deviation = 4.20

Coefficient of Variation
$= 4.20 \div 24 = 0.1750$

Mean = 30

Standard Deviation = 5.48

Coefficient of Variation
$= 5.48 \div 30 = 0.1827$

Probability

Number of Injuries per Year

- - - - - Probability of Injury Without Seminar ——— Probability of Injury With Seminar

[DA02649]

The chart in the exhibit shows the frequency distributions of back injuries both with and without the educational seminar in order to demonstrate the estimated effect of this loss prevention measure. The frequency distribution without the educational seminar has a mean of 30, a standard deviation of 5.48, and a coefficient of variation of 0.1827.

The frequency distribution with the educational seminar has a lower mean of 24, a lower standard deviation of 4.20, and a lower coefficient of variation of 0.1750. Based on these figures, the consultant's educational seminar would not only reduce the expected frequency of back injuries, but also it would reduce their variability from year to year, which would allow Etchley to budget more effectively for those injuries that do occur.

Generally, a loss prevention measure is implemented before a loss occurs in order to break the sequence of events that leads to the loss. Because of the close link between causes of loss and loss prevention, determining effective loss prevention measures usually requires carefully studying how particular losses are caused.

For example, according to Heinrich's domino theory, described in the exhibit, most work-related injuries result from a chain of events that includes an unsafe act or an unsafe condition. Workplace safety efforts have therefore focused on trying to eliminate specific unsafe acts or unsafe conditions to break this chain of events and prevent injuries. See the exhibit "Heinrich's Domino Theory."

Heinrich's Domino Theory

In 1931, H. W. Heinrich published the first thorough analysis of work injuries caused by accidents. He determined that work injuries were actually a result of a series of unsafe acts and/or mechanical or physical hazards (dominoes) that occurred in a specific order. Furthermore, he concluded that if any one of these dominoes could be removed from the chain, the work injury could be prevented. Heinrich's theory included the following five dominoes: (1) social environment and ancestry, (2) the fault of persons, (3) personal or mechanical hazards, (4) the accident, and (5) the injury. For example, if risk control measures could minimize mechanical hazards, the domino chain would be broken and fewer injuries would occur. Many of the principles that Heinrich outlined in his publication became the basis of modern risk control measures.

H.W. Heinrich, Industrial Accident Prevention, 4th edition (New York: McGraw-Hill, 1959). [DA02650]

As is the case with avoidance, a loss prevention measure may reduce the frequency of losses from one loss exposure but increase the frequency or severity of losses from other loss exposures. For example, a jewelry store that installs security bars on its windows would likely reduce the frequency of theft. These same bars, however, might make it impossible for firefighters to enter the building through the windows or might trap employees inside the store if a fire occurs.

Loss Reduction

Loss reduction

A risk control technique that reduces the severity of a particular loss.

Automatic sprinkler systems are a classic example of a **loss reduction** measure; sprinklers do not prevent fires from starting, but they can limit or extinguish fires that have already started. Some loss reduction measures can prevent losses as well as reduce them.

For instance, using burglar alarms is generally considered a loss reduction measure because an alarm is activated only when a burglary occurs. However, because burglar alarms also act as a deterrent, they can prevent loss as well as reduce it.

As an example of a loss reduction measure, assume the consultant Etchley hired to conduct the educational seminars suggested that Etchley provide back braces for all of its employees because the braces help prevent back injuries and reduce the severity of back injuries that do occur. See the exhibit "Example of a Loss Reduction Measure: Etchley Manufacturing."

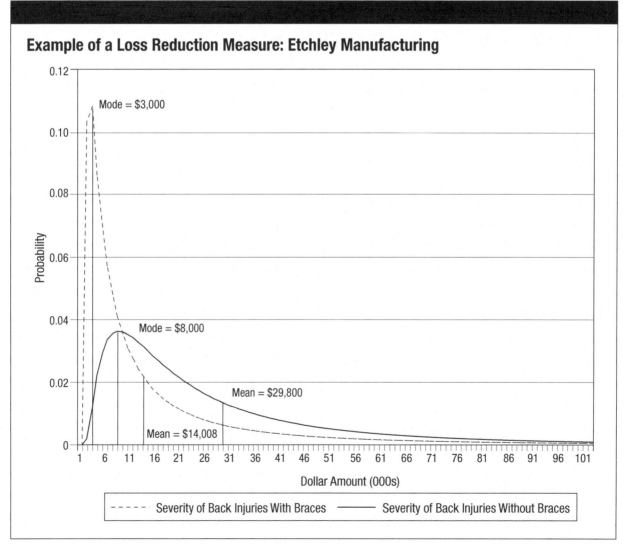

Example of a Loss Reduction Measure: Etchley Manufacturing

Mode = $3,000

Mode = $8,000

Mean = $29,800

Mean = $14,008

Probability

Dollar Amount (000s)

- - - - - Severity of Back Injuries With Braces   ——— Severity of Back Injuries Without Braces

The exhibit contains the original severity distribution for Etchley and the new severity distribution with all employees using back braces. As with most severity distributions, the one for back injuries is not symmetrical, but skewed. Most back injuries are grouped in the left portion of the distribution (lower severity values), with some very serious injuries grouped as outliers to the right. This positively skewed distribution pulls the tail of the distribution to the right and increases the mean.

Note the difference between the means and modes with and without back braces. The use of back braces lowers the average severity (mean) by $15,792 ($29,800 – $14,008 = $15,792) as well as the severity of the injuries that would occur most often (mode) by $5,000 ($8,000 – $3,000 = $5,000).

The two broad categories of loss reduction measures are pre-loss measures, which are applied before a loss occurs, and post-loss measures, which are applied after a loss occurs. The aim of pre-loss measures is to reduce the amount or extent of property damaged and the number of people injured or the extent of injury incurred from a single event.

For example, Etchley's use of back braces is a pre-loss measure; erecting fire walls to limit the amount of damage and danger that can be caused by a single fire is also a pre-loss measure.

Post-loss measures typically focus on emergency procedures, salvage operations, rehabilitation activities, public relations, or legal defenses to halt the spread or to counter the effects of loss. An example of a post-loss loss reduction measure is to temporarily move an organization's operations to a new location following a fire so that operations can continue while the damaged property is repaired, thus reducing loss severity.

Disaster recovery planning is a specialized aspect of loss reduction. A disaster recovery plan, also called a catastrophe recovery plan or a contingency plan, is a plan for backup procedures, emergency response, and post-disaster recovery to ensure that critical resources are available to facilitate the continuity of operations in an emergency situation. For many organizations, disaster recovery planning is especially important in addressing the risks associated with those systems without which the organization could not function. Disaster recovery plans typically focus on property loss exposures and natural hazards, not on the broader array of risks and associated loss exposures that may also threaten an organization's survival.

USING SEPARATION, DUPLICATION, AND DIVERSIFICATION

Before a specific risk control technique is recommended to an organization or individual, several available options should be considered.

In some situations, avoiding risk or preventing a loss is not feasible, either for logistical or financial reasons. Three risk control techniques allow an organization or individual to accept unavoidable risk by making losses potentially less severe and more predictable:

- Separation
- Duplication
- Diversification

Separation

Separation

A risk control technique that isolates loss exposures from one another to minimize the adverse effect of a single loss.

Separation is appropriate if an organization can operate with only a portion of separate units intact after a loss. For example, if an organization produces its products at two factories in different locations, the portion of the activity or assets at one factory must be sufficient for operations to continue if the other factory is damaged, destroyed, or otherwise forced to shut down. Otherwise, separation has not achieved its risk control goal.

Separation is rarely undertaken for its own sake, but is usually a byproduct of another management decision. For example, few organizations build a second warehouse simply to reduce the potential loss severity at the first warehouse. However, if an organization is considering constructing a second warehouse to expand production, the risk control benefits of a second warehouse could support the argument in favor of the expansion.

The intent of separation is to reduce the severity of an individual loss at a single location. However, by creating multiple locations, separation most likely increases loss frequency. For example, using two distantly separated warehouses instead of one reduces the maximum possible loss at each individual location, but increases loss frequency, because two units are exposed to loss. The insurance or risk management professional should be confident that the benefits of reduced loss severity from separation more than offset the increased loss frequency.

As an example of separation, consider a hypothetical organization, Ryedale Shipping Company (Ryedale), which has to decide between these options for shipping its clients' products:

- Option A—use one central warehouse
- Option B—use two warehouses

Under Option A, the central warehouse would contain $500,000 worth of merchandise and have a 5 percent chance of experiencing a fire in any given year. For simplicity, assume that only one fire per year can occur and that if a fire occurs, all of the warehouse's merchandise is completely destroyed. Under Option B, the two warehouses would each have the same probability of a fire (5 percent), but would each house $250,000 worth of merchandise. For simplicity, assume that the two locations are independent of one another. See the exhibit "Example of Separation: Ryedale Shipping Company."

Example of Separation: Ryedale Shipping Company

Option A

	Central Warehouse
Value of merchandise	$500,000
Probability of a fire	.05

Severity distribution (maximum loss in a fire)	$500,000
Probability of a fire in the central warehouse	.05
Expected loss (.05 × $500,000)	$25,000

Option B

	Warehouse 1 (W1)	Warehouse 2 (W2)
Value of merchandise	$250,000	$250,000
Probability of a fire	.05	.05

Severity distribution (maximum loss in a fire)	$250,000
Probability of fire at W1 and fire at W2 (.05 × .05)	.0025
Probability of fire in W1 but not W2 [.05 × (1 − .05)]	.0475
Probability of fire in W2 but not in W1 [(1 − .05) × .05]	.0475
Probability of one fire in either W1 or W2 (.0475 + .0475)	.095
Probability of zero fires (1 − .05) × (1 − .05)	.9025
Expected loss [(.0025 × $500,000) + (.095 × $250,000)]	$25,000

[DA02652]

The exhibit shows the severity distributions for these options and how the expected loss is calculated.

Under Option A, the severity distribution is just the single outcome of a loss of $500,000. There are two possible outcomes in any one year: a fire at the central warehouse or no fire at the central warehouse. Given a probability of fire of .05 (5 percent), Ryedale would expect a $500,000 loss 5 percent of the time and a $0 loss 95 percent of the time. Therefore, the expected loss in any given year is $25,000 (.05 × $500,000 = $25,000).

Under Option B, only $250,000 worth of merchandise is at risk in any one fire. Therefore, having two warehouses reduces Ryedale's severity distribution from $500,000 to $250,000.

Increasing the number of warehouses increases the number of possible outcomes. One of these situations will occur:

- No fire at either location.
- There will be a fire at the first warehouse (W1) but not at the second warehouse (W2).
- There will be a fire at W2 but not at W1.
- There will be a fire at both W1 and W2.

The probability of each of these possible outcomes is shown in the exhibit. Given a probability of fire of .05, Ryedale would expect these outcomes:

- $500,000 loss (fires at both W1 and W2) 0.25 percent of the time
- $250,000 loss at W1 4.75 percent of the time
- $250,000 loss at W2 4.75 percent of the time
- $0 loss 90.25 percent of the time

The expected loss remains $25,000, but the likelihood of suffering a $500,000 loss has fallen from 5 percent to 0.25 percent, whereas the likelihood of suffering a $250,000 loss has increased from 0 percent to 9.5 percent.

This results in a total claims distribution for Option B that has a lower standard deviation than the total claims distribution for Option A. The standard deviation of losses under Option A is $108,973, and the standard deviation for Option B falls to $77,055.18. Therefore, losses under Option B are more predictable than losses under Option A.

Duplication

Duplication

A risk control technique that uses backups, spares, or copies of critical property, information, or capabilities and keeps them in reserve.

Duplication is a risk control technique that involves actions such as maintaining duplicate records, spare parts for machinery, or copies of keys. Duplication differs from separation in that duplicates are not a part of an organization's daily working resources. Duplication is only appropriate if an entire asset or activity is so important that the consequence of its loss justifies the expense and time required to maintain the duplicate.

For example, an organization may make arrangements with more than one supplier of a key raw material. That alternative supplier would be used only if a primary supplier could not provide needed materials because of, for example, a major fire at the primary supplier's plant.

Like separation, duplication can reduce an organization's dependence on a single asset, activity, or person, making individual losses smaller by reducing the severity of each loss. Duplication is not as likely as separation to increase loss frequency because the duplicated unit is kept in reserve and is not as exposed to loss as is the primary unit. For example, a secondary vehicle that is ordinarily kept garaged is not as vulnerable to highway accidents as the primary vehicle.

Duplication is likely to reduce the average expected annual loss from a given loss exposure because it reduces loss severity without increasing loss frequency significantly. Similar to separation, duplication can also make losses more predictable by reducing the dispersion of potential losses.

There are several measures an organization can implement that are similar to duplication and that incorporate nonowned assets.

One option is for an organization to contractually arrange for the acquisition of equipment or facilities in the event that a loss occurs. For example, a plant that manufactures aircraft can pay an annual fee for a contract in which a supplier agrees to deliver within thirty days the hydraulic tools and scaffolding required to continue operations in a rented hangar if the manufacturer's assembly plant incurs a loss. In this way, the aircraft manufacturer can continue operations with minimal business interruptions and avoid the expense associated with owning or storing duplicate equipment.

Diversification

Although **diversification** closely resembles the risk control techniques of duplication and separation, it is more commonly applied to managing business risks, rather than hazard risks.

Organizations engage in diversification of loss exposures when they provide a variety of products and services that are used by a range of customers. For example, an insurer might diversify its exposures by type of business and geography by selling both personal and commercial insurance and both property-casualty and life insurance in multiple regions. Investors employ diversification when they allocate their assets among a mix of stocks and bonds from companies in different industry sectors.

An investor might diversify investments by purchasing stock in a bank and stock in a pharmaceutical manufacturer. Because these are unrelated industries, the investor hopes that any losses from one stock might be more than offset by profits from the other.

As with separation and duplication, diversification has the potential to increase loss frequency, because the organization has increased the number of loss exposures. However, by spreading risk, diversification reduces loss severity and can make losses more predictable.

Organizations implement risk control techniques and the measures that support them to address one or more specific loss exposures. Each measure should be tailored to the specific loss exposure under consideration. Furthermore, the application of risk control techniques should serve to support an organization's overall goals, pre-loss and post-loss risk management goals, and risk control goals.

Diversification
A risk control technique that spreads loss exposures over numerous projects, products, markets, or regions.

RISK CONTROL GOALS

Different risk control measures will help an organization achieve its risk financing goals with varying degrees of effectiveness and efficiency. Therefore, when assisting others in selecting appropriate risk control measures, risk professionals must first seek to understand the risk control goals the organization is trying to achieve.

Because risk control is an integral part of a risk management program, risk control goals should support risk management program goals. Common risk control goals include these:

- Implement effective and efficient risk control measures
- Comply with legal requirements
- Promote life safety
- Ensure business continuity

Implement Effective and Efficient Risk Control Measures

An organization generally undertakes risk control measures that have a positive financial effect. Most risk control measures are implemented at a cost to the organization. These costs are typically cash outlays, like the costs of the losses they aim to control, and are considered part of the cost of risk. However, so that risk control does not unduly increase the cost of risk, one of the goals of risk control is to employ measures that are effective and efficient.

A measure is effective if it enables an organization to achieve desired risk management goals, such as the pre-loss goals of economy of operations, tolerable uncertainty, legality, and social responsibility or the post-loss goals of survival, continuity of operations, profitability, earnings stability, growth, and social responsibility.

Some risk control measures will be more effective than others. For example, both a sprinkler system and employees patrolling a warehouse with fire extinguishers may be effective risk control measures. However, a sophisticated sprinkler system with heat and flame sensors will likely be more effective than employee patrols.

The effectiveness of various risk control measures is often based on both quantitative and qualitative standards. For example, determining whether measures to ensure worker safety are effective may rely not only on statistics regarding workers compensation claims, but also on employee satisfaction with the measures taken.

As well as being effective, a risk control measure should be efficient. A measure is efficient if it is the least expensive of all possible effective measures. This does not necessarily mean an organization should choose the measure that entails the least initial cash outlay.

The long-term effects should also be examined to determine which measure can be implemented with the least overall cost to the organization. For example, consider an organization that needs to improve security at night. The organization's risk manager determines that a new security system and stationing a night security guard are both equally effective measures from a financial perspective, but needs to determine which of these methods is most efficient.

There are several methods available for this comparison, one of which is cash flow analysis. Given a loss exposure and the effective alternative risk control measures, the risk manager can use cash flow analysis to determine which measure will be most efficient. See the exhibit "Using Cash Flow Analysis to Determine the More Efficient Risk Control Measure."

In this example, both the security system and the security guard are equally effective; they both reduce annual losses by $40,000. Cash flow analysis shows that although the security system requires a larger initial investment, it costs less to operate and maintain each year.

If the risk manager examines these choices over a ten-year period, the annual cost of the security guard over multiple years eventually exceeds the initial investment required for the security system, making the security system ultimately more efficient.

The major advantage of using cash flow analysis for selecting risk control measures is that it provides the same basis of comparison for all value-maximizing decisions and thereby helps the organization achieve its value-maximization goal. It is also very useful for not-for-profit organizations that want to increase their efficiency by reducing unnecessary expenditures on risk control.

The disadvantages of cash flow analysis include the weaknesses of the assumptions that often must be made to conduct the analysis and the difficulty of accurately estimating future cash flows. Moreover, cash flow analysis works on the assumption that the organization's only goal is to maximize its economic value and does not consider any of the nonfinancial goals or selection criteria. For example, legality and social responsibility goals are not directly considered in cash flow analysis.

Comply With Legal Requirements

An organization may be required to implement certain risk control measures if a state or federal statute mandates specific safety measures, such as protecting employees from disability or safeguarding the environment against pollution. These risk control measures are a means of implementing the risk control techniques of avoidance, loss prevention, and loss reduction and they also support the risk management program pre-loss goal of legality. The cost of adhering to legal requirements becomes part of the cost of risk.

Many laws and regulations require organizations to implement specific risk control measures. For example, the fire safety code mandates certain fire safety

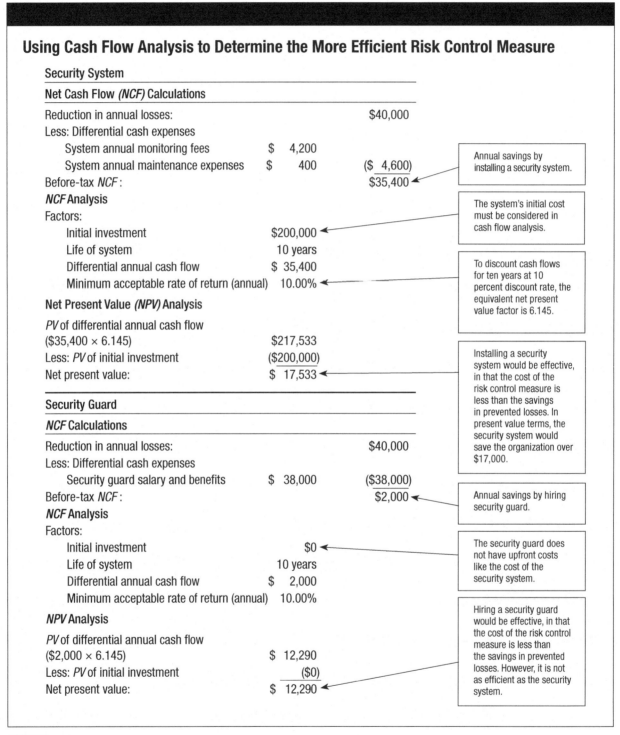

Using Cash Flow Analysis to Determine the More Efficient Risk Control Measure

Security System

Net Cash Flow (NCF) Calculations

Reduction in annual losses:		$40,000
Less: Differential cash expenses		
System annual monitoring fees	$ 4,200	
System annual maintenance expenses	$ 400	($ 4,600)
Before-tax NCF:		$35,400

Annual savings by installing a security system.

NCF Analysis

Factors:	
Initial investment	$200,000
Life of system	10 years
Differential annual cash flow	$ 35,400
Minimum acceptable rate of return (annual)	10.00%

The system's initial cost must be considered in cash flow analysis.

To discount cash flows for ten years at 10 percent discount rate, the equivalent net present value factor is 6.145.

Net Present Value (NPV) Analysis

PV of differential annual cash flow	
($35,400 × 6.145)	$217,533
Less: PV of initial investment	($200,000)
Net present value:	$ 17,533

Installing a security system would be effective, in that the cost of the risk control measure is less than the savings in prevented losses. In present value terms, the security system would save the organization over $17,000.

Security Guard

NCF Calculations

Reduction in annual losses:		$40,000
Less: Differential cash expenses		
Security guard salary and benefits	$ 38,000	($38,000)
Before-tax NCF:		$2,000

Annual savings by hiring security guard.

NCF Analysis

Factors:	
Initial investment	$0
Life of system	10 years
Differential annual cash flow	$ 2,000
Minimum acceptable rate of return (annual)	10.00%

The security guard does not have upfront costs like the cost of the security system.

NPV Analysis

PV of differential annual cash flow	
($2,000 × 6.145)	$ 12,290
Less: PV of initial investment	($0)
Net present value:	$ 12,290

Hiring a security guard would be effective, in that the cost of the risk control measure is less than the savings in prevented losses. However, it is not as efficient as the security system.

[DA02647]

procedures, environmental regulations govern the nonuse or use and disposal of toxic material, workers compensation laws require employers to provide a safe working environment, and disability laws require organizations to make certain accommodations for people with disabilities. These laws could require risk control measures that support avoidance (such as a ban of some toxic substances), loss prevention (such as safety procedures for machinery usage), and loss reduction (such as fire suppression systems).

Some laws and regulations are amended frequently, so it is important for risk professionals to be aware of these amendments. Failure to comply with legal requirements exposes the organization to additional fines, sanctions, or liability.

Promote Life Safety

Safeguarding people from fire has grown in importance from a risk control perspective because of the emphasis legislative bodies have placed on health and safety issues and because of the increasing frequency and severity of liability claims. In the context of risk control, **life safety** is the aspect of fire safety that focuses on the minimum building design, construction, operation, and maintenance requirements necessary to assure occupants of a safe exit from the burning portion of the building.

Life safety must consider both the characteristics of the people who occupy buildings and the types of building occupancies (such as residential, office, or manufacturing). Consideration of the general characteristics of both building occupants and occupancy has led to the development of specific fire safety standards for buildings. These standards are codified in NFPA 101: Life Safety Code® published by the National Fire Protection Association (NFPA).[1]

Promoting life safety can be expanded beyond fire safety to incorporate any cause of loss that threatens the life of employees, customers, or others. Therefore, organizations must be concerned about other causes of loss, such as product safety, building collapse, industrial accidents, environmental pollution, or exposure to hazardous activities that may create the possibility of injury or death. For example, a toy manufacturer should have an established product recall procedure in the event that a safety issue arises with one of its toys. Similarly, a car manufacturer should install appropriate safety guards on machinery, equip employees with appropriate safety gear, and give employees sufficient training to enable them to carry out their jobs in reasonable safety.

Ensure Business Continuity

In addition to implementing effective and efficient measures, complying with legal requirements, and promoting life safety, risk control should aim to ensure business continuity—that is, minimize or eliminate significant business interruptions, whatever their cause. Business continuity is designed to meet both the primary risk management program post-loss goal of survival and the post-loss goal of continuity of operations.

Loss exposures and their associated losses vary widely by industry, location, and organization. Some organizations are more susceptible to terrorism, some

Life safety

The portion of fire safety that focuses on the minimum building design, construction, operation, and maintenance requirements necessary to assure occupants of a safe exit from the burning portion of the building.

are more susceptible to information technology problems, and others are more susceptible to natural disasters. Because each organization is unique in its potential losses, each must also be unique in its application of risk control measures to promote business continuity.

For example, many causes of loss, such as fire and explosion, can be prevented through appropriate loss prevention measures. If left untreated, these causes of loss could result in a significant business interruption. However, there are other causes of loss (including natural disasters such as hurricanes or earthquakes) that an organization may not be able to avoid or prevent. Nonetheless, the organization may be able to minimize any business interruption resulting from a natural disaster through appropriate loss reduction techniques.

SELECTION OF RISK CONTROL TECHNIQUES

After considering alternative risk control techniques, risk professionals decide which techniques are appropriate for particular loss exposures.

In performing this part of the risk management process, risk professionals can benefit from knowing which risk control techniques are usually applicable to each of these loss exposures:

- Property
- Liability
- Personnel
- Net income

Property Loss Exposures

The risk control techniques commonly selected for property loss exposures vary by the type of property and the cause of loss threatening the property. Risk control measures used to prevent or reduce fire losses, for example, are substantially different from those used to prevent or reduce theft losses. Avoidance, loss prevention, loss reduction, separation, and duplication can all be applied in some way to the broad array of property loss exposures.

An example will help to show how different risk control techniques might be selected for a particular loss exposure. Commercial property underwriters commonly assess fire loss exposures for buildings and their contents based on each building's construction, occupancy, protection, and external exposure (referred to as COPE factors). As demonstrated in the exhibit, each COPE factor can be addressed through the application of various risk control techniques. See the exhibit "Application of Risk Control Techniques to COPE."

Application of Risk Control Techniques to COPE

COPE Factor	Description	Risk Control Technique
Construction	Construction materials and techniques range from simple frame construction (least resistive to fire) to fire-resistive construction (most fire resistive), with a wide variety of choices in between.	Loss prevention and loss reduction through construction designed to minimize frequency and severity of losses.
Occupancy	There are several different classifications of occupancy, ranging from residential to industrial, with each classification presenting its own risk to real property.	Loss reduction through safety training and emergency evacuation procedures.
Protection	There are two categories of protection, internal or external. Internal protection refers to what the organization does to protect its own real property. External protection refers to what fire departments and other public facilities do to safeguard the general public.	Two loss reduction measures used for internal fire protection are fire detection and suppression. External protection could involve selecting a building site near a highly rated fire department.
External Exposure	A building is exposed to fire hazards from outside sources, such as neighboring buildings. COPE factors are used to evaluate neighboring buildings' fire risk and the risk of a fire spreading to the organization's property.	The loss prevention and reduction measures may include relocation away from external hazards or removing combustible materials from the space separating the protected building from a neighboring building.

[DA02643]

Liability Loss Exposures

To select effective risk control for liability loss exposures, individuals and organizations need to understand the various ways in which their activities or operations can result in their becoming legally liable to others and what measures can be effective in preventing such incidents or reducing the damages for which they are held liable. Three risk control techniques can be used to control liability losses: (1) avoid the activity that creates the liability loss exposure, (2) decrease the likelihood of the losses occurring (loss prevention), and (3) if a loss does occur, minimize its effect on the organization (loss reduction). The other risk control techniques of separation, duplication, and diversification are not as effective in treating liability loss exposures.

Although avoidance is sometimes an effective risk control technique for liability losses, it is often either not practicable or not possible to avoid undertaking the activity or activities that can lead to liability losses. Therefore, loss prevention and loss reduction measures are more typically used.

The most common loss prevention measure is to control hazards (conditions that increase loss frequency or severity). Limiting the number or magnitude of hazards surrounding the loss exposures can prevent losses from occurring.

For example, to limit liability claims arising from employee or customer injuries that occur in a parking lot, an organization could implement loss prevention measures such as clearing ice and snow, providing adequate signs, repairing potholes and cracks in walking surfaces, or conducting periodic inspections.

After a liability loss has occurred, individuals and organizations can implement loss reduction measures to reduce the severity of the liability loss. Such measures can include these:

- Consulting with an attorney for guidance through the legal steps necessary to resolve liability claims.
- Properly responding to the liability claim and to the claimant in order to avoid feelings of ill will that may increase the claimant's demands.
- Participating in alternative dispute resolution. Litigation is a long and costly process. Some forms of alternative dispute resolution, such as mediation or arbitration, often help to resolve liability claims more quickly and more economically than litigation.

Personnel Loss Exposures

Personnel loss exposures are unavoidable, because all organizations have key employees. These loss exposures can arise from events both inside and outside the workplace.

The risk control measures that organizations find most cost-effective are those that can be instituted in the workplace. Therefore, most risk control measures regarding personnel loss exposures involve preventing and reducing workplace injury and illness.

Loss prevention measures used to control work-related injury and illnesses typically involve education, training, and safety measures. An organization may also attempt to prevent personnel causes of loss that occur outside the workplace by controlling key employees' activities through employment contracts; for example, placing restrictions on hazardous activities such as sky diving, flying personal aircraft, riding motorcycles, and so on. Alternatively, organizations may use a form of separation, such as restricting the number of key employees who can travel on the same aircraft.

Loss reduction measures include emergency response training and rehabilitation management. Although all organizations must comply with federally mandated safety measures issued by OSHA (the Occupational Safety and Health Administration), additional training and safety precautions are often cost-effective.

Net Income Loss Exposures

Net income loss exposures can be associated with property, liability, or personnel loss exposures. Therefore, any of the risk control measures that control these three categories of loss exposures also indirectly control net income loss exposures. For example, to prevent a net income loss associated with a property loss exposure, an organization needs to prevent the property loss from occurring.

In addition to reducing the immediate effect of property, liability, or personnel losses on net income, risk control efforts must also control long-term effects, such as a loss of market share that can result from the net income loss. For example, if a manufacturer conducts a product recall, that manufacturer loses sales in the short term, causing a temporary loss of revenue. If the manufacturer's customers switch to purchasing products from other organizations, permanent market share could be lost, which is a long-term effect that translates into permanent revenue loss.

Two risk control techniques that are directly aimed at reducing the severity of net income losses are separation and duplication. Separation and duplication enable an organization to reduce net income losses by maintaining operations or quickly resuming operations following a loss. Diversification is also a viable risk control technique for many because it helps to ensure that an organization's entire income is not dependent on one product or customer.

HOW SMART PRODUCTS APPLY TO RISK MANAGEMENT

Historically, risk managers' assessments of the probability of adverse events were limited by the boundaries of human perception. Today, however, previously imperceptible risk factors, such as a worker's hydration level, the presence of a hazardous chemical in the air, or the catastrophic intersection of seemingly disconnected financial transactions, can be factored into risk management decision making.

This new world of risk assessment data has been revealed by smart products that sense their environment, process data, and communicate with other smart products and smart operations. These interactions generate **big data**—to which advanced analytics can be applied, ultimately reducing the uncertainty associated with predicting future events.

Big data
Sets of data that are too large to be gathered and analyzed by traditional methods.

As technology evolves, the availability and sophistication of smart products that can help refine risk management techniques continue to grow. Here are just a few examples:

- Wearables such as helmets that monitor fatigue or wristwatches that measure vital signs can sense, monitor, report, and analyze workers' health or well-being and their surrounding environments. Data generated by wearables may be specific to one employee or aggregated for a project, team, or organization.

- Drones can be used in surveillance and aerial photography; being unmanned and highly versatile makes them ideal for assessing conditions or risks in dangerous or unknown areas. The data generated by drones relies heavily on other technologies, such as computer vision, image recognition, and artificial intelligence, to mine the data collected and form conclusions about detected objects.

- In addition to performing activities and capturing information from sensors in a workplace, robots can measure, respond to, and produce data for monitored hazards or changing environmental conditions. For example, sensors in conjunction with high-definition cameras can scan and inspect bridges for erosion or other unsafe conditions.

Smart products have introduced a new dimension of depth and precision to risk assessment and control in a variety of contexts, including these:

- Property management
- Supply chain management
- Transportation management
- Catastrophe management
- Workplace safety management
- Construction and engineering management

Property Management

Wireless sensor network (WSN)

A wireless network consisting of individual sensors placed at various locations to exchange data.

Property managers can use **wireless sensor networks (WSNs)** to detect and respond to leaks and malfunctions or prevent on-site falls and injuries. For example, temperature and water sensors can monitor heat irregularities and detect the first signs of leakage before tenants (especially lower-level ones in multistory buildings) sustain water damage to drywall, carpets, furniture, or other belongings. Temperature sensors provide alerts before a pipe freezes and are particularly useful in vacant or temporarily unoccupied buildings. Light sensors monitor illumination and provide lighting when needed around the perimeter of buildings, in parking lots, on stairs, and in underground parking garages, eliminating hazards that could lead to liability claims and lawsuits. Motion sensors and surveillance cameras can deter crime before it occurs and document suspicious activities. Thermal sensors, current sensors, and smoke detectors assess impending fire conditions so that first responders can be notified before a fire begins or actions can be taken to lessen the extent and cost of damage if one does occur.

Because the sensors in a WSN work together, multiple buildings can be remotely managed, producing data that shows real-time and historical maintenance reports and service records, as well as comparisons among properties or units, floors, or departments within a property. Some sensors only need to be placed in the desired locations and activated. Many applications allow further monitoring or interaction opportunities. And surveillance cameras, enabled with computer vision, capture images that can be analyzed for additional insights, allowing for loss prevention and reduction and ensuring continuous climate control, controlled power consumption, and compliance with building codes.

Supply Chain Management

Supply chain management involves the risk of not only product, service, or shipment disruptions caused by unforeseen events but also the downstream effects that interruptions cause to other products, services, or shipments. Risk assessment, which involves identifying potential or actual disruptions, and risk control, which involves preventing or reducing disruptions, use many emerging technologies to manage supply chain risks.

For example, radio frequency identification (RFID), which uses radio frequency to identify objects, wireless protocols, and the Global Positioning System (GPS), is particularly important to managing supply chain risks. Supply chain assets were previously tracked using standard bar codes, which must be in close proximity to a reader. In contrast, RFID tags identify assets and compile their characteristics without human intervention.

RFID technology is wireless, supports an automated process, does not require the reader to be in close proximity to the asset, and provides specific information on each asset to facilitate logistics and transport. This technology, especially when used with GPS for additional location tracking, enables a mixed shipment of freight to be identified and tracked without the need to remove any external wrapping. Furthermore, each item of freight can be easily cataloged by the reader according to description and condition, manufacture and expiration dates, arrival location and time, and relationship to current inventory. When a shipment is incomplete or damaged, RFID technology can be used to assess the risk, automatically call for replacements, and manage the replacement process.

Additionally, RFID tags provide unique identifiers, which offer real-time, accurate record storage and retrieval in a closed-loop system. With this readily available, detailed data on supply chain assets, companies can immediately identify discrepancies and interruptions and quickly prevent and reduce supply chain risk. Furthermore, RFID's process-automation capability can generate real-time alerts for those who need to receive the information and oversee remediation.

Other kinds of sensors can empower more precise supply chain management. For example, sensor data can inform a supply chain manager that weather conditions have interrupted the production of parts or that cargo has been stolen.

Transportation Management

Transportation management that facilitates risk assessment and control involves incorporating technologies from the **Internet of Things (IoT)** to connect vehicles and their drivers with solutions for awareness, safety, efficiency, and reliability. These same technologies also help organizations manage their vehicle fleets.

Internet of Things (IoT)
A network of objects that transmit data to and from each other without human interaction.

Some of these technologies even provide driver assistance. Examples include crash avoidance; self-parking; cameras on the back of trucks to facilitate lane changing; and, in some cases, full autonomous driving capabilities enabled by cameras that use computer vision to discern people from other objects or vehicles, as well as to recognize changes in pavement types or abrupt lane changes in construction zones.

Smart transportation
The integration of strategic vehicle management solutions with innovative technologies.

Smart transportation is also key to transportation management. As with many smart operations in a variety of contexts, it can be described as a series of layers:

- A sensing layer, which uses a variety of sensors, cameras, and data-collection capabilities to make (or help the driver to make) necessary corrections and provide information to others

- A communications layer that provides data transmission to and from drivers and managers using wireless protocols that ensure necessary capabilities, such as recording, data uploading, navigating, video recording, and centralized monitoring for both the sensing layer and the service layer

- A service layer, which employs applications using data processing, cloud computing, and storage and analysis of large amounts of the data captured by vehicle sensors and provided by drivers

The results of this interaction among layers are improved remote diagnostics, prompt driver response from real-time analysis of his or her driving habits or physical condition, fuel and/or vehicle repair savings because of implemented corrections, preventive maintenance alerts before a costly mechanical breakdown, and customizable products and services (such as comparisons of nearby hotels and restaurants) to make rides easier for drivers and more enjoyable for passengers.

These advancements are also attributable to the photos, images, diagnostics, trip logs, and other vast amounts of data and statistics created by the sensing layer, analyzed by the service layer, and supported by the communications layer. The resulting data is, in turn, used to monitor performance and further refine the processes.

For example, accelerometers, devices that measure acceleration, motion, and tilt, are combined with special software to detect and measure linear motion. Through **telematics**, accelerometer technology can generate information about vehicle fleets, such as operator acceleration and braking. It can also be used for many other applications, such as to detect excessive vibration in an industrial machine that is about to explode and may injure workers and/or damage property.

Additionally, augmented reality technology can integrate a digital experience into a user's physical environment. One such example, head-up displays in or near aircraft and car windshields, reduces distractions for pilots and drivers by displaying information, such as speed and warning signals, within their lines of sight.

Telematics
The use of technological devices to transmit data via wireless communication and GPS tracking.

Catastrophe Management

Sensors and WSNs are also used in catastrophe management. As long as a sensor can withstand a harsh environment, it can continuously monitor an area for light, temperature, specific gases, and more. Alternatively, a sensor or WSN can measure local changes when a catastrophe is predicted or has occurred.

By continuously sensing the environment, sensors and WSNs can detect and analyze changes over time and help predict a catastrophe and allow for adequate preparation. For example, an accelerometer can continuously monitor earth movements to determine where an earthquake will occur, and underwater pressure sensors can measure water weight on sensors to help determine how fast and in which direction a tsunami will travel. In fire-prone areas, gas sensors, thermal sensors, and anemometers can be strategically placed on the outer proximity of an area to warn of approaching forest fires.

Lidar is a technology used to, among other things, improve the performance and accuracy of autonomous vehicles. It can work with optical sensors, such as high-definition cameras, to detect images, even through shadows or blinding sunshine. Lidar has applications to catastrophe management, both before and after a natural disaster:

Lidar
A sensor similar to radar that uses infrared light to detect nearby objects.

- It provides images even under lighting conditions that are inadequate because of cloudiness, intense sunshine, or shadows. Furthermore, its high-definition three-dimensional mapping technology provides more realistic and usable data than two-dimensional mapping.
- It can capture and produce accurate elevation data, enhancing the mapping of flood-prone areas before a flood and helping to determine the flood levels that will be reached based on current water levels in surrounding rivers. It can also help identify regions, neighborhoods, or even individual structures that may need to be evacuated before a flood.
- Furthermore, lidar images after a flood, and the additional data it collects on air pressure, temperature, wind turbulence, and location, provide

information that assists in prioritizing rescue and remediation efforts. This information can also be used to analyze and compare various flood events.

- Lidar can help determine the optimal location for emergency communications equipment after a disaster disrupts cell or internet service. Models produced using lidar images identify the optimal locations for placing mobile Wi-Fi terminals (linked to satellites) to provide a signal for up to a thirty-mile radius. After a catastrophe such as a tsunami or an earthquake, lidar can provide street-by-street or even structure-by-structure analysis of locations with the highest risk, thus helping rescue and remediation resources be deployed efficiently.

Workplace Safety Management

Many smart products ultimately may be used to improve workplace safety and productivity:

- Wearables allow workers to wear sensors in comfortable and familiar ways (such as in safety vests or work boots) and still have their hands free to do their jobs.
- Drones provide information and help assess and control risks by going into unknown and potentially dangerous areas without putting humans at risk; they can accomplish this on the ground, in the air, or underwater.
- Robots—no longer clunky, human-like machines—operate in close proximity to workers but do more of the repetitive and heavy-lifting jobs. This allows workers to better use their skills and for humans and machines to be better integrated in the workplace.

Construction and Engineering Management

Mechanical sensors detect and measure a physical quantity and produce a signal that is readable by the user or another device. They are generally used with machinery and have many applications in construction and engineering:

- Motion sensors have many applications, including surveillance and security.
- Pressure sensors are similar to strain sensors, which convert pressure or tension into a measurement of electrical resistance.
- Current sensors are useful in protecting electronic systems and batteries from heat buildup.
- Position sensors are used when components are to be activated only when they are in the optimal places for a particular process to continue. They are used, for example, in car-wash machinery that senses the size of vehicles and adapts the cleaning process accordingly.
- Proximity sensors, slightly different from position sensors, respond when an object reaches a threshold area within range of the sensor. For

example, proximity sensors in smartphones can sense the presence of an ear and turn off the backlight and touch-screen functions to save power.

- An inertial measurement unit (IMU) tracks an object's position using accelerometers and gyroscopes. IMUs are used in navigation systems, as orientation (location) sensors in personal devices, and to measure motion in fitness trackers and gaming systems. They are also key sensors for autonomous vehicles.

BUSINESS CONTINUITY PLANNING

An organization can develop a detailed plan of action to mitigate risk and maintain operations regardless of external and internal events that could otherwise prove disastrous.

Over half of all businesses subjected to a catastrophic event fail immediately. Of those businesses that survive a catastrophe, half fail within two years. While government agencies may not fail immediately, a catastrophe could result in the reassessment of their effectiveness and mission, a change of leadership, or reorganization, leading to further disruption.

The development of a business continuity plan (BCP) is an important component of business continuity management (BCM). A BCP allows an organization to analyze all possible eventualities to determine the critical functions that must continue during a disruption so that the organization survives, recovers, and resumes growth. The development and implementation of a BCP entails seven steps:

1. Understanding the business
2. Conducting a business impact analysis (BIA)
3. Performing a risk assessment
4. Developing the continuity plan
5. Implementing the continuity plan
6. Building a BCM/BCP culture
7. Maintaining and updating the plan

While BCP and BCM contain the word "business," both terms refer to securing continuity of operations. Thus, applying the concept to other than for-profit entities can be accomplished by considering the "business of the agency" or the "business of the charity," for example. Thus, "business" considers the mission, vision, and strategy of the enterprise in addition to its survival.

Understanding the Business

To complete a business continuity plan, an organization must first understand all aspects of its business. This includes determining key objectives and how and when they will be met, as well as the internal and external parties involved in achieving them.

Once the organization determines its key objectives (for example, a key objective may be "continuing to manufacture and sell widgets"), it must examine how it uses its facilities, materials supply chain, human resources, communications, information systems, processes, distribution channels, and customers to achieve them. This allows the organization to identify the key processes that will constitute the basis for its BIA.

Conducting a Business Impact Analysis

An organization conducts a BIA to identify and assess the risks that may affect it. A BIA assesses what events may occur, when they may occur, and how they could affect achievement of key objectives. The BIA also measures the financial and nonfinancial effect of risks and explores organizational vulnerabilities, critical elements in developing strategies to protect organizational resources.

The analysis also distinguishes between critical and noncritical processes. This allows the organization to use the BIA to determine its recovery time objective, which is the time period within which a critical process must be recovered in order for the organization to resume operations after a disruption of operations.

Various international standards, such as ISO 31000:2009, take different approaches or use different terminology for the BIA. In some standards, the BIA and the risk assessment are combined. In other standards, the BIA goes beyond a more traditional risk assessment, which often focuses only on hazard risks and fails to assess the full impact of risk on all aspects of the operation.

Performing a Risk Assessment

An organization performs a risk assessment to identify and evaluate potential exposures and the probability that certain events will occur. It also indicates how susceptible the organization may be to particular disruptions. This helps the organization prioritize its BCM strategy and risk controls and assists management in making decisions regarding organizational risk appetite. A thorough risk assessment will reveal exposures and can assist in establishing methods for future risk mitigation efforts. Finally, the risk assessment helps the organization determine an action plan.

Assessments can be conducted at various levels. Convergys Corporation, for example, conducts three levels of assessment:[2]

- Enterprise assessment—a global assessment of risks that could affect the enterprise's overall business goals
- Site assessment—an assessment by risk owners at risk centers of risks associated with particular sites or locations or even specific geographies
- Program or project assessments—an assessment of a project's capabilities, resources, and limitations in relationship to a viable recovery strategy

Developing the Continuity Plan

After it has conducted the BIA and performed a risk assessment to establish recovery time objectives, an organization can begin to develop strategies to maintain critical functions during disruptions. Organizations may use one strategy or a combination of strategies to ensure resiliency:

- Active backup model—The organization establishes a second site that includes all of the necessary production equipment housed at the primary site. Staff may be relocated to the second site if operations are disrupted at the primary site.
- Split operations model—In this model, an organization maintains two or more active sites that are geographically dispersed. Capacity at each site is sufficient to handle total output in the event of a disruption at either site.
- Alternative site model—An organization that uses this strategy maintains a production site and an active backup site that functions as the primary site as needed.
- Contingency model—This strategy involves the organization's developing an alternate way to maintain production, perhaps using manual processes.

All of these strategies involve three levels of planning:[3]

- BCM organizational strategy
- BCM process level strategy
- BCM resource recovery strategy

These planning levels require the organization to examine its basic processes, determine potential points of failure, and create alternate operational methods.

Strategic choices for addressing a disruption of operations include these options:

- An insurance policy—This allows the organization to recover some of its financial losses if it suffers an insurable loss.
- Transfer processing—This entails the organization's entering reciprocal arrangements with another company or division to perform a necessary function in the event of a disruption of operations.

- Termination—With this strategy, an organization ceases production of the affected product or service.
- Loss mitigation—This entails implementation of risk controls and plans to reduce, minimize, or divert any loss.
- Do nothing—If an organization does nothing in the event of a disruption of operations, it absorbs the potential loss. This represents an increase of its risk appetite.

Implementing the Continuity Plan

Senior management must impress upon the organization that the BCP is integral to its survival and success. The business continuity coordinator (BCC) assists and directs each department in formulating a departmental plan. This ensures that the organization's component parts work effectively for the entire organization.

Each department's plan must include these elements:[4]

- Statement of acceptable level of functioning
- Recovery time objectives, resources needed, and potential failure points
- Tasks and activities required
- Procedures or processes
- Supporting documentation and information
- Structure to support the plan
- Description of division teams—purpose, team members, mission
- Explanation of interdependencies among the various division teams

The BCC presents the drafted BCP to senior management for approval. Once the BCP is approved, the BCC and senior management begin to influence the organization's culture to accept, practice, and maintain the BCP.

Building a BCM/BCP Culture

Senior management provides the vision statement and support for the BCP. It must also set expectations and objectives for middle management concerning maintenance of departmental plans. See the exhibit "Business Continuity Management (BCM) Encompasses All Divisions."

Staff must be educated on the importance of maintaining the BCP. One way management can achieve this is to hold semiannual exercises in which staff members react to a hypothetical disaster scenario by using the plan to maintain operations. If successful, these exercises may find "holes" in the BCP that need to be addressed. Exercises also provide opportunities to amend the BCP as new processes are introduced and used.

External suppliers and customers should know that the organization has a BCP and be encouraged to provide their own contingency plans. When key

Business Continuity Management (BCM) Encompasses All Divisions

Risk Management	Facilities Management	Human Capital Management	Technology Management
Intellectual Property Management	Reputation Management	Market Share Management	Supply and Distribution Management

[DA03892]

suppliers and customers are prepared for a disruption of operations, their relationship with the organization is improved.

Maintaining and Updating the Plan

Organizational environments, processes, and products change rapidly in today's business environment, and so too should the BCP. A BCP is effective only if it is kept fresh and updated. The BCP should be reviewed in detail and amended as internal or external conditions warrant. Analyzing the written BCP is essential and should be done semiannually or when a significant change has occurred in product line, processes, or management. An organization must also determine how best to store its BCP. Companies often maintain electronic copies of the BCP on a secure server accessible from several locations, while written copies are also maintained by key members of the organization.

Business continuity planning may not be effective in all cases. When an organization's survival is threatened, strategic redeployment planning is required.

SUMMARY

Risk control is a conscious act or a decision not to act that either reduces the frequency and/or severity of losses or avoids losses altogether. Three methods of risk control are avoidance, loss prevention, and loss reduction.

In some situations, avoiding risk or preventing a loss is not feasible, either for logistical or financial reasons. Three risk control techniques allow an organization or individual to accept unavoidable risk by making losses potentially less severe and more predictable. The first, separation, isolates loss exposures from one another to minimize the chances of one large loss. Duplication involves securing backup copies of records, keys, or important equipment so operations can continue in the event of a loss, and diversification spreads loss exposures over several projects, products, markets, or regions.

Common risk control goals, which support risk management program goals, include these:

- Implement effective and efficient risk control measures
- Comply with legal requirements
- Promote life safety
- Ensure business continuity

The risk control techniques most applicable to property loss exposures vary based on the type of property as well as the cause of loss. Loss prevention and loss reduction are the risk control techniques most commonly used for liability loss exposures. Most risk control measures for personnel loss exposures involve preventing and reducing workplace injury and illness. Net income exposures can be controlled by the measures that control the property, liability, or personnel losses that cause net income losses.

Smart products can be used to enhance risk assessment and control in a variety of contexts, including these:

- Property management
- Supply chain management
- Transportation management
- Catastrophe management
- Workplace safety management
- Construction and engineering management

BCM is a strategic and operational approach designed to maintain business operations in the event of a catastrophe. Its purpose is to analyze potential risks and determine the most effective solutions the organization may employ to mitigate the risk and resulting damage. An important component of the BCM process is the business continuity plan, which entails these steps:

1. Understanding the business
2. Conducting a BIA
3. Performing a risk assessment
4. Developing the continuity plan
5. Implementing the continuity plan
6. Building a BCM/BCP culture
7. Maintaining and updating the plan

ASSIGNMENT NOTES

1. NFPA 101: Life Safety Code is a registered trademark of the National Fire Protection Association, Quincy, Mass., 02169.

2. Adapted from an unpublished manuscript, Carol A. Fox and Michael S. Epstein, "Why Is Enterprise Risk Management (ERM) Important for Preparedness?" (Convergys Corporation, 2009).

3. PAS 56: 2003, Guide to Business Continuity Management, The Business Continuity Institute, March 2003, p. 14.

4. PAS 56: 2003, Guide to Business Continuity Management, p. 18.

5

Selecting Risk Financing Techniques

Educational Objectives

After learning the content of this assignment, you should be able to:

▷ Describe common risk financing goals for organizations.

▷ Describe the following aspects of retention and transfer:

- Retention funding measures

- Limitations on risk transfer measures

- The advantages of both retention and transfer

▷ Explain how the following factors influence the ability of a risk financing measure to meet an individual's or organization's risk financing goals:

- The mix of retention and transfer

- Loss exposure characteristics

- Characteristics of the individual or organization

▷ Explain how guaranteed cost insurance operates and how effectively it meets risk financing goals.

▷ Explain how self-insurance operates and how effectively it meets risk financing goals.

▷ Explain how large deductible plans operate and how effectively they meet risk financing goals.

▷ Explain how captive insurers operate and how effectively they meet risk financing goals.

▷ Explain how finite risk insurance plans operate and how effectively they meet risk financing goals.

▷ Explain how pools operate and how effectively they meet risk financing goals.

▷ Explain how retrospective rating plans operate and how effectively they meet risk financing goals.

5

▶ Explain how hold-harmless agreements operate and how effectively they meet risk financing goals.

▶ Explain how these capital market solutions operate and how effectively they meet risk financing goals:

- Securitization

- Hedging

- Contingent capital arrangements

Selecting Risk Financing Techniques

5

RISK FINANCING GOALS

To manage its risk and maintain a tolerable level of uncertainty, an organization should pursue risk financing goals.

Risk financing goals must support both the organization's risk management and financial goals. Determining how to achieve these goals leads to selection of the most appropriate risk financing techniques.

To achieve the financial goal of maximizing market value, most publicly traded organizations should pursue risk financing goals. (Although their overall goals may differ, privately held and not-for-profit organizations should also do this.) Common risk financing goals include these:

- Pay for negative financial consequences of an event
- Maintain liquidity
- Manage uncertainty
- Comply with legal and regulatory requirements
- Minimize the "cost of risk"

Organizations must choose the goals that best support their overall business goals.

Pay for Negative Financial Consequences of an Event

Risk financing makes funds available to pay for the negative consequences of an event, which can be sudden or gradual. An example of the latter is an organization that suffers a decline in customer loyalty. Risk financing, when thought of in its broadest sense, can provide a source of funds to take action that offsets this decline. However, risk financing is usually related to offsetting the negative financial consequences of a sudden event, such as a flood or an earthquake.

Further, the availability of funds may be important when operations have been disrupted, such as when damaged property must be replaced. However, paying for the negative consequences of an event is also important from a public relations perspective, among others. For example, an organization does not want to tarnish its reputation by not paying liability losses that result from legitimate third-party claims.

Maintain Liquidity

Liquid asset
Property that can be quickly and easily converted into cash.

Liquid assets are essential to providing funds to meet or modify the negative financial consequences of events. A **liquid asset** can easily be converted into cash at its fair market value. For example, marketable securities are liquid because they can be readily sold in the stock or bond market. Some assets, such as machinery and equipment, are not liquid because they would be difficult to sell quickly.

When an organization retains its financial risk, it must determine the amount of cash it needs to pay for the consequences of an event, as well as determine the timing of those cash payments. In deciding how to make financial resources available to pay for its retained risk, an organization must consider its various sources of liquidity: the liquidity of its assets, the strength of its cash flows, its borrowing capacity, and (for a publicly traded organization) its ability to issue stock.

The higher an organization's retention, the greater its need for liquidity. Likewise, organizations that retain risk and experience greatly varying consequences—and, therefore, greater uncertainty—also need substantial liquidity.

Manage Uncertainty

Managing uncertainty is needed to achieve the main financial goal of most publicly traded organizations, which is to maximize market value by maximizing the present value of expected future cash flow. Future cash flow is a projection of the amount of cash that will flow into an organization in a given period less the amount of cash that will flow out of the organization during that same period. The present value of the future cash flow is derived by a calculation (called discounting) that accounts for the time value of money.

In theory, investors value a publicly traded organization by projecting the size of its future cash flow. To estimate the organization's current market value, they use a discount rate to adjust the expected cash flow to the present.

The higher the uncertainty associated with future cash flow, the greater the discount rate. The greater the discount rate, the lower the present value of an organization's cash flow and the lower the current market value that investors assign the organization. Therefore, increased uncertainty in an organization's cash flow reduces the organization's market value.

Risk management framework
A foundation for applying the risk management process throughout the organization.

Achieving the risk financing goal of managing the uncertainties of an organization's cash flow and more can be challenging. For example, an organization often has difficulty determining the maximum level of uncertainty it can tolerate. To do so, it can apply a risk management process that has been integrated into an organization's overall governance, strategy, reporting processes, values, and culture through a **risk management framework**.

Comply With Legal and Regulatory Requirements

Legal and regulatory requirements come from a variety of government entities. For example, the United States Securities and Exchange Commission (SEC) is an agency of the U.S. government that is responsible for enforcing federal securities laws such as the Sarbanes-Oxley Act of 2002. Sarbanes-Oxley sets stringent standards for all U.S. public company boards. Such standards include requirements that senior executives take personal responsibility for the accuracy and completeness of corporate financial reports by certifying and approving the integrity of their reports quarterly. Sarbanes-Oxley also modifies reporting requirements for financial transactions, including off balance sheet transactions, pro-forma figures, stock transactions of corporate officers, and timely notice of material changes in financial condition.

Another example of legal and regulatory compliance in the U.S. concerns organizations that raise funds by issuing bonds. These organizations are legally required to purchase insurance. For example, an organization may be subject to a covenant imposed by the bond purchasers that requires it to insure its property for a specific amount. The insurance laws of most states require organizations to purchase liability insurance for their vehicles or, alternatively, to qualify as self-insurers.

Similarly, state workers compensation statutes require most employers to purchase workers compensation insurance or to qualify as self-insurers.

Minimize the Cost of Risk

Cost of risk is a concept applied to **hazard risk**—that is, the possibility of accidental loss arising from property, liability, personnel, and net income loss exposures. Hazard risk contrasts with business risk (also called speculative risk), which presents not only the possibility of loss but also the possibility of gain.

Hazard risk
Risk from accidental loss, including the possibility of loss or no loss.

Managing the cost of risk involves minimizing the cost per unit of risk transferred and retaining risk when a sufficient return would result. The return from retaining risk can be measured by the savings in risk transfer costs, assuming the organization has the option to transfer its risk.

Although managing cost of risk is only one of several risk financing goals, it is the primary measure used by many organizations to gauge the effectiveness of their risk management programs. Likewise, cost of risk serves, at least in part, as a personal performance measure for many risk management professionals.

An organization usually seeks to minimize its cost of risk because any reduction in hazard risk expenses increases its net income. The following expenses form part of the cost of risk, regardless of whether losses are retained or transferred:

- Administrative expenses
- Loss control expenses

- Retained losses
- Transfer costs

Administrative Expenses

Administrative expenses include an organization's costs of internal administration and purchased services, such as claim administration and risk
management consulting. Administrative expenses also include any insurance
premium taxes paid.

An organization should incur administrative expenses to the extent necessary
to properly manage its risk financing program. Often, an organization can save
administrative expenses by modifying procedures or eliminating unnecessary
tasks. For example, some firms with a loss retention program save expenses by
outsourcing the claim administration function.

Loss Control Expenses

Loss control expenses are incurred to prevent losses or reduce the severity of
losses that do occur. An organization can best analyze its loss control expenditures by conducting a cost-benefit analysis.

Resources should be allotted to a loss control measure as long as the marginal
benefit exceeds marginal cost. However, moral and ethical issues also influence the choice of taking loss control measures—such as equipping corporate
vehicles with anti-lock brakes and side-curtain air bags.

Retained Losses

Retained losses are a major part of an organization's cost of risk. When deciding whether to retain a loss, an organization can compare the projected cost of
retaining the loss with the cost of transferring it.

Retaining some types of losses that have significant delays in claim reporting and settlement offers an additional benefit. Such losses, which include,
for example, workers compensation claims, are known as long-tail losses.
Long-tail losses are not paid to claimants immediately but instead are paid
over time. Therefore, an organization can invest those amounts until losses
are paid.

An organization should measure the value of such deferred loss payments
when analyzing the cost of its loss retention program. Deferring loss payments
lowers the organization's cost of risk.

When deciding whether to retain or transfer its losses, an organization should
also take into account the value of the cash flow benefit from retaining losses.
A premium paid to an insurer to transfer losses is usually due at the beginning
of the policy period, whereas retained losses are paid at later dates, generating a cash flow benefit to the organization and, therefore, lowering its present
value costs.

Transfer Costs

Transfer costs are the amounts an organization pays to outside organizations to transfer loss consequences. In the context of hazard risk, transfer costs often include insurance premiums. In return for the premium, the insurer accepts the uncertainty of the cost of the insured's covered losses and agrees to reimburse the insured for covered losses or to pay covered losses on the insured's behalf.

By minimizing its transfer costs, an organization can maximize the net present value of its cash flow. It can minimize its transfer costs by employing an effective insurance broker or negotiating directly with insurers and other organizations that agree to pay for its loss consequences.

Apply Your Knowledge

Frank is a risk manager for a real estate management company. He has been asked to study whether the company should invest in additional exterior lighting around the buildings it manages to prevent crime. How should Frank decide whether resources should be spent on the lighting?

Feedback: Frank should know an organization can best analyze its loss control expenditures by conducting a cost-benefit analysis. Resources should be allotted to the loss control measure of adding exterior lighting as long as the marginal benefit exceeds marginal cost. Employees, tenants, and customers are likely to feel safer with the additional lighting, which could increase sales and net income. Employees may have fewer workers compensation injuries as well, which would also increase net income. Fewer crime victims could result in fewer liability claims alleging the company should have installed better exterior lighting. Frank should also consider the loss control measure for humanitarian reasons: his employer may allocate resources to install the exterior lighting so that people are not victims of preventable crimes, regardless of the cost-benefit analysis.

RETENTION AND TRANSFER

While retention and transfer are separate risk management techniques, most risk financing measures involve both retention and transfer. Therefore, after setting risk financing goals, an individual or organization should determine the best mix of retention and transfer for meeting those goals.

Determining this mix requires understanding how both retention and transfer operate, the advantages of each, and how each enables an individual or organization to meet risk financing goals. This information can be combined with consideration of the specific loss exposure characteristics, plus any characteristics specific to the individual or organization, to determine the most appropriate levels of retention and transfer.

Retention and Transfer in Same Risk Financing Measure

Retention

A risk financing technique by which losses are retained by generating funds within the organization to pay for the losses.

Transfer

In the context of risk management, a risk financing technique by which the financial responsibility for losses and variability in cash flows is shifted to another party.

Because most risk financing measures involve elements of both **retention** and **transfer**, the distinction between the two is eroding. Therefore, it is more appropriate to view pure retention and pure transfer as the extreme points on a continuum of risk financing measures, with almost all risk financing measures, including insurance, falling somewhere between the two extremes. That is, most risk financing measures are risk-sharing mechanisms, part retention and part transfer.

Whether any specific risk financing measure involves more retention or more transfer depends on the measure. For example, the "Insurance Risk Sharing" exhibit shows that an individual or organization that purchases an insurance policy (the insured) retains the deductible amount and any losses above the policy limit. The insured transfers to the insurer losses that are above the deductible but below the policy limit. In the example in the exhibit, the majority of the risk financing measure involves transfer. See the exhibit "Insurance Risk Sharing."

Retention

Retention can be the most economical form of risk financing. However, it also exposes the individual or organization to the most cash flow uncertainty. Retention can be either planned or unplanned.

Provided loss exposures have been adequately identified and analyzed (assessed), retention is an intentional form of risk financing and is called planned retention. Planned retention allows the risk professional to choose the most appropriate retention funding measure.

Unplanned retention occurs when either losses cannot be insured or otherwise transferred or an individual or organization fails to correctly identify or assess a loss exposure. In these two situations, retention becomes the risk financing method of last resort, which is why retention is often called the default risk financing technique. Unplanned retention can have a severe effect on risk financing goals and limits the choice of retention funding techniques.

Insurance Risk Sharing

Cara has just purchased a homeowners policy from Radley Insurance with a $1,000 deductible and a $300,000 limit. It would cost Cara $350,000 to rebuild her home today using the same construction materials. Assuming a total loss of the home from fire, Cara would retain the first $1,000 in loss because of her deductible. Radley would then pay the next $300,000 (risk transfer) in losses. Cara would be responsible for the last $49,000 in losses, as she would retain any losses above the limit. With the maximum retained amount of the losses being $50,000 and the maximum transferred amount of the losses being $300,000, this example of risk financing is closer to pure transfer than pure retention.

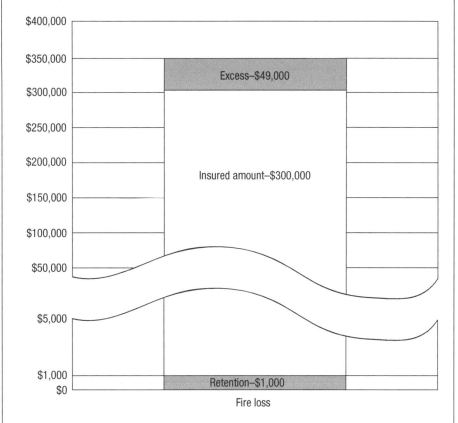

Cara can adjust the levels of retention and transfer in this example by adjusting her deductible and policy limit. Cara can decrease (increase) her retention by reducing (increasing) her deductible and raising (lowering) her policy limit.

[DA02693]

Retention Funding Measures

Retention funding measures rely on funds that originate within the organization. In order of increasing administrative complexity, these four planned retention funding measures are available to an organization:

- Current expensing of losses
- Using an unfunded reserve
- Using a funded reserve
- Borrowing funds

Current expensing of losses is the least formal funding measure (and therefore the least expensive to administer), but it also provides the least assurance that funds will be available, especially to pay for a major loss. Current expensing relies on current cash flows to cover the cost of losses.

This strategy may be feasible for losses with a low expected value but becomes less advisable as the expected value of the loss increases. Generally, the larger the potential loss an organization wants to retain relative to its cash flows, the more formal and better funded the type of retention should be.

An unfunded loss reserve appears as an accounting entry denoting potential liability to pay for a loss. Although this reserve recognizes in advance that the organization may suffer a loss, the organization does not support that potential for loss with any specific assets.

A typical example of an unfunded loss reserve is the reserve for uncollectible accounts. Organizations establish this reserve based on an estimation of the portion of accounts receivable that will not be paid.

In contrast to an unfunded loss reserve, a funded loss reserve is supported with cash, securities, or other liquid assets allocated to meet the obligations that the reserve represents. For example, a reserve for taxes payable at the end of the coming calendar quarter is usually supported by cash to pay them when they become due.

Funded loss reserves can be fairly informal, such as identifying assets that would be sold in the event of a loss, or highly complex transactions such as forming a captive insurer.

Although borrowing funds does not appear to be a retention measure, when individuals or organizations use borrowed funds to pay losses, they suffer a resulting reduction in their line of credit or ability to borrow for other purposes. This reduction ultimately depletes their resources.

Consequently, the individuals or organizations are indirectly using their own resources to pay for losses and, in time, use their own earnings to repay the loan. In the short term, the external source of capital is paying for the loss. In the long term, however, the individuals or organizations pay the entire loss.

Advantages of Retention

The advantages of using retention as a risk financing technique include these:

- Cost savings
- Control of claims process

- Timing of cash flows
- Incentives for risk control

The primary advantage that retention offers an individual or organization is cost savings. Retention is typically the most economical risk financing alternative and can generate cost savings in several ways. For example, suppose that an organization is deciding whether to retain its commercial auto liability loss exposures or transfer them through a commercial auto insurance policy. If the organization chooses to retain the risk of auto liability, then it can save money by avoiding the costs that are often included in insurance premiums:

- Administrative costs—Underwriting, claims, and investment costs incurred by the insurer as well as the additional amounts added to these costs in order to generate the profit needed by the insurer.
- Premium taxes—Taxes on insurance premiums imposed by many states.
- Moral hazard costs—Costs that are often included in underwriting and claims to verify information submitted or claims filed (often included with administrative costs).
- Social loading costs—If the state funds a residual pool through which high-risk individuals or organizations are able to purchase insurance that was unavailable from insurers, the insurers who sell insurance in that state will pass the costs of the residual pool on to all insureds who have purchased policies.
- Adverse selection costs—Cost of being pooled with high-risk policyholders. (This applies only to individuals and organizations that typically have losses below average losses.)

In addition to cost savings, retention allows an organization to maintain control of the claims process. This control allows greater flexibility in investigating and negotiating claims settlements. For example, an organization that is very concerned with its reputation may want to litigate liability claims against it, whereas an insurer may be more willing to settle the claim to reduce the payout that may be required on its part.

Another advantage of retention is the timing of cash flows. Most transfer measures require the individual or organization to make an up-front payment (such as a premium for an insurance policy). At some point after the loss occurs, the individual or organization is reimbursed by the other party.

Retention avoids the up-front payment and can shorten the delay between the time of the loss and the payment by the other party. It also allows the individual or organization to maintain any use of the funds that would have otherwise been paid. These funds can either be used in day-to-day operations or invested to generate additional income.

Retention also has the advantage of being an incentive for risk control. When individuals or organizations directly pay for their own losses, they have a strong incentive to prevent and reduce those losses. This encourages risk control in order to maximize the reduction in loss frequency and loss severity.

Although not without consequences in terms of the cost of risk control measures, these efforts should ultimately reduce loss costs. See the exhibit "Industry Language—Self-Insurance and Retention."

Industry Language—Self-Insurance and Retention

The term "self-insurance" is sometimes used to describe a risk financing plan for which a person or an organization retains its own losses—or simply decides not to buy insurance. Used this way, the term "self-insurance" is interchangeable with the term "retention."

Some argue that self-insurance is an inaccurate term because insurance involves a transfer of risk, thereby making it impossible to insure one's self. Others assert that certain forms of self-insurance are not insurance at all and that the label "self-insurance" should be applied only to a formal program in which an organization keeps records of its losses and maintains a system to pay for them. This text uses "self-insurance" in this context, that is, when an organization uses a formal program to record and pay for losses.

Insurance professionals should be aware that some statutes, regulations, and contracts use "self-insurance" and "retention" interchangeably. In addition, "self-insurance" and "retention" are also used together: self-insured retention. Self-insured retentions are similar to deductibles. A self-insured retention (SIR) is defined as a risk financing measure in which the insured organization adjusts and pays its own losses up to the self-insured retention limit.

[DA05016]

Transfer

The opposite of pure retention is pure transfer. A pure transfer shifts the responsibility for the entire loss from one party (transferor) to another party (transferee). However, most, if not all, transfer arrangements contain limitations that prevent them from being regarded as pure transfers.

Limitations on Risk Transfer Measures

There are two main limitations on the risk transfer measures available to individuals and organizations.

First, risk transfer measures (including insurance) are not typically pure transfers but are some combination of retention and transfer. Most, if not all, risk transfer measures involve some type of limitation on the potential loss amounts that are being transferred. These limitations can be deductibles, limits, or other restrictions so that the transferor pays at least some portion of the loss.

Second, the ultimate responsibility for paying for the loss remains with the transferor. Risk financing does not eliminate the transferor's legal responsibility for the loss if the transferee fails to pay.

For example, if an employee suffers a work injury covered by the applicable workers compensation act, the employer's workers compensation insurer would pay for the medical bills of the injured employee. If the workers compensation insurer cannot or will not pay the medical bills for some reason, the employer is still responsible for paying the bills.

Therefore, the transferor is reliant on the good faith and financial strength of the transferee as well as on the judicial enforceability of the transfer agreement. The transferee might not pay because of lack of funds, a dispute about whether the loss falls within the transfer agreement's scope or financial limits, or as a result of a successful court challenge to the agreement's enforceability.

Advantages of Transfer

Despite the limitations, there are significant advantages to using risk transfer measures as part of a risk financing program:

- Reducing exposure to large losses
- Reducing cash flow uncertainty
- Providing ancillary services
- Avoiding adverse employee and public relations

The principal advantage of risk transfer measures is that they reduce an individual's or organization's exposure to large losses. Retaining large loss exposures increases the probability that the individual or organization will incur financial distress. Financial distress can have negative effects on relationships with suppliers and customers and may ultimately lead to bankruptcy.

Retaining large loss exposures also increases the probability that the individual or organization will need to either raise funds from external sources, such as a stock or bond issue, or borrow funds, which can be costly. Risk transfer measures can help lessen cash flow uncertainty by reducing the effect of losses associated with retaining large loss exposures.

Many publicly traded organizations try to reduce uncertainty about cash flows and earnings on those cash flows because investors dislike uncertainty about cash flows. Therefore, as well as achieving the risk financing goal of managing cash flow uncertainty, risk transfers can increase an organization's attractiveness to investors and thereby potentially increase the overall value of the organization.

Risk transfer has the advantage that ancillary services can be included in the transfer arrangement; for example, insurers often offer risk assessment and control services as well as claims administration and litigation services. Being able to access these services can be a major factor in deciding to transfer some loss exposures.

The level of efficiency and expertise that some organizations, such as insurers, have developed in these areas often makes the risk transfer agreement very appealing to organizations that cannot provide these services efficiently.

Although it is possible to obtain these ancillary services outside of transfer arrangements through third-party providers, this can be expensive.

Finally, risk transfer can have the advantage of avoiding adverse employee and public relations because as well as transferring responsibility for the loss itself, the organization can transfer responsibility for the claims administration process. Therefore, any issues with claims administration are less likely to harm the reputation of the organization and consequently are less likely to generate adverse employee and public relations.

Because most risk financing measures involve elements of both retention and transfer, selecting a risk financing measure involves determining how much of a particular loss exposure the individual or organization is willing to retain.

SELECTING APPROPRIATE RISK FINANCING MEASURES

To select the appropriate risk financing measures to be used in a risk management program, an individual or organization needs to evaluate the relative advantages of all the available measures and consider the ability of each to meet the risk financing goals.

The major factors influencing the ability of a risk financing measure to meet an individual's or organization's risk financing goals are these:

- The mix of retention and transfer
- Loss exposure characteristics
- Characteristics of the individual or organization

Mix of Retention and Transfer

An organization's risk financing program needs to balance retention and transfer in light of the specific risk financing goals that the organization is trying to accomplish. This balance can be achieved through the appropriate mix of risk financing measures.

Some loss exposures may be fully retained, others mostly transferred, and the remainder addressed with risk financing measures that balance retention and transfer. See the exhibit "Ability of Retention and Transfer to Meet Risk Financing Goals."

Because retention can be the most economical risk financing measure, it enables an organization to meet its risk financing goal of minimizing the cost of risk. However, depending on the magnitude of the actual losses sustained, retention programs may have difficulty paying for losses.

The ability to pay for the negative financial consequences of an event (or losses) depends on the structure of the retention measure implemented and

Ability of Retention and Transfer to Meet Risk Financing Goals

Risk Financing Goal	Retention	Transfer
Pay for Negative Financial Consequences of an Event	Depends on magnitude of losses and structure and management of retention measure, as well as the relative strength of cash flows	Primary benefit of transfer measures
Maintain Liquidity	Depends on magnitude of losses and structure and management of retention measure, as well as the relative strength of cash flows	Generally reduces the level of liquidity needed
Manage Uncertainty	Typically exposes the individual or organization to more variability in cash flows	Important benefit of transfer measures
Comply With Legal and Regulatory Requirements	Depends on structure and management of retention measure	Secondary benefit of transfer measures
Minimize the Cost of Risk	Primary benefit of retention	Rarely the most cost-effective option

[DA02694]

the relative strength of the individual's or organization's cash flows. For example, if a loss exposure suffers a substantial loss that was retained, the ability to pay for the loss depends on whether the retention measure was pre-funded (such as funded reserve) or post-funded (such as cash flows or borrowing), how large the loss is relative to what was expected when the retention decision was made, and how large the loss is relative to cash flows or assets of the individual or organization.

Retention also generates the highest level of cash flow uncertainty and may threaten an organization's liquidity level. Often, how an organization structures and manages its retention determines how effective it is at achieving risk financing goals compared with transfer.

Risk transfer measures typically offer the greatest certainty regarding the ability to pay losses, offer the greatest cash flow certainty, and are useful in preventing liquidity problems, but they may be costly to arrange. Furthermore, some organizations are required by statute or contractual obligation to transfer some loss exposures to insurers.

For example, most mortgage lenders require that the property owner carry adequate limits of property insurance coverage. Similarly, many states require that motor vehicle owners have auto liability coverage. These requirements add to the overall cost of transfer and may therefore affect the benefit of transfer relative to retention.

Loss Exposure Characteristics

The frequency and severity of losses associated with each loss exposure are vital to determining whether a loss exposure should be fully retained or whether some form of transfer is appropriate. See the exhibit "The Effect of Frequency and Severity on the Retention or Transfer Decision."

The Effect of Frequency and Severity on the Retention or Transfer Decision

	Low Frequency	High Frequency
Low Severity	Retain	Retain
High Severity	Transfer	Avoid (if possible) Retain (last resort)

[DA02695]

The high-frequency, high-severity quadrant covers losses that occur frequently and are severe. These loss exposures should be avoided. Neither retention nor transfer is adequate to handle these types of loss exposures. If risk control measures can be applied to reduce the frequency or severity of the losses (or both), the loss exposure can be reclassified into the appropriate quadrant to be re-evaluated in terms of risk financing options.

The exhibit indicates that risk financing through retention is the appropriate technique for most loss exposures. It is only for loss exposures with low-frequency, high-severity losses that risk transfer measures are appropriate.

Characteristics of the Individual or Organization

The optimal balance between retention and transfer varies for each individual or organization, depending on specific characteristics. Therefore, individuals and organizations will make different decisions in selecting the appropriate risk financing measures. Even if two organizations have the same set of loss exposures, differences between the organizations may result in vastly different selections. The individual- or organization-specific characteristics that can affect the selection of appropriate risk financing measures include these:

- Risk tolerance
- Financial condition
- Core operations
- Ability to diversify
- Ability to control losses
- Ability to administer the retention plan

Risk Tolerance

Individuals and organizations vary widely in their willingness to assume risk. A risk-averse organization may decide not to produce a certain type of product because of the high instance of associated product liability claims, whereas another organization's primary source of revenue could be that same product.

The level of risk an organization is willing to assume directly affects its optimal balance between retention and transfer. All else being equal, the higher an individual's or organization's willingness to accept risk, the higher the likelihood that more risk will be retained.

Financial Condition

The financial condition of the individual or organization has a significant effect on ability to retain risk. The more financially secure an individual or organization is, the more loss exposures can be retained without causing liquidity or cash flow problems.

However, even financially secure individuals or organizations need to be careful. They may experience short-term liquidity problems if a significant loss has been retained and short-term cash flow or liquid assets are not sufficient to cover the loss.

Core Operations

An organization is often better able to retain the loss exposures directly related to its core operations because it has an information advantage regarding those operations. That is, the organization knows and understands its core operations and the loss exposures associated with them better than any outside party, including insurers. Because of this information advantage, an outside party would likely need higher compensation to enter into a transfer agreement.

Ability to Diversify

If an organization can diversify its loss exposures, similar to the way many individuals and organizations diversify their investment portfolios, it can gain the advantage of offsetting losses that arise from one loss exposure with the absence of losses associated with the other loss exposures. The organization is then better able to accurately forecast future losses. This increased level of loss accuracy would reduce uncertainty about losses and therefore allow the organization to retain more loss exposures.

Ability to Control Losses

Because risk control reduces loss frequency and/or loss severity, the more risk control an organization is able to undertake, the more loss exposures it is typically able to retain. All else being equal, the reductions in frequency and/or severity make it more likely that the organization will have the ability to fund the retention of that particular loss exposure.

Ability to Administer the Retention Plan

Risk retention requires more administration than risk transfer. Such administration may include claim administration, risk management consulting, or retention fund accounting. Organizations that have a better ability to fulfill these administrative requirements are able to use retention more efficiently.

Determining the optimal balance between risk transfer and risk retention measures keeps the risk financing program aligned with the individual's or organization's overall risk management goals. For the portion of those loss exposures that an individual or organization decides to transfer, a variety of risk financing measures are available.

USING GUARANTEED COST INSURANCE

Guaranteed cost insurance, in which a specified premium is paid for predetermined amounts of coverage, is the type of insurance most people are familiar with. And as a main risk financing measure used by organizations, it is one with which insurance and risk management professionals should be wholly familiar.

Guaranteed cost insurance operates by transferring the financial consequences of loss exposures from the insured to an insurer. However, it can be difficult to meet all of a large organization's risk financing needs through a single insurance policy. By layering coverage, an organization can meet many of its risk financing goals.

How Guaranteed Cost Insurance Operates

This section uses the term "guaranteed cost insurance" to refer to insurance policies in which the premium and limits are specified in advance. The premium is guaranteed in that it does not depend on the losses incurred during the coverage period.

Designed to cover property, liability, personnel, and net income loss exposures from various causes of loss, guaranteed cost insurance policies have been widely offered by the insurance industry for many years. Insurance is a funded risk transfer measure: the insurance buyer (insured) transfers the potential financial consequences of certain loss exposures to an insurer.

The insured pays the insurer a relatively small, established financial cost in the form of an insurance premium. In exchange, the insurer agrees to pay for all of the insured's losses that are covered by the insurance policy, typically subject to a deductible and policy limit. The insurer also agrees to provide necessary services, such as claims handling and liability-claim defense.

Organizations that have large loss exposures often have difficulty finding a single insurer that is willing or able to supply adequate guaranteed cost insurance coverage. These organizations often purchase multiple guaranteed cost insurance policies as part of their overall insurance program, which is typically divided into two or more layers: a primary layer and one or more excess layers.

The **primary layer** is also referred to as the working layer because it is the layer used most often to pay losses.

An **excess layer** can help insureds who want more coverage than is offered by the primary layer. Insurance policies issued to provide coverage in excess layers are often referred to as **excess coverage**.

In between primary and excess layers in an insurance program, an organization may use an **umbrella policy**. A **buffer layer** is used when the umbrella policy requires underlying coverage limits that are higher than those provided by the primary layer.

As an example of using layers of coverage, consider a large hotel chain that uses a layered liability insurance program to insure its large liability loss exposures:

- The primary layer of the insurance program consists of three primary (underlying) policies covering general liability, commercial auto liability, and employers' liability.

- Coverage above the primary layer is provided by an umbrella policy, which provides coverage for all three areas of liability.

- For the auto liability coverage, the umbrella policy requires a buffer layer above the primary layer because the primary auto liability policy limits are below the umbrella policy's minimum requirements.

- Finally, the hotel chain has three layers of excess insurance above the umbrella policy, providing layers of coverage for loss exposures not covered by the umbrella policy.

The exhibit illustrates the hotel chain's multilayered liability insurance program. See the exhibit "Multilayered Liability Insurance Program Including a Buffer Layer."

Primary layer

The first level of insurance coverage above any deductible.

Excess layer

A level of insurance coverage above the primary layer.

Excess coverage

Insurance that covers losses above an attachment point, below which there is usually another insurance policy or a self-insured retention.

Umbrella policy

A liability policy that provides excess coverage above underlying policies and may also provide coverage not available in the underlying policies, subject to a self-insured retention.

Buffer layer

A level of excess insurance coverage between a primary layer and an umbrella policy.

Multilayered Liability Insurance Program Including a Buffer Layer

Excess layer 3
Excess layer 2
Excess layer 1
Umbrella policy

General liability (primary layer)	Buffer layer	Employers' liability (primary layer)
	Auto liability (primary layer)	

[DA02696]

The number of layers the insured purchases depends on both the limits the insured desires and the limits that are available from insurers. The premium per $100 of coverage (the rate) usually decreases for each layer of coverage (for example, in the preceding exhibit, excess layer 3 would probably be cheaper than excess layer 2) because of the corresponding decreased probability that losses will be large enough to reach higher layers.

Ability to Meet Risk Financing Goals

Before using guaranteed cost insurance for risk financing, an organization should assess the extent to which such insurance meets the organization's risk financing goals. An additional benefit offered by guaranteed cost insurance is that a business can generally deduct insurance premiums for tax purposes. See the exhibit "Ability of Guaranteed Cost Insurance to Meet Risk Financing Goals."

USING SELF-INSURANCE

Organizations that wish to employ their own system for retaining and paying losses may adopt self-insurance. Many organizations use self-insurance for loss exposures, such as workers compensation, that result in losses paid over a period of time.

Self-insurance is a type of **alternative risk transfer (ART)**. It can play an important part of an organization's ability to meet its risk financing goals.

Self-insurance

A form of retention under which an organization records its losses and maintains a formal system to pay for them.

Alternative risk transfer (ART)

Those risk financing measures that do not fall into the category of guaranteed cost insurance.

Ability of Guaranteed Cost Insurance to Meet Risk Financing Goals

Risk Financing Goal	How Guaranteed Cost Insurance Meets the Goal
Pay for Negative Financial Consequences of an Event	Insurance can meet this goal, provided the loss exposures are covered by the guaranteed cost insurance policies.
Maintain Liquidity	Insurance can meet this goal because the organization requires less liquidity with guaranteed cost insurance compared with retention or other risk financing measures.
Manage Uncertainty	Insurance can meet this goal because much of the uncertainty about future losses is transferred to the insurer.
Comply With Legal and Regulatory Requirements	Insurance can meet this goal, especially regarding loss exposures that are required (by law or contractual obligation) to be transferred.
Minimize the Cost of Risk	Insurance can meet this goal, but it is not ideal because insurance premiums are designed to cover not only expected losses, but also insurer administrative costs, adverse selection and moral hazard costs, premium taxes, and any social loadings.

[DA12702]

How Self-Insurance Operates

Self-insurance is a formal retention plan. In contrast, an informal retention plan allows an organization to pay for its losses with its cash flow or current (liquid) assets, without any established payment procedures or method of recording losses.

Self-insurance is particularly well-suited for financing losses that are paid out over a period of time, thereby providing a cash flow benefit (compared with guaranteed cost insurance) to the organization retaining its losses. Accordingly, workers compensation, general liability, and automobile liability loss exposures are often self-insured because they have claim payouts that extend over time.

Self-insurance is usually combined with transfer, such as an excess insurance policy that covers infrequent, high-severity losses. It is typically used to finance high-frequency losses because it is more efficient than filing numerous small claims with an insurer.

To function effectively amid a large volume of claims transactions, self-insurance requires claims administration services similar to those provided by an insurer. Such services include these:

- Recordkeeping—A self-insured organization needs a recordkeeping system to track its self-insured claims.

- Claims adjusting—As with an insured plan, claims must be investigated, evaluated, negotiated, and paid.

- Loss reserving—A self-insured organization must determine reserve amounts needed for estimated future payments on self-insured losses that have occurred. The reserves for self-insured loss payments can be funded or unfunded.

- Litigation management—This involves controlling the cost of legal expenses for claims that are litigated, such as evaluating and selecting defense attorneys, supervising them during litigation, and keeping records of their costs. It also involves techniques including auditing legal bills and experimenting with alternative fee-billing strategies.

- Regulatory requirements—In most states, an organization must qualify as a self-insurer before it can self-insure workers compensation or auto liability loss exposures. The qualification requirements specify items such as financial security requirements; filing fees, taxes, and assessments that must be paid; excess coverage requirements; and periodic reports that the organization must submit to the regulatory body to qualify as a self-insurer.

- Excess insurance—Many states require a self-insurer to purchase excess insurance. Some states specify conditions for purchasing this coverage, while in others, a state agency reviews each applicant and decides whether to require excess insurance.

Ability to Meet Risk Financing Goals

Before adopting a self-insurance plan, an organization should evaluate whether the plan can meet its risk financing goals. See the exhibit "Ability of a Self-Insurance Plan to Meet Risk Financing Goals."

Ability of a Self-Insurance Plan to Meet Risk Financing Goals

Risk Financing Goal	How a Self-Insurance Plan Meets the Goal
Pay for Negative Financial Consequences of an Event	Self-insurance can help meet this goal if an organization carefully chooses the loss retention level, purchases appropriate excess coverage, and has sufficient cash flow or liquid assets.
Maintain Liquidity	Self-insurance can help meet this goal if an organization carefully chooses the loss retention level, purchases appropriate excess coverage, and accurately forecasts paid amounts for retained losses.
Manage Uncertainty	With self-insurance, retained loss outcomes are uncertain. The higher the retention, the higher the degree of uncertainty of retained loss outcomes.
Comply With Legal and Regulatory Requirements	A self-insurer must meet certain legal requirements. In most states, an organization must quality as a self-insurer for workers compensation and auto liability.
Minimize the Cost of Risk	A self-insured organization must administer its own claims (either with its own staff or a third-party administrator) but can save insurer operating expenses, profits, and risk charges. These significant savings are the primary benefits of self-insurance.

[DA12712]

USING LARGE DEDUCTIBLE PLANS

For organizations that are able to retain financial consequences of loss up to or in excess of $100,000 per occurrence, large deductible plans can be ideal. In return for a large deductible, an organization receives a lower premium (avoiding a potentially unaffordable one for certain loss exposures) and still benefits from the insurer's claims handling and other services.

Similar to self-insurance, large deductible plans are more common for certain loss exposures than others. Before adopting a large deductible plan, organizations should carefully consider whether they can guarantee the payment of losses under the deductible amount and how the plan will address their risk financing goals.

How Large Deductible Plans Operate

Large deductible plan

A rating plan whereby the insured assumes a substantial per accident or per occurrence deductible, generally ranging from $100,000 up to $1 million.

Both self-insurance and large deductible plans are common for workers compensation, auto liability, and general liability policies. A **large deductible plan** is similar to a self-insurance plan combined with excess coverage insurance in that it exposes the organization to a relatively large amount of loss. In exchange for this exposure, the insurer provides a premium reduction relative to guaranteed cost insurance.

A key difference between self-insurance and large deductible plans is that with self-insurance, the insured is responsible for adjusting and paying its own losses up to the attachment point of the excess coverage insurance. Under a large deductible plan, the insurer adjusts and pays all claims, even those below the deductible level. The insurer then seeks reimbursement from the insured for those claims that fall below the deductible. In effect, the insurer is guaranteeing the payment of all claims. The insured usually must provide the insurer with a form of financial security (such as a letter of credit) to guarantee payment of covered losses up to the deductible.

Ability to Meet Risk Financing Goals

Before adopting a large deductible plan, an organization should evaluate the plan's ability to meet the organization's risk financing goals. The exhibit describes how a large deductible plan can meet these goals. See the exhibit "Ability of a Large Deductible Plan to Meet Risk Financing Goals."

Ability of a Large Deductible Plan to Meet Risk Financing Goals

Risk Financing Goal	How a Large Deductible Plan Meets the Goal
Pay for Negative Financial Consequences of an Event	The plan meets this goal because the insurer pays for losses as they become due, including losses less than the deductible for which the insured eventually reimburses the insurer.
Maintain Liquidity	The plan meets this goal because liquidity is maintained if the deductible level is carefully selected. The liquidity needed is lower with a large deductible plan than with retention, but higher than the liquidity needed with guaranteed cost insurance.
Manage Uncertainty	The plan meets this goal because the organization can effectively manage cash flow uncertainty if the deductible amount is chosen carefully. The plan will meet this goal better than self-insurance but not as well as guaranteed cost insurance.
Comply With Legal and Regulatory Requirements	The plan meets this goal because it can meet legal requirements for purchasing insurance because an insurer issues a policy guaranteeing that all covered claims will be paid.
Minimize the Cost of Risk	The plan may meet this goal because the insurer administers the claims process, even for the small claims the insured has retained. The plan will meet this goal better than guaranteed cost insurance but not as well as retention plans.

[DA12716]

USING CAPTIVE INSURERS

Organizations that are willing to retain a significant share of their own losses in exchange for greater flexibility often form their own insurer, called a captive insurer, or captive. However, before an organization decides to use a captive, it should determine whether this method of risk financing will address its needs.

Specifically, insurance professionals and organizations can familiarize themselves with these considerations:

- Single-parent versus group captives
- How captive insurers operate
- Special types of group captives
- Captives' ability to meet risk financing goals

Single-Parent Versus Group Captives

Captive insurer, or captive
A subsidiary formed to insure the loss exposures of its parent company and the parent's affiliates.

A **captive insurer, or captive**, can be owned by a single parent or multiple parents. Single-parent captives, also called pure captives, typically operate as a formalized retention plan and only provide insurance coverage for their parent or sibling organizations, known as affiliated business.

A captive owned by multiple parents is called a group captive. Group captives typically operate as formalized pools in which several organizations group together to share the financial consequences associated with their collective loss exposures. Because of the sharing of loss exposures with other parents, group captives act more like transfer measures.

If a significant portion of the captives' revenues are generated by underwriting loss exposures from unrelated, third-party organizations (unaffiliated business), captives operate much more as a transfer measure than as a retention measure. Captives also have the potential to transfer the financial consequences of some of the insured loss exposures to other insurers through a variety of arrangements, including reinsurance.

How Captive Insurers Operate

A captive requires an investment of capital by its parent(s) to pay losses and manage its accounting, auditing, legal, and underwriting expenses. Just as any other insurer does, a captive collects premiums, issues policies, invests assets, and pays covered losses. Over 7,000 captive insurers operate worldwide, with many large organizations using one or more captives to finance their loss exposures.

Deciding how a captive will operate involves these considerations:

- What types of loss exposures the captive will insure
- Where the captive will be domiciled
- Whether the captive will accept unaffiliated business

Similar to self-insurance, captives are commonly used to cover loss exposures that substantially drain cash flow, such as workers compensation, general liability, and automobile liability. An advantage to covering these types of losses through a captive is that the captive can earn investment income on the substantial loss reserves necessary for these exposures.

Captives are also used to cover property loss exposures that are difficult to insure in the primary insurance market, as well as loss exposures that fall under specialized types of business, such as products liability and environmental liability.

The decision about types of loss exposures covered by the captive is often made before the captive's formation. In such cases, the captive is specifically formed to handle particular loss exposures for the parent. Once in operation, many captives expand their operations to manage a wider variety of loss exposures.

Many jurisdictions, known as domiciles, encourage captives to locate within their territories by offering favorable regulations and low (or no) taxes. These domiciles see captive insurance as an industry that boosts their economies by providing employment and income, such as annual registration fees.

Examples of these domiciles are overseas locations including Barbados, Bermuda, Dublin, Isle of Man, Guernsey, Singapore, and the Cayman Islands, as well as United States locations such as Colorado, Hawaii, Tennessee, and Vermont.

Although a captive insurer can be domiciled anywhere in the world, most organizations choose a domicile that is favorable toward the formation and operation of captives. Corporate governance concerns about the transparency of financial transactions have increased the appeal of onshore captive domiciles and offshore domiciles that offer reputable regulatory oversight.

When selecting the domicile for a captive, the captive's parent should consider these factors:

- Initial capital requirements, taxes, and annual fees
- Reputation and regulatory environment
- Premium and investment restrictions
- Support of infrastructure in terms of accountants, bankers, lawyers, captive managers, and other third-party service providers within the domicile

Some organizations operate a captive not only to underwrite their own loss exposures but also to insure third-party business—that is, business that is not directly related to the captive's parent and affiliates. Some organizations use their captives in this way to enable them to operate in the insurance business. Others have found a benefit to writing third-party business over which they have some control, such as warranties on the products they sell.

There are several considerations when deciding whether to insure third-party business. For example, many domiciles have different capital and regulatory requirements for captives that are involved in such business. These requirements are much more restrictive than those for captives that are writing only affiliated business.

Furthermore, writing third-party business may require additional actuarial, underwriting, and marketing expertise that the captive does not currently offer. Finally, insuring third-party business adds risk to the captive resulting from the possibility of adverse results from that business.

Special Types of Group Captives

In addition to the single-parent and group captive structures discussed previously, there are several special types of group captives. These are the most common ones:

- **Risk retention group** (RRG)
- **Rent-a-captive**
- **Protected cell company** (PCC)

The Liability Risk Retention Act allows the formation of RRGs to provide liability coverage other than personal insurance, workers compensation, and employers liability. RRGs were formed in response to the lack of liability insurance coverage available in insurance markets during the mid-1980s.

A rent a captive arrangement allows an organization to use a captive without supplying its own capital to establish such a company. Each insured keeps its own premium and loss account, so no risk transfer occurs among members. However, unlike in a PCC structure, no statutory separation of capital and assets exists in a rent-a-captive structure. Because of this, the capital rented by the insured in a rent-a-captive structure could be diminished by losses of another insured in the structure.

A PCC is otherwise similar in structure to a rent-a-captive. An organization pays premiums to the PCC and receives reimbursement for its losses while also receiving credit for underwriting profit and investment income.

As with a rent-a-captive, each organization keeps its own premium and loss account in a separate cell from those of other members. Because the PCC is required by statute to be separated into cells, each member is assured that other members and third parties cannot access its assets in the event that any of those other members becomes insolvent. This protection is not necessarily provided by a rent-a-captive.

Ability to Meet Risk Financing Goals

Before forming a captive, an organization should evaluate the captive insurer plan's ability to meet the organization's risk financing goals. See the exhibit "Ability of a Captive Plan to Meet Risk Financing Goals."

Risk retention group

A group captive formed under the requirements of the Liability Risk Retention Act of 1986 to insure the parent organizations.

Rent-a-captive

An arrangement under which an organization rents capital from a captive, to which it pays premiums and receives reimbursement for its losses.

Protected cell company (PCC)

A corporate entity separated into cells so that each participating company owns an entire cell but only a portion of the overall company.

Ability of a Captive Plan to Meet Risk Financing Goals

Risk Financing Goal	How a Captive Plan Meets the Goal
Pay for Negative Financial Consequences of an Event	The captive can meet this goal if properly capitalized and managed.
Maintain Liquidity	The captive can meet this goal if it is properly capitalized.
Manage Uncertainty	The captive can meet this goal by charging level premiums to the parent and affiliates and by retaining earnings in the years with lower losses to pay for higher losses in the other years.
Comply With Legal and Regulatory Requirements	The captive can be structured to meet all legal requirements, although captives are rarely licensed to operate as a primary insurer in the United States.
Minimize the Cost of Risk	The captive can reduce an organization's costs over time if properly funded and managed, despite large start-up costs.

[DA12721]

USING FINITE RISK INSURANCE PLANS

A finite risk insurance plan is often used for especially hazardous loss exposures (such as those leading to environmental liability and earthquake damage) for which insurance capacity is limited or unavailable.

To fully understand this form of alternative risk transfer (ART), risk professionals need to be familiar with the advantages and disadvantages of how a finite risk insurance plan operates and its ability to meet organizations' risk financing goals.

How Finite Risk Insurance Plans Operate

Finite risk insurance differs from guaranteed cost insurance in that a large part of the insured's premium under a finite risk insurance agreement creates a fund (experience fund) for the insured's own losses. The remaining amount of the premium is used to transfer a limited portion of risk of loss to the insurer. The insurer under a **finite risk insurance plan** usually shares with the insured a large percentage of its profit from the plan.

Unlike a guaranteed cost insurance policy, the premium for a finite risk insurance plan is a very high percentage of the policy limits. For example, an

Finite risk insurance plan

A risk financing plan that transfers a limited (finite) amount of risk to an insurer.

insurer might provide a limit of $10 million for a $7 million premium. The insurer's risk is limited because the most it would ever have to pay is $10 million, and it has the opportunity to earn investment income on the $7 million premium until losses are paid. By charging a substantial premium for the risk and applying a relatively low policy limit, the insurer has only a small chance that its losses and expenses will exceed its premium and earned investment income.

As with most ART measures, finite risk insurance combines many of the advantages of both risk retention and risk transfer. An insured that can control its losses receives profit sharing, including investment income, on the cash flow of the experience fund. In addition, the insured is protected by a limited amount of risk transfer in the event that losses are much higher than expected.

A finite risk plan often enables an insured to obtain higher limits than it could get using guaranteed cost insurance. Underwriters are willing to provide the higher limits because premiums and limits are combined over several years under a single plan. In addition, by using a finite risk plan, an insured can certify to third parties that it has insurance that might not otherwise be available.

Ability to Meet Risk Financing Goals

Before adopting a finite risk plan, an organization should evaluate the plan's ability to meet the organization's risk financing goals. See the exhibit "Ability of a Finite Risk Plan to Meet Risk Financing Goals."

Ability of a Finite Risk Plan to Meet Risk Financing Goals

Risk Financing Goal	How a Finite Risk Plan Meets the Goal
Pay for Negative Financial Consequences of an Event	The plan can meet this goal because the insurer pays for losses as they become due. However, because of the limited risk transfer, the insured ultimately pays for almost all of its own losses.
Maintain Liquidity	The plan cannot meet this goal because premium payments are usually paid upfront.
Manage Uncertainty	The plan can meet this goal because cash flows are smoothed over multiple periods; however, large premiums may be due at outset.
Comply With Legal and Regulatory Requirements	The plan can meet this goal because the insurer issues a policy guaranteeing that all covered claims will be paid.
Minimize the Cost of Risk	The plan can meet this goal because the profit-sharing feature encourages and rewards successful risk control efforts and thereby reduces an organization's cost of risk.

[DA12717]

USING POOLS

Participating in a pool can be a cost-effective alternative to guaranteed cost insurance for organizations. Pools are particularly common for workers compensation loss exposures, and the pool will process and pay workers compensation claims on behalf of its member organizations.

To determine whether an organization should join a **pool**, the pool's operation and ability to meet risk financing goals should be examined.

Pool
A group of organizations that band together to insure each other's loss exposures.

How Pools Operate

A pool is made up of member organizations. Each insured member of the pool contributes premium based on its loss exposures. In exchange, the pool pays for each insured's covered losses. In some pools, the members also contribute capital.

Pools can be organized in a variety of ways, including as a stock insurer or as a not-for-profit unincorporated association governed by its members. However, the structure of most pools is less formal than the structure of a group captive.

A pool operates like an insurer by collecting premiums, paying losses, purchasing excess insurance or reinsurance, and providing other services such as risk control consulting. Pools can be formed to cover various types of loss exposures and are well-suited for organizations that are too small to use a captive insurer.

For example, in the United States, workers compensation pools are common and permitted in most states. The individual states regulate the formation and operation of these pools. Public entities are commonly members of workers compensation pools.

Pools achieve savings through economies of scale in administration, claims handling, and the purchase of excess insurance or reinsurance. Each pool member might realize a savings in premium compared with guaranteed cost insurance, yet still benefit from risk sharing with the other pool members. A suitably designed pool can reduce an organization's cost of risk and keep cost uncertainty associated with retained losses at a tolerable level.

Ability to Meet Risk Financing Goals

Before joining a pool, an organization should evaluate the pool's ability to meet that organization's risk financing goals. See the exhibit "Ability of a Pool to Meet Risk Financing Goals."

Ability of a Pool to Meet Risk Financing Goals

Risk Financing Goal	How a Pool Meets the Goal
Pay for Negative Financial Consequences of an Event	A pool can meet this goal because there is risk sharing with other members of the pool. However, ultimately, the pool must pay for its own losses.
Maintain Liquidity	A pool can meet this goal if adequately funded and managed, reducing an organization's necessary level of liquidity.
Manage Uncertainty	A pool can meet this goal through risk sharing with the other members. This risk sharing can be a major benefit of a pool if it has enough loss exposures to benefit from the law of large numbers.
Comply With Legal and Regulatory Requirements	A pool can meet this goal if organized and managed within state regulations.
Minimize the Cost of Risk	A pool can meet this goal through economies of scale in administration.

[DA12719]

USING RETROSPECTIVE RATING PLANS

Retrospective rating plans provide an opportunity for organizations to receive a lower premium when they do not experience as many losses as anticipated. This provides an incentive for organizations to prevent and control losses. However, it also requires them to pay additional premium if their actual losses exceed expected losses.

Several aspects of a retrospective rating plan's operation should be considered, including optional loss limits, minimum and maximum premiums, administration, and the overall benefits. After these are considered, an organization can determine whether a retrospective rating plan can meet its risk financing goals.

How Retrospective Rating Plans Operate

A **retrospective rating plan** is a type of risk financing plan. Under it, an organization buys insurance subject to a rating plan that adjusts the premium rate after the end of the policy period based on a portion of the insured's actual losses during the policy period. See the exhibit "Comparison of Retrospective Rating and Experience Rating Plans."

Retrospective rating plan
A rating plan that adjusts the insured's premium for the current policy period based on the insured's loss experience during the current period; paid losses or incurred losses may be used to determine loss experience.

Comparison of Retrospective Rating and Experience Rating Plans

Retrospective rating is frequently confused with experience rating because both consider the insured's loss experience. Experience rating adjusts the premium for the current policy period to recognize the loss experience of the insured during past policy periods. In contrast, retrospective rating adjusts the premium for the current policy period to recognize the insured's loss experience during the *current* policy period.

[DA05019]

Retrospective rating plans are used to finance low-to-medium-severity losses and are generally combined with other risk financing plans (such as excess liability insurance) to cover high-severity losses. An organization must have a substantial insurance premium, usually amounting to several hundred thousand dollars per year, to benefit from a retrospective rating plan.

At its inception, a retrospective rating plan appears to operate in the same way as a guaranteed cost insurance plan. The insured pays a premium (the deposit premium) at the beginning of the policy period, and the insurer issues an insurance policy and agrees to pay covered losses up to the policy limit. However, in a retrospective rating plan, the insured's losses during the policy period are considered in calculating a major portion of the premium.

The insurer (using a rating formula agreed on at policy inception) adjusts the premium after the end of the policy period to include a portion of the insured's covered losses that occurred during the policy period. If the premium due is more than the original deposit premium, the insurer will collect additional premium from the insured.

If the premium due is less than the deposit premium, the insurer will issue a refund to the insured. Because the premium is adjusted upward or downward based directly on a portion of covered losses, the insured is, in effect, retaining a portion of its own losses.

Organizations commonly use retrospective rating plans for losses covered by their workers compensation, auto liability, and general liability insurance policies. Organizations also use retrospective rating plans to finance auto physical damage and crime losses.

Loss Limit

Loss limit

The level at which a loss occurrence is limited for the purpose of calculating a retrospectively rated premium.

Retrospective rating plan premiums may be calculated using a **loss limit**. The loss limit can vary and is negotiated by the insurer and the insured. For example, the loss limit under a retrospective rating plan might be $100,000 per occurrence. In this case, the first $100,000 of each covered loss occurrence is included in the retrospective premium, and the amount of each loss occurrence that exceeds $100,000 and is less than the policy limit is transferred to the insurer.

Minimum and Maximum Premiums

The adjusted premium under a retrospective rating plan is subject to a minimum and maximum amount, called the minimum premium and the maximum premium, respectively. For example, a retrospective rating plan might have a minimum premium of $200,000 and a maximum premium of $1 million. If the insured experiences no losses during the policy period, the minimum premium of $200,000 still applies. If, during the policy period, the insured experiences a total of $1.4 million in losses subject to the policy's loss limit, the premium is limited to the maximum premium of $1 million.

Because the premium for a retrospective rating plan includes a portion of the insured's covered losses during the policy period and is subject to maximum and minimum amounts, an insured retains a portion of its losses. If an insured incurs higher-than-average losses during a policy period, the final adjusted premium under a retrospective rating plan is higher than the premium that the insured would pay under a guaranteed cost insurance plan to cover the same losses.

The opposite is true if losses are lower than average. The portion of losses not retained is transferred to the insurer, which is compensated through risk transfer premium charges that are built into the retrospective rating plan premium. The retrospective rating plan premium also includes charges for other components, such as residual market loadings, premium taxes, and insurer overhead and profit. Such charges are also found in guaranteed cost insurance policies.

Administration

Retrospective rating plans require only a moderate amount of administration by the insured. The insured's responsibility is limited to making premium payments and arranging for any required security, such as a letter of credit, to guarantee future payments. The insurer is responsible for many of the administrative tasks, such as adjusting claims, making necessary filings with the states, and paying applicable premium taxes and fees. Because a portion of the premium includes the insured's covered losses, the insured should periodically audit the insurer's claims handling, loss payment, and loss reserving practices. Often, a broker or a risk management consultant performs this audit on the insured's behalf.

Benefits of Retrospective Rating Plans

An organization can save certain expenses by retaining a portion of losses under a retrospective rating plan instead of transferring all losses under a guaranteed cost insurance plan. One significant expense saved is insurer risk charges, which are extra charges that an insurer includes as part of its risk transfer premium to cover the chance that losses will be higher than expected.

Retrospective rating plans encourage risk control. With a retrospective rating plan, an organization that is able to prevent and/or reduce its losses quickly realizes a premium savings compared with what it would pay under a guaranteed cost insurance plan. This direct link between losses and premium is a major incentive for an insured to control its losses.

If designed correctly, a retrospective rating plan also provides financial stability. If the loss limit and the maximum premium are set so as to reduce the uncertainty of the insured's premium adjustments to a level that it can tolerate, then the insured benefits from the relative stability that the retrospective rating plan provides for its earnings, net worth, and cash flow. If a retrospective rating plan covers more than one type of loss exposure, then the insured also benefits from the stability provided through diversification by retaining losses from different types of loss exposures under a single plan.

Ability to Meet Risk Financing Goals

A retrospective rating plan can help an organization meet its risk financing goals by providing an appropriate balance between risk retention and risk transfer. Before adopting a retrospective rating plan, an organization should evaluate the plan's ability to meet the organization's risk financing goals. See the exhibit "Ability of a Retrospective Rating Plan to Meet Risk Financing Goals."

Ability of a Retrospective Rating Plan to Meet Risk Financing Goals

Risk Financing Goal	How a Retrospective Rating Plan Meets the Goal
Pay for Negative Financial Consequences of an Event	The plan can meet this goal because, as with any insurance plan, the insurer pays for losses as they become due.
Maintain Liquidity	The plan can meet this goal if the loss limit and maximum premium are chosen carefully.
Manage Uncertainty	The plan can meet this goal because it helps manage some cash flow uncertainty, but because of the retrospective nature of the premium, some cash flow uncertainty remains.
Comply With Legal and Regulatory Requirements	The plan can meet this goal because an insurer issues a policy guaranteeing that all covered claims will be paid.
Minimize the Cost of Risk	The plan can meet this goal because it includes a significant amount of retention and can reduce an organization's cost of risk over the long run.

[DA12718]

USING HOLD-HARMLESS AGREEMENTS

Businesses often use hold-harmless agreements to transfer the financial consequences of risk to another party that is not an insurer. They are commonly included in various types of contracts or agreements, such as construction contracts, maintenance contracts, rental and lease agreements, purchase orders, and sales agreements.

Because hold-harmless agreements are widespread in business transactions, risk professionals must understand how they operate and how they can help a particular organization meet its risk financing goals.

How Hold-Harmless Agreements Operate

Hold-harmless agreements are a noninsurance risk transfer measure. A hold-harmless agreement can be a stand-alone contract or a clause within a contract. An example of the latter is inclusion of this language in a lease of premises: "To the fullest extent permitted by law, the lessee shall indemnify, defend, and hold harmless the lessor, agents, and employees of the lessor from and against all claims arising out of or resulting from the leased premises."

Hold-harmless agreements are commonly used to assign responsibility for losses arising out of a particular relationship or activity. For example, it is common for manufacturers to enter into hold-harmless agreements with distributors whereby the manufacturer agrees to assume the liability losses the distributor suffers as a result of distributing the manufacturer's products. This type of hold-harmless agreement is a risk financing measure that transfers the financial responsibility for liability losses from the distributor to the manufacturer.

The party that uses a hold-harmless agreement to transfer the financial consequences of loss to another party is commonly referred to as the **indemnitee**, and the other party, which agrees to indemnify the indemnitee, is referred to as the **indemnitor**. To increase the likelihood that the indemnitor will have the financial resources to perform its duty to indemnify, the contract or agreement may require the indemnitor to demonstrate proof of financial responsibility, such as a certificate of insurance showing that the indemnitor has a specified amount of insurance that will cover the liability assumed under the hold-harmless agreement.

Indemnitee
Party in a hold-harmless agreement whose legal liability is assumed by the indemnitor.

Indemnitor
Party in a hold-harmless agreement who assumes the other party's liability.

Ability to Meet Risk Financing Goals

Before using a hold-harmless agreement as a risk financing measure, an organization should ascertain that the agreement is not affected by any statute that forbids certain types of hold-harmless agreements in the state where the agreement is made. If the hold-harmless agreement would be legally enforceable, the organization should then evaluate its ability to meet its risk financing goals. See the exhibit "Ability of a Hold-Harmless Agreement to Meet Risk Financing Goals."

Ability of a Hold-Harmless Agreement to Meet Risk Financing Goals

Risk Financing Goal	How a Hold-Harmless Agreement Meets the Goal
Pay for Negative Financial Consequences of an Event	The agreement can meet this goal provided the loss exposures are covered by the agreement and the other party has the financial ability to pay losses subject to the agreement.
Maintain Liquidity	The agreement can meet this goal because the organization requires less liquidity with a hold-harmless agreement compared with retention or other alternative risk transfer measures.
Manage Uncertainty	The agreement can meet this goal subject to the extent of the agreement.
Comply With Legal and Regulatory Requirements	The agreement can meet this goal, especially regarding loss exposures that are required (by law or contractual obligation) to be transferred.
Minimize the Cost of Risk	The agreement can meet this goal subject to any other contractual demands the other party requires before accepting the hold-harmless agreement.

[DA12715]

USING CAPITAL MARKET SOLUTIONS

In a capital market, bonds and other financial assets with a maturity of more than one year are bought and sold. Innovative approaches to risk financing have used capital market solutions as additional alternative risk transfer measures.

Capital market
A financial market in which long-term securities are traded.

Because these **capital market** solutions involve significant time and expense to implement, only a few large organizations (including insurers and reinsurers) have used them to finance risk. For example, insurers have used capital market solutions to finance catastrophe loss exposures, such as the possibility of large earthquake or hurricane losses. However, these products can be used to finance any type of insurable risk.

Three examples of capital market solutions are securitization, hedging, and contingent capital arrangements.

How Securitization Operates

An organization can use **securitization** to exchange income-producing assets for cash provided by the purchaser of the security. For example, a bank might securitize its mortgage receivables and sell them through an intermediary (called a special purpose vehicle, or SPV) to investors following this process:

1. The bank (mortgagee) lends money to both individuals and organizations (mortgagors) to purchase real property.

2. The mortgagors make a promise to repay the mortgage through periodic payments to the bank. These mortgage payments are mortgage receivables to the bank.

3. The bank, through an SPV, may sell a mortgage-backed security to investors.

4. The bank collects money from the investors and transfers the mortgage receivables to the investors.

In this type of transaction, the bank is no longer exposed to any risk of non-payment by the mortgagors. That risk has been transferred from the bank to the investors through the mortgage-backed securities. These securities appeal to investors when they offer a sufficiently attractive return for the perceived risk of nonpayment by the mortgagor. The bank exchanges one asset for another. It sells its mortgage receivables, which are subject to the possibility of default and other risks, and it receives the investors' money in exchange. Through securitization, risk inherent in the mortgage receivables is transferred from the bank to the investors.

Insurance securitization is a unique form of securitization. The cash flows that arise from the transfer of insurable risks are similar to premium and loss payments under an insurance policy.

The most common insurance securitizations are catastrophe bonds. Insurers or reinsurers sell insurance policies that cover losses related to natural catastrophes.

For example, insurance policies may cover property damage caused by hurricanes or earthquakes. Because of the catastrophic nature of these loss exposures, insurers and reinsurers may have difficulty using pooling and the law of large numbers to adequately mitigate the catastrophic risk. One solution is to transfer that risk to the capital markets where investors holding diversified portfolios have a larger pool of assets to absorb catastrophic losses.

Similar to mortgage-backed securities, insurers and reinsurers can purchase insurance from an SPV, which will use premiums to sell catastrophe bonds to investors. Investors, in turn, pay the principal to the SPV.

At the end of the bond term (typically one to three years), provided no covered catastrophe has occurred, an investor receives both the principal and interest payment from the SPV. If a catastrophe did occur, the investor receives less in return.

Securitization

The process of creating a marketable investment security based on a financial transaction's expected cash flows.

Insurance securitization

The process of creating a marketable insurance-linked security based on the cash flows that arise from the transfer of insurable risks.

Depending on the terms of the bond issue, the investor may receive only the principal with no interest income, or only a portion of the principal. The premiums paid by the insurer are used by the SPV to offset the cost of bond issue and to cover any interest payments (payment to the investor) promised by the bond.

The payoff on catastrophe bonds is linked to the occurrences of major catastrophes during the bond's term. For example, suppose an investor purchases a bond from an SPV that provides a rate of return higher than a similarly rated corporate bond or a U.S. Treasury bond of comparable maturity. The investor assumes the risk that a hurricane might occur during the bond's term in exchange for a higher rate of return.

If a hurricane does occur and causes losses that exceed a specified dollar threshold, the investor's return on the bond is reduced. If total property losses are high enough to trigger a reduced return on the bond, either the investor's interest income or the interest income and principal repayments on the bond may be lowered, depending on the terms of the bond and the extent of the losses.

The SPV uses the savings in interest and principal repayments to pay cash to the issuing insurer or reinsurer, which uses the cash to offset its hurricane losses. Through the process of insurance securitization, the risk of loss caused by a hurricane has been securitized by linking it with the returns provided to investors in a marketable security.

Securitization passes on to investors some of the catastrophe risk that an insurer has accumulated through its insurance policies, thereby reducing the insurer's overall risk. From the investor's perspective, insurance-linked securities help diversify the investor's portfolio because the insurable risk embedded in insurance-linked securities is not closely correlated with the risks normally involved in other investments.

How Hedging Operates

Hedging
A financial transaction in which one asset is held to offset the risk associated with another asset.

To deal with the consequences of risk to which it is exposed, an organization can use **hedging**. One asset—often a contract, such as an option or futures contract—is held to offset the risk of another asset. Hedging as a risk financing measure is well suited to business risks created by price changes.

Commodities (such as energy, metal, or agricultural), foreign exchange rates or currencies, and interest rates are all frequently hedged. The risk transferred is the exposure to loss from declines or increases in an asset's market price. The asset concerned is one that the hedging party holds for an extended period as a normal part of doing business.

For example, suppose a manufacturer knows that it is going to require a substantial quantity of oil to support its manufacturing activities. If the manufacturer is concerned about the volatility in oil prices, it can hedge against changes in oil prices by entering a contract to buy the oil at a certain price and time at some point in the future. This type of hedging of speculative business risks allows an organization to protect itself against possible price-level losses by sacrificing potential price-level gains.

As another example, suppose that a soybean farmer is exposed to loss if the market price of soybeans drops significantly between when the crop is planted and when the harvest is sold. Although the farmer is exposed to loss if the market price decreases, soybean consumers, such as a soy milk manufacturer, may profit from such a price decrease. If the market price were to rise, the farmer would profit, but the manufacturer would be exposed to a loss.

To manage this market price risk, the farmer could enter into a soybean hedge with the manufacturer during the soybean growing season, locking in a future sales price via a futures contract before bringing the soybeans to market. Changes in market prices—whether increases or decreases—would no longer affect the farmer's anticipated revenue on a per-unit basis, just as they would no longer affect the manufacturer, because the price has already been agreed upon. Both manufacturer and farmer are insulated from gains or losses associated with market price changes.

Any price or other financial value that is uncertain in the future and that can be objectively measured, such as a stock market index, common stock price, commodity price, or consumer or industrial price index, can be the basis for a hedge. Those prices or financial values are called underlying assets. The hedging contracts that are based on those underlying assets are called **derivatives**.

For a derivative contract to be a successful hedging contract, two parties must be willing to hedge the underlying asset. For example, the soybean farmer (exposed to loss when prices decrease) would not be able to hedge the soybean prices for the harvest if no consumers (such as the soy milk manufacturer) were exposed to loss when prices increased. There are several exchanges in which derivative contracts are traded that are easily accessible by organizations seeking to hedge.

One advantage of hedging is that hedging against possible net income losses from price changes can reduce an organization's business risk loss exposures. Consequently, an organization that uses hedging has a greater capacity to bear both business risks and hazard risks while also reducing its dependence on traditional financial and insurance markets for its risk transfer needs.

A disadvantage of hedging is that it can destabilize not only an organization's general risk financing plans but also its entire financial structure. If an organization's retained earnings or capital is seriously jeopardized by unwise speculative investments in hedging instruments, the earnings or capital may no longer reliably pay for retained losses. Consequently, the financial security that they provide could be greatly impaired. The goal of reducing an organization's cost of risk for losses by generating high returns for loss reserves must be balanced against the goal of ensuring that funds will be available when needed to pay for losses.

Derivative
A financial contract that derives its value from the value of another asset.

Finally, the value of the derivative contract might not correspond exactly with organizations' losses. As hedging contracts are based on some general measure or index, if the general measure or index does not provide a payout that is highly correlated with an organization's losses, the risk financing measure does not provide the needed protection.

How Contingent Capital Arrangements Operate

Contingent capital arrangement

An agreement, entered into before any losses occur, that enables an organization to raise cash by selling stock or issuing debt at prearranged terms after a loss occurs that exceeds a certain threshold.

In a **contingent capital arrangement**, an organization pays a capital commitment fee to a party that agrees in advance to purchase the debt or equity after a loss, thereby allowing the organization to raise cash. The organization does not transfer its risk of loss to investors. Instead, it receives a capital injection in the form of debt or equity after a loss occurs to help it pay for the loss. Because the terms are agreed to in advance, the organization generally receives more favorable terms than it would receive if it were to try to raise capital after a large loss, when it is likely to be in a weakened capital condition.

For example, a publicly traded pharmaceutical manufacturer may have a contingent capital arrangement with an investment bank that requires the investment bank to purchase a specified number of the manufacturer's shares at a predetermined price if the manufacturer suffers a significant property loss at its main manufacturing plant for which it was unable to acquire property insurance.

The manufacturer pays the investment bank a fee at the beginning of the agreement. If the loss occurs, the investment bank purchases the shares at the predetermined price, providing the manufacturer with the capital necessary to rebuild the plant. If no loss occurs, the agreement expires without any stock sale occurring. Similar agreements for bond issues have also been structured.

Ability to Meet Risk Financing Goals

Before using capital market solutions as risk financing measures, an organization should evaluate their ability to meet the organization's risk financing goals. See the exhibit "Ability of Capital Market Solutions to Meet Risk Financing Goals."

Ability of Capital Market Solutions to Meet Risk Financing Goals

Risk Financing Goal	How Capital Market Solutions Meet the Goal
Pay for Negative Financial Consequences of an Event	They can meet this goal because some of the financial consequences of the losses are transferred to investors.
Maintain Liquidity	They can meet this goal because capital market solutions can reduce the necessary level of liquidity that an organization needs to maintain.
Manage Uncertainty	They can meet this goal because some of the financial consequences of the losses are transferred to investors.
Comply With Legal and Regulatory Requirements	They can meet this goal if correctly structured.
Minimize the Cost of Risk	They cannot typically meet this goal. Capital market solutions are expensive relative to other risk financing measures.

[DA02708]

SUMMARY

Risk management professionals use risk financing goals to guide them in selecting appropriate risk financing techniques. Risk financing goals should support an organization's risk management and financial goals. Common risk financing goals include paying for the negative financial consequences of an event, maintaining an appropriate level of liquidity, managing uncertainty, complying with legal and regulatory requirements, and managing the cost of risk.

The four planned retention funding techniques are current expensing of losses, using an unfunded reserve, using a funded reserve, and borrowing funds. The advantages of using retention as a risk financing technique include cost savings, control of claims process, timing of cash flows, and incentives for risk control. Most transfer methods limit the loss amounts that can be transferred, and the ultimate responsibility for paying losses remains with the transferor. The advantages of transfer include reducing the exposure to large losses, reducing cash flow uncertainty, providing ancillary services, and avoiding adverse employee and public relations.

When selecting appropriate risk financing methods, one must evaluate the relative advantages of the available measures and their ability to meet risk financing goals. The main factors to consider are these:

- The mix of retention and transfer needed to meet the goals
- Loss exposure characteristics
- Characteristics of the individual or organization

Under a guaranteed cost insurance policy, an insured pays an insurer a premium, and the insurer agrees to pay for all of the organization's losses that are covered by the insurance policy. To meet their risk financing goals, many organizations purchase multiple guaranteed cost insurance policies as part of an overall insurance program.

For many organizations, self-insurance is an appropriate risk financing technique for losses that are paid out over a period of time, such as those related to workers compensation, general liability, and automobile liability. Often, organizations must meet certain financial requirements to self-insure. In all cases, an organization should carefully consider whether self-insurance meets its risk financing goals.

Under a large deductible plan, an organization retains losses under a certain high deductible amount in exchange for a lower premium. Large deductible plans give organizations the benefits of insurer claims handling services on all claims, not only those covered by the plan.

Some organizations benefit from using captive insurers to insure loss exposures—particularly those loss exposures that substantially drain cash flow. A captive can be owned by a single parent or multiple parents, and several special types can be formed to meet organizations' varying risk financing goals.

Finite risk plans work by transferring only a limited amount of risk to an insurer. While the insured must typically pay a very high premium, these plans can be particularly useful for organizations that have difficult-to-insure loss exposures.

Through a pool, an organization shares risks with other members of the pool. If adequately funded and managed, a pool can provide a practical risk-financing solution for many organizations, particularly those that are too small to use a captive insurer.

Organizations with substantial insurance premiums may benefit from retrospective rating plans, which adjust premium for the current policy period based on the insured's loss experience during the current period. Such rating plans are used to finance low-to-medium-severity losses and are usually combined with other risk financing plans to cover high-severity losses.

A hold-harmless agreement is a noninsurance risk transfer measure that allows one party (the indemnitee) to transfer liability to another (the indemnitor). Before using a hold-harmless agreement, an organization should evaluate how the agreement would meet its risk financing goals and whether any statutory restrictions apply to hold-harmless agreements in the particular situation.

Many large organizations use capital market solutions to finance risk. Three common examples of capital market solutions are securitization, hedging, and contingent capital arrangements.

6

Data Analytics

Educational Objectives

After learning the content of this assignment, you should be able to:

▷ Describe the evolution of big data and technology and its impact on the property-casualty insurance business.

▷ Categorize the various characteristics and sources of big data available for insurance and risk management applications.

▷ Describe data mining and the data mining process.

▷ Explain how data-driven decision making applies to risk management and insurance.

Data Analytics

BIG DATA AND TECHNOLOGY—THE FUTURE OF INSURANCE

Technology has transformed our lives in how we communicate, learn, and do business. It also continues to evolve at a rapid pace. For example, self-driving cars, once thought to be a subject of science fiction, are now a reality. Technology has already changed the insurance industry, and these changes have only just begun. The convergence of big data and technology has started a transformation of the property-casualty insurance business.

Insurance would not be feasible without data. The ability of insurers to provide coverage for a variety of risk exposures is based on the law of large numbers. Traditionally, the data insurers use has come from loss histories. By analyzing large numbers of claims, insurers could reasonably predict the probable cost of future claims.

However, as technology evolves, the sources and amount of data available to insurers are increasing rapidly. To effectively use this data, insurers must continue to develop new methods of obtaining, processing, and analyzing it.

Strategic Opportunities From Big Data and Technology

Why would an insurance professional who is not an actuary or a data scientist want to learn about data analytics? The most comprehensive reason is that big data and technology are central to the future of the insurance industry. The evolution of this area has already disrupted the traditional ways in which insurers market, underwrite, and analyze their products. This disruption will only gain momentum with such changes on the horizon as self-driving cars, sensors in products ranging from bridges to jeans, and computers that teach themselves without human intervention.

Another, more practical reason is that insurance professionals, such as those in underwriting and claims, must be able to communicate with the data scientists in their organizations. Those who are engaged in the typical work of an insurer may serve on multifunctional teams to assist in the design of approaches to data analytics. Additionally, professionals in traditional insurance functions will need to understand how to use the techniques developed by data scientists to make decisions. Also, as the application of data analytics to insurance continues to evolve, professionals in areas such as underwriting and claims will be valuable in evaluating the results of the new techniques. Communication between those who perform the daily work of an insurer and those designing data analytics is important for success.

Data-driven decision making has been proved to produce better business results than other types of decision-making. For example, the credit industry was using data to select clients and determine credit lines. The data was obtained from loss histories, and the goal was to determine the probability of default. Signet Bank, a small bank, wanted to determine which potential clients would be profitable; however, it did not have that data available. Signet decided to accept a certain cost to obtain the data—the bank began providing credit randomly; losses increased significantly, and this was the cost of data acquisition. However, the data the bank acquired enabled its data scientists to develop predictive models that identified the characteristics of the most profitable clients. The bank then used the results to develop a strategy regarding which credit products to offer to which clients at what level of credit and interest rate. Signet Bank became Capital One.

Apply Your Knowledge

Why would claims, underwriting, or risk management professionals study data analytics?

a. To become data scientists

b. To be able to communicate with data scientists

c. To make high-level strategic decisions for their insurers

d. To learn how to design models to obtain data

Feedback: b. Claims or underwriting professionals typically study data analytics to be able to communicate with data scientists in their organizations. Although claims, underwriting, or risk management professionals may use the results of data analytics in their decision making, they would not usually make high-level decisions for insurers. They also would not be expected to become data scientists or to learn how to design models to obtain data.

Big Data

Although insurers have always gathered and analyzed large amounts of data to make business decisions, the amount of data available has increased exponentially and is therefore referred to as big data. Two types of big data are available to insurers. The first is their own internal data, and the second is data from external sources.

Why would insurers' own internal data now be considered advancements that require new methods of analysis? The answer is based on techniques such as **data mining** and text mining. An example of data mining is using a new technique to identify previously unknown factors that are common to an insurer's most profitable auto insurance customers. Other advanced techniques can enable innovative ways to market to those customers. Text mining can be used to analyze claims adjusters' notes to identify fraud indicators.

New external sources of big data are constantly evolving. An example of an external source that some insurers are using is telematics. The data provided by telematics is analyzed to determine the driving patterns that lead to accidents as well as reflect safe driving. This information can result in a real-time change in premium if the auto owner agrees. A safe driver could receive a discount, while an unsafe driver may receive a premium increase and/or be required to attend a remedial driving program. The information obtained from telematics can also be applied to an insurer's online application and selection process.

Technology

Technology is constantly providing innovative products that are changing risk management and insurance. Similar to telematics devices, sensors can provide a stream of data to insurers regarding risk. Heat sensors can provide information about fire risk to both the customer and the insurer. Sensors on machinery can indicate a malfunction or the removal of a safety device. Sensors are now being included in clothing, which are referred to as wearables. Wearables in uniforms can provide valuable ergonomic information to improve safety.

An emerging area of technology is the Internet of Things (IoT). Although this technology is still being explored for its potential in insurance, it is likely to evolve rapidly. The IoT is similar to telematics, home sensors, and wearable technology, but its potential is more extensive. The potential involves machine-to-machine communication and **machine learning**. The IoT may eventually be able to identify the next asbestos-type problem before it occurs by analyzing data from wearables, sensors, and text mining. For example, nanotechnology is a relatively new type of process, and its eventual effects are still unknown. The IoT could help insurers monitor risks associated with this process.

Drones are a new technological source of information, and they can produce data for underwriting or claims management. Instead of sending adjusters to a disaster scene, insurers are now testing the use of drones to provide detailed data about property damage. Drones, along with other technological tools such as cell phones and the Internet, can assist in gathering risk data for underwriting property coverage in wildfire-prone areas. Results from modeling data already obtained have provided the new, valuable insight that a well-constructed, well-maintained property in a high-risk area can be a better risk than a poorly maintained one in a moderate-risk area.

Data mining
The analysis of large amounts of data to find new relationships and patterns that will assist in developing business solutions.

Machine learning
Artificial intelligence in which computers continually teach themselves to make better decisions based on previous results and new data.

Artificial Intelligence (AI)

Computer processing or output that simulates human reasoning or knowledge.

Social media is a rich source of data. Google and Facebook target advertisements to people who are likely to be interested in a particular product based on their profiles on social media sites. Google, Facebook, and Apple are also developing **artificial intelligence (AI)** to solve problems and introduce new products and services. For example, Google uses AI to find answers to rare search inquiries. All these organizations are researching techniques that will provide and analyze information from voice recordings, photos, and videos.

AI has significant potential for insurers. For example, claims adjusters often take recorded statements from claimants. AI techniques could be applied to recognize voice patterns that may indicate the possibility of fraud. There could also be applications related to photos of accidents or natural catastrophes. However, whether and to what extent insurers can use social media, such as videos posted on Facebook, is subject to regulatory and privacy concerns.

Data Science

Data science

An interdisciplinary field involving the design and use of techniques to process very large amounts of data from a variety of sources and to provide knowledge based on the data.

Data science is a new field that arose from the need to link big data and technology in ways that provide useful knowledge. As discussed earlier, big data, by definition, is an amount of data too large to be analyzed by traditional methods. Data scientists have interdisciplinary skills in mathematics, statistics, computer programming, and sometimes engineering that allow them to perform data analytics on big data.

Data scientists use various techniques to organize and analyze data. Machine learning is one example. Traditional techniques, such as probability, are often combined with newer techniques to obtain the most relevant knowledge from the data. A major concept in data science is that the data organization and analysis are automated rather than performed by an individual.

However, human evaluation of automated data analysis is critical. First, analysis performed by computers is not always accurate. An example is weather forecasting. Different models interpret meteorological data differently and produce varying forecasts. Experienced meteorologists must evaluate all of the model analyses and use their professional judgment to make a decision. Second, the automated analysis may be correct but irrelevant to a given business problem. For example, an automated analysis of claims information indicating that teenaged male drivers are more likely to have accidents would not be relevant to a deeper understanding of auto accident risk because the information about teenaged male drivers is already known. And third, just as technology is rapidly evolving, so are the physical, political, economic, and business environments. Unless the automated method can take those factors into account, the results of the automated analysis may not be helpful if the environment suddenly changes.

For data science to be useful to an insurer or to specific functional areas, such as underwriting or claims, it is usually important to define the business problem to be solved, such as improving claims or underwriting results. In the future, data analytics may be used to forecast unforeseen, or "black swan," events. However, this is still an area for exploration rather than application to business decisions.

Strategic Applications to Insurance

Insurers and risk managers should determine which investments in big data and technology will provide the best fit for their business. For example, an insurer that provides only personal lines of coverage may not be interested in wearables. A company that operates a fleet of vehicles may be more interested in telematics than building sensors. Insurers and risk managers also need to decide on the computers and software to process the increasing amounts of data.

After the data has been obtained and processed, insurance analytics must be applied to make data-driven decisions and develop strategy. This involves not only the big data, technology, and data science techniques but also people who can evaluate the results of the analytics.

Insurance professionals in areas such as underwriting, claims, and risk management should have input into the types of data that they know would be helpful to their decision making, such as fraud indicators. These professionals should also have input into how well the analytics are working to produce relevant and practical information or to improve efficiency.

At more senior levels of an insurer, the information obtained from data analytics can guide decisions such as which lines of coverage management wants to increase or decrease, countries where it would like to expand or reduce operations, and even investment decisions. See the exhibit "Process of Developing Strategy With Data Analytics."

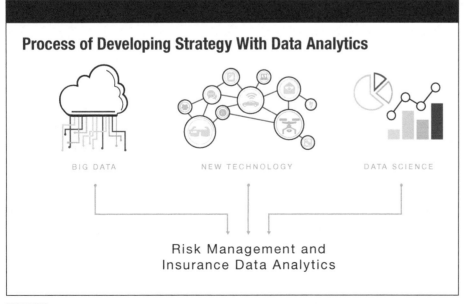

[DA11928]

Evolution of Big Data

Big data and technology can be regarded in stages of evolution. The first is Big Data 1.0, which is the stage at which many organizations are now. The next stage is Big Data 2.0. Some organizations are already at this stage. There will certainly be future stages as the technology continues to evolve.

Big Data 1.0

In Big Data 1.0, organizations began using the Internet to conduct business and compile data about their customers. Insurers developed online insurance applications. They also used the data from applications, as well as claims history, to improve underwriting efficiency and to provide customer information for product development and marketing.

Other industries were performing similar functions in Big Data 1.0. For example, retail investment firms, such as E*Trade, could use the Internet to provide new products to customers. Computers could place stock and bond trades much more efficiently than previous methods.

Big Data 2.0

Because of rapid advances in data science, we have reached the stage of Big Data 2.0. This stage allows organizations to obtain and aggregate vast amounts of data very quickly and extract useful knowledge from it.

For example, investment firms have computers that can scan the Internet instantly for news and information about products, prices, economic and geopolitical developments, and consumer trends. This data is then provided to computer trading algorithms that conduct automated trading of stocks and bonds at high speeds. Many people in the financial industry believe that computer trading has completely altered the world's major stock markets. There are questions regarding whether traditional forms of investing that individual investors use, such as selecting particular stocks, can be effective in the new trading environment of Big Data 2.0.

Big Data 2.0 also allows organizations to process and analyze data from sources such as vehicles, homes, and wearable technology. Sensors can be built into products, and data science provides methods to process and analyze the data that comes from those sensors. Big Data 2.0 is evolving quickly. Some insurers are already actively involved in this phase, while others are lagging. It is not an exaggeration to say that insurers that can adapt quickly and effectively to the convergence of big data and technology will have significant competitive advantages.

BIG DATA CHARACTERISTICS AND SOURCES

Insurers' traditional data is organized into databases with defined fields. Insurance professionals can produce reports that show results from this data.

Risk managers can usually access their insurers' data to produce reports about claims they are handling. Big data has introduced different types and sources of data than those traditionally used.

It is important for risk management and insurance professionals to understand the different types of big data. The varieties, volume, and sources of data are rapidly increasing. For example, risk managers can obtain new types of data on safety from sources such as sensors on employees. Underwriters can obtain new data on risks from drones and social media. Claims adjusters can better identify fraud by identifying patterns in internal and external data. Risk management and insurance professionals increasingly work with data scientists to determine the types of data that are useful to make business decisions.

To better understand big data, these categories will be discussed:

- Data characteristics
- Internal and external data
- Structured and unstructured data

Data Characteristics

The term "big data" implies large quantities of data. Although this is true, big data is also different from traditional data in other respects.

These are characteristics that differentiate big data from traditional data:

- Volume—There is an enormous amount of data that is now available, and the amount continues to increase. To use an analogy, traditional data is like the planet earth, and big data is like the solar system. Eventually, big data could increase to the infinite size of the universe.

- Variety—Traditionally, insurers used **structured data**. Big data also includes structured data in larger volume than traditional data. However, because big data comes from multiple sources, much of it is **unstructured data**.

- Velocity—This is the constantly increasing speed at which data arrives at an insurer. Velocity also includes the growing rate of change in the types of data.

- Veracity—This refers to the completeness and accuracy of data. Unstructured big data is more likely to have less veracity than structured data. However, even traditional structured data will not be perfect. Also, insurers can often gain useful information from big data, even if it has lower veracity.

- Value—Value is derived from the results of data analysis to help insurers make better business decisions. Big data has great potential to add value, but it must be obtained and analyzed with techniques that provide meaningful results. This is the goal of data science.

Structured data

Data organized into databases with defined fields, including links between databases.

Unstructured data

Data that is not organized into predetermined formats, such as databases, and often consists of text, images, or other nontraditional media.

Internal and External Data

Data science allows insurers access to increasingly larger and more varied data, referred to as big data. Some of this data is received directly by the insurer or the risk manager's organization. Other data is obtained from outside sources.

Internal Data

Insurers have always relied on data, and they possess large quantities of it. Certain types of data, such as risk factors, losses, premium, rating factors, rates, and customer information, have been traditionally used to make business decisions. Much of this data is also reported to state rating bureaus. Similarly, risk managers also have relied on data about losses and premium, in addition to safety statistics that are reported to the Occupational Safety and Health Administration (OSHA).

Internal data

Data that is owned by an organization.

However, risk managers and insurers have vast quantities of **internal data** that they have not used because of its volume and/or a lack of techniques to access it. For example, an insurer may not analyze computer claims codes about claimants' preexisting medical conditions—traditional internal data that could be useful if data science techniques are applied to it.

Data science also provides techniques to use nontraditional internal data. For example, voice analysis can be applied to recorded statements of claimants to identify vocal characteristics associated with fraud, such as gaps in the claimant's version of the accident or a defensive tone. Underwriters often obtain photos of property, and claims adjusters often obtain photos of an accident scene. Artificial intelligence can analyze these photos to find information that may be missed by a human analysis, such as potential environmental hazards around a property or, through facial recognition, the identity of a witness to an accident.

External Data

External data

Data that belongs to an entity other than the organization that wishes to acquire and use it.

There is sometimes a blurring of the boundary between internal and **external data**. For example, data from telematics is obtained from a device that is installed on a customer's vehicle. The insurer owns the device, but the customer owns the vehicle. Because of the customer's ownership of the vehicle and the nature of the data provided—the customer's personal driving habits—telematics should probably be categorized as external data.

Another source of data with a blurred boundary is a wearable sensor used by an employee while working. The employer provides the sensor, but it is placed on the employee's person and transmits information about the individual. This information could be considered internal data because it is used in the workplace and because the sensor is owned by the employer. However, it could also be considered external data because it is obtained from and about an individual.

Other sources of external data include sensors in customers' homes or commercial buildings, photos of a catastrophe obtained by drones, and the Internet—especially social media. For insurers to access information from sensors on customers' property, customers must first grant permission. Regulators have already approved the use of drones by insurers to inspect catastrophe scenes. However, there may be other regulations governing what information can be used and how it can be used.

Privacy issues are a legal and regulatory concern in obtaining mass information from public sources, including social media. This is particularly true with data science because it is used to discover and analyze previously unknown data relationships. For example, an insurance company might access individual items of data on a claimant from both internal and external sources. While the data from each source by itself might not violate the claimant's privacy, combining all the data might lead to conclusions that harm the claimant's privacy in a way that he or she did not anticipate. As a result, privacy regulations have been passed by various states and countries. See the exhibit "The National Association of Insurance Commissioners' Insurance Consumer 'Cybersecurity Bill of Rights'."

Other sources of external data include statistical plan data, other aggregated insurance industry data, competitors' rate filings, and third-party data. The most commonly used types of third-party data are **economic data** and **geodemographic data**. Additionally, insurers obtain and use credit ratings for both personal and commercial lines of insurance where permitted by law.

Economic data

Data regarding interest rates, asset prices, exchange rates, the Consumer Price Index, and other information about the global, the national, or a regional economy.

Geodemographic data

Data regarding classifications of a population.

Structured and Unstructured Data

As mentioned above, data can be either structured or unstructured. The traditional data that insurers use for underwriting and claims management is structured. This data is organized into databases that are often linked to each other. For example, an underwriter could query one database regarding a customer's claims history and another database regarding the customer's premium history. The underwriter could receive this information in the same report because the databases are linked. Telematics provide an example of structured external data. There are predetermined fields in a database for the driving information that insurers receive from telematics, such as distance traveled, braking, and left turns.

Unstructured data is not organized. Adjusters' notes are an example of internal unstructured data. Although the notes are contained in individual claims files identified by numbers, there is no database that categorizes the data contained in the notes and provides results. Unstructured external data includes information from the Internet, such as social media.

Data science is used for both structured and unstructured data, but it is especially useful for unstructured data. Data scientists use various techniques to gather, categorize, and analyze unstructured data. This process may or may not produce useful results. For example, if an insurer is concerned about an

The National Association of Insurance Commissioners' Insurance Consumer 'Cybersecurity Bill of Rights'

As an insurance consumer, you have the right to:

1. Know the types of personal information collected and stored by your insurance company, agent or any business it contracts with (such as marketers and data warehouses).

2. Expect insurance companies/agencies to have a privacy policy posted on their websites and available in hard copy, if you ask. The privacy policy should explain what personal information they collect, what choices consumers have about their data, how consumers can see and change/correct their data if needed, how the data is stored/protected, and what consumers can do if the company/agency does not follow its privacy policy.

3. Expect your insurance company, agent or any business it contracts with to take reasonable steps to keep unauthorized persons from seeing, stealing or using your personal information.

4. Get a notice from your insurance company, agent or any business it contracts with if an unauthorized person has (or it seems likely he or she has) seen, stolen or used your personal information. This is called a data breach. This notice should:

- Be sent in writing by first-class mail or by e-mail if you have agreed to that.

- Be sent soon after a data breach and never more than 60 days after a data breach is discovered.

- Describe the type of information involved in a data breach and the steps you can take to protect yourself from identity theft or fraud.

- Describe the action(s) the insurance company, agent or business it contracts with has taken to keep your personal information safe.

- Include contact information for the three nationwide credit bureaus.

- Include contact information for the company or agent involved in a data breach.

5. Get at least one year of identity theft protection paid for by the company or agent involved in a data breach.

6. If someone steals your identity, you have a right to:

- Put a 90-day initial fraud alert on your credit reports. (The first credit bureau you contact will alert the other two.)

- Put a seven-year extended fraud alert on your credit reports.

- Put a credit freeze on your credit report.

- Get a free copy of your credit report from each credit bureau.

- Get fraudulent information related to the data breach removed (or "blocked") from your credit reports.

- Dispute fraudulent or wrong information on your credit reports.

- Stop creditors and debt collectors from reporting fraudulent accounts related to the data breach.

- Get copies of documents related to the identity theft.

- Stop a debt collector from contacting you.

"NAIC Roadmap for Cybersecurity Consumer Protection," National Association of Insurance Commissioners, 2015, www.naic.org/documents/committees_ex_cybersecurity_tf_related_roadmap_cybersecurity_consumer_protections. pdf (accessed March 7, 2015). [DA11943]

increase in the frequency and severity of windstorm losses, it may want to gather data about weather patterns. Obtaining and analyzing unstructured information from news and weather reports on the Internet may provide a result the insurer already knows, namely that windstorms are increasing in frequency and severity. However, in another example, if an insurer wants to develop a more accurate profile of a claimant who commits insurance fraud, obtaining and analyzing unstructured internal data from adjusters' notes and external data from social media may provide information that can be used to develop a profile for claims investigations. See the exhibit "Big Data Categories and Examples."

Big Data Categories and Examples

	Structured	Unstructured
External	Telematics	Social media
	Financial data	News reports
	Labor statistics	Internet videos
Internal	Policy information	Adjuster notes
	Claims history	Customer voice records
	Customer data	Surveillance videos

[DA11944]

DATA MINING

Big data can be very useful to insurers and other organizations. However, it is only useful if it can be properly processed and analyzed.

Data mining is the application of various techniques to big data. Data mining and the data mining process allow organizations to analyze large amounts of internal and external data from various sources.

Data Mining Techniques

Data mining is closely related to the fields of **statistics**, machine learning, and **database** management.

Although data analysts use different approaches, depending on the nature of the data and the business problem, these are the basic techniques of data mining:

- Classification—Assigning members of a dataset into categories based on known characteristics. For example, an insurer wants to predict which insureds in its mid-size commercial lines of business are unlikely to

Statistics

A field of science that derives knowledge from data; it provides a root understanding of useful approaches to data analysis.

Database

A collection of information stored in discrete units for ease of retrieval, manipulation, combination, or other computer processing.

renew their policies. Each insured could be classified as likely to renew or unlikely to renew based on specific characteristics, such as size, location, and types of coverage. The insurer could then develop solutions to increase renewals among those customers identified as unlikely to renew.

- Regression analysis—A statistical technique that predicts a numerical value given characteristics of each member of a dataset. For example, an insurer might want to learn the percentage of premium increase that would lessen a customer's likelihood of renewing an auto policy. By analyzing customers using the variables of nonrenewal and percentage of premium increase, the insurer could develop a regression model to analyze customers and provide a probability score.

Algorithm

An operational sequence used to solve mathematical problems and to create computer programs.

- Association rule learning—Examining data to discover new and interesting relationships. From these relationships, **algorithms** are used to develop rules to apply to new data. An insurer can explore data to find relationships among its products purchased. For example, through data mining, the insurer might discover that customers who purchase more than $250,000 in homeowners policy limits have a high probability of purchasing an umbrella policy. Rules for a computer program can then be developed to identify new customers who might be interested in purchasing both a homeowners and an umbrella policy.

- Cluster analysis—Using statistical methods, a computer program explores data to find groups with common and previously unknown characteristics. The results of the cluster analysis may or may not provide useful information. For example, an insurer may learn that drivers who watch more hours of television have more accidents, but this information is not likely to be useful to the insurer. However, cluster analysis may identify possibilities for new insurance products.

Classification and regression analysis are data mining techniques that are applied when an insurer knows what information it wants to predict. In the examples above, an insurer knows that it wants to predict which customers are unlikely to renew their policies or the probability that a customer will not renew if the premium is increased by a certain percentage. The insurer also knows the specific characteristics of the data it plans to analyze to find the answers to these questions. See the exhibit "Data Mining."

Association rule learning and cluster analysis are used to explore data to make discoveries. Insurers, like other businesses, might apply cluster analysis to discover customer needs that could lead to new products. Unlike classification and regression analysis, there are no known characteristics of the data beforehand. The purpose of association rule learning and cluster analysis is to discover relationships and patterns in the data and then determine whether that information is useful for making business decisions.

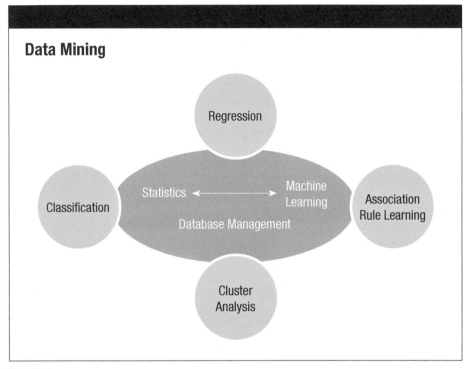

Data Mining

Regression

Statistics ⟷ Machine Learning

Classification

Database Management

Association Rule Learning

Cluster Analysis

[DA11958]

Apply Your Knowledge

An insurer wants to predict which claims may be fraudulent and target them for additional investigation. It wishes to do this based on the known fraud indicators of a claimant threatening to hire an attorney immediately after an accident and having a history of similar claims. Which one of the following data mining techniques would the analyst be likely to use?

a. Classification
b. Regression analysis
c. Association rule learning
d. Cluster analysis

Feedback: a. Classification is likely to be used because the insurer is predicting the category into which a member of a dataset belongs—namely the category that indicates the likely existence of fraud. The insurer intends to use characteristics known beforehand: threatening to hire an attorney immediately after the accident and having a history of similar claims with the insurer.

Association rule learning and cluster analysis are exploratory techniques and do not rely on categorizing members of a dataset based on known data characteristics. Regression analysis is used to predict a numerical value based on known data characteristics rather than a category.

Developing a Predictive Model

A data mining technique is applied to a set of data. The result of this is a model that can be applied to new data. In the example about determining whether a claim might be fraudulent, a classification technique can be used to categorize each claim. After the results are evaluated and validated, the model is used on new claims data to indicate if the claim needs to be sent for further analysis. As the model is applied over time, machine learning refines the model by analyzing the newly added data to revise the algorithms to better predict results. See the exhibit "Data Mining Used to Develop a Model."

The Data Mining Process

In 1999, a consortium of individuals who worked in the emerging field of data mining at DaimlerChrysler, NCR, and SPSS received funding from the European Union to develop a data mining process standard. The result was the **Cross Industry Standard Process for Data Mining (CRISP-DM).**[1] See the exhibit "The Cross Industry Standard Process for Data Mining (CRISP-DM)."

Cross Industry Standard Process for Data Mining (CRISP-DM)

An accepted standard for the steps in any data mining process used to provide business solutions.

A fundamental feature of this standard is the circle that surrounds the process diagram. This circle indicates that data mining is a continuous process that involves continually evaluating and refining the model.

The first step in the process is to understand what a business wants to achieve by applying data mining to one or more sets of data. For example, does an insurer wish to retain more customers or better identify fraudulent claims? Does a risk manager want to find out if a wearable sensor can reduce injuries?

The next step is to understand the types of data that are being used. Is the insurer using only its own claims data, or is it also using data from a statistical rating agency? Is the risk manager only using data from sensors and its own claims data, or is the organization partnering with an insurer to obtain and analyze data?

After the data is selected and its source(s) understood, it must be prepared. This involves cleaning the data as much as possible to eliminate missing or inaccurate data. The purpose of the data mining determines to what extent the data must be cleaned. For example, if it is being used to price insurance, the data should be of high quality. However, if an insurer is exploring social media data to look for opportunities for new products, the data may be usable even if it is of lower quality.

After these steps, data mining techniques are applied to develop a model to analyze the data. The results are evaluated to determine whether they are reasonable and meet the business purpose. Even if they do not meet this pur-pose, the data mining may still be of use. The data might be better prepared or the model adjusted to produce the desired result. Even if the model produces useful information, machine learning will continue to refine that model to

Data Mining Used to Develop a Model

Step One

Historical Data		
Threatening to Hire Attorney	Prior Claims	Fraudulent
Y	Y	Y
N	N	N

Step Two

Data Mining Applied to Historical Data

Step Three

Develop a Predictive Model

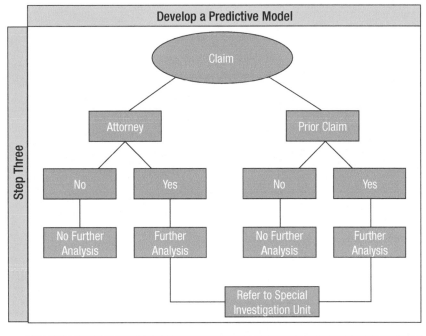

Step Four

Deploy the Model
Identify claims for further analysis

[DA11963]

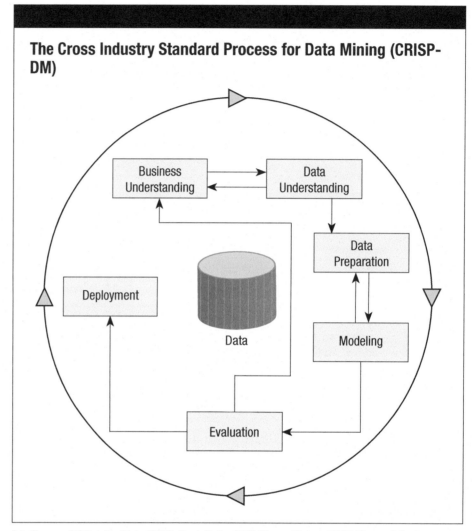

The Cross Industry Standard Process for Data Mining (CRISP-DM)

Pete Chapman (NCR), Julian Clinton (SPSS), Randy Kerber (NCR), Thomas Khabaza (SPSS), Thomas Reinartz (DaimlerChrysler), Colin Shearer (SPSS), and Rüdiger Wirth (DaimlerChrysler), CRISP-DM 1.0, SPSS, Inc., 2000, p. 10, https://the-modeling-agency.com/crisp-dm.pdf (accessed February 22, 2016). [DA11959]

produce increasingly better and more accurate information after the model is deployed to analyze new data.

DATA-DRIVEN DECISION MAKING

Risk managers and insurers have traditionally made many decisions based on data. Insurers use their own and industry loss data to price insurance products. Risk managers use accident data to reduce losses. However, data analytics can improve the types of data, methods of analysis, and results by applying **data-driven decision making**.

Risk management and insurance were previously dependent on human analysis of data. Computers increasingly were able to provide data, such as

Data-driven decision making

An organizational process to gather and analyze relevant and verifiable data and then evaluate the results to guide business strategies.

losses and premiums, that could be segmented based on the business need. For example, if a risk manager or underwriter wanted to know the previous year's losses at a particular location, a computer could provide the data. The risk manager or underwriter would then analyze the data to arrive at a business decision, such as whether to renew a policy. Data science provides more advanced methods of aggregating and analyzing data.

Data Science and Data-Driven Decision Making

Data science can help insurers and risk managers improve their business results through data-driven decision making. These are several ways to achieve improvements:

- Automating decision making for improved accuracy and efficiency—For example, many insurers provide online quotes for personal auto insurance based on a computer algorithm.

- Organizing large volumes of new data—For example, an insurer could organize data according to multiple characteristics, such as the information provided by telematics, which can include speed, braking patterns, left turns, and distance traveled.

- Discovering new relationships in data—For example, a risk manager could identify the characteristics of workers who have never had a workplace accident and use that information to identify how to improve safety for all workers.

- Exploring new sources of data—An insurer could use text mining to analyze claims adjusters' notes for various purposes, such as developing an automated system to predict a claim's severity and assign the appropriate resources to those claims predicted to become severe.

Across all types of businesses, perceived improvement in companies using big data has increased by 26 percent and is expected to increase by 41 percent in the next few years.[2] Currently, insurers process only approximately 10 to 15 percent of the available structured data.[3]

The data about using big data and data science for decision making is compelling. Insurers and risk managers have access to a wealth of existing data they are not tapping. Additionally, there is a rapidly growing quantity of external data from various sources, such as the Internet at large and the Internet of Things.

Insurers, as well as other organizations, acquire data engineering and processing technology that can manage big data, which is too large for most conventional systems. Models can then be developed to gather and analyze data in the context of an insurer's areas of interest, with results ultimately provided to the data analytics team or the manager who requested the data analysis. The appropriate person(s) can make data-driven decisions accordingly. See the exhibit "An Example of a Data-Driven Decision-Making Process: Automated Underwriting for Personal Auto Insurance."

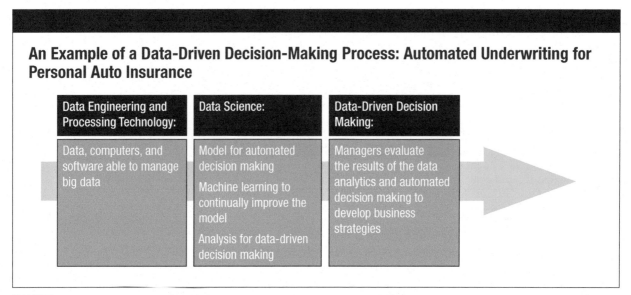

An Example of a Data-Driven Decision-Making Process: Automated Underwriting for Personal Auto Insurance

Data Engineering and Processing Technology:	Data Science:	Data-Driven Decision Making:
Data, computers, and software able to manage big data	Model for automated decision making Machine learning to continually improve the model Analysis for data-driven decision making	Managers evaluate the results of the data analytics and automated decision making to develop business strategies

[DA11977]

Data-driven decision making can be applied across an insurer's or risk manager's enterprise to solve a variety of business problems, achieve greater efficiency, and provide a competitive advantage. There are two basic approaches to data-driven decision making: descriptive and predictive.

The Descriptive Approach

The descriptive approach is applied when an insurer or risk manager has a specific problem. Data science is intended to be used to provide data that will help solve the problem. Insurers or risk managers do not continue to use data-driven decision making beyond the specific problem.

For example, to increase market share, an insurer changed its underwriting guidelines for auto insurance one year ago. It reduced applicants' required time period without an accident to be accepted for coverage from five years to three years.

The insurer now wants to obtain data regarding the accident rates for insureds who were accepted for coverage during the past year and who qualified based on three years without an accident. The insurer also wants to compare those insureds with those accepted for coverage during the past year based on five years without an accident. Additionally, the insurer wants to compare these new customers with its previous customers. It wants data regarding previous customers' accident experience both prior to and after becoming insured.

The insurer intends to use the results of this analysis to determine if its new three-year guideline is producing acceptable results. Using data-driven decision making, executives will decide whether to continue the three-year guideline or return to the five-year guideline. This is a one-time problem for data-driven decision making, and the analysis will not be repeated.

The Predictive Approach

A predictive approach to data analytics involves providing a method that can be used repeatedly to provide information for data-driven decision making by humans, computers, or both.

For example, automated underwriting for personal auto insurance is a predictive approach that is used each time a person applies for insurance. The computer makes the underwriting decision and issues a price quote.

In another example, a risk manager may receive data from sensors regarding which employees are using required safety equipment. The risk manager will make a decision about how to address the problem of employees who are not using their safety equipment.

In an additional example, predictive analytics can be used to assign claims to an adjuster. However, the claims manager may have authority to reassign a claim that the computer assigns as a minor claim if the claim turns out to be severe.

A Model for Data-Driven Decision Making in Risk Management and Insurance

Following the process outlined in the decision-making model will help ensure the best results. The important first step is to define the risk management or insurance problem. Without a business context, modeling and analyzing data is unlikely to be effective. For example, a risk manager for a large national retailer observes that customer slips and falls are increasing in both frequency and severity. The risk manager wants to determine why this increase is occurring and develop a solution for the problem. This involves a descriptive approach because the problem requires a one-time analysis. The analytical method used for this problem will not be repeated. See the exhibit "Risk Management and Insurance Data Analytics Decision-Making Model."

The risk manager decides to focus first on the increase in frequency. The problem is clearly defined, which is the most important step in data-driven decision making. It is often useful to have input from professionals working in the area of the business where the problem is occurring. If the problem is not clearly defined, it may not be possible to make a data-driven decision.

After defining the problem, quality data must be gathered to obtain information about the customer accidents. The risk manager, who has access to the liability insurer's claims system, decides to use the insurer's claims data. The variables to be used are date of accident; store location; area of store property in which the accident occurred, such as a parking lot or entrance; weather data; and sales volume at the store on the date of accident. The risk manager runs a report to identify missing or obviously inaccurate data, such as a date of loss stated as January 1, 1898. The risk manager eliminates claims with missing or inaccurate data from the dataset.

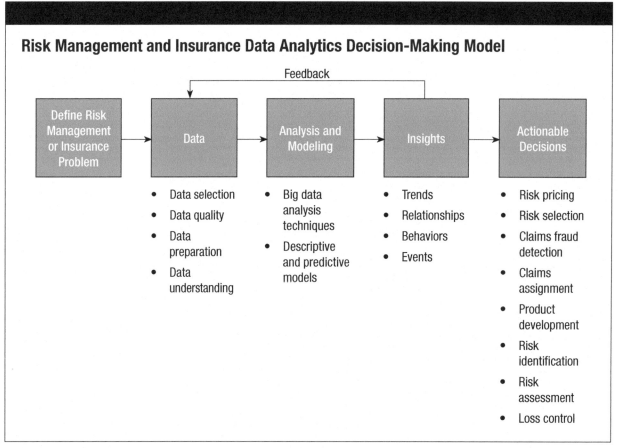

Risk Management and Insurance Data Analytics Decision-Making Model

[DA11978]

The risk manager then meets with the data analytics team to discuss a process that will find any correlations or patterns that might be useful in analyzing the losses and the reason for the increase. Using a cluster technique, the analytics team discovers several patterns in the data: There was a spike in falls at the retailer's stores in northeastern locations in December during snowstorms. Sales volume was higher because of the holiday shopping season. Also, there was an increase in falls at the retailer's stores in Florida in August during tropical storms. Sales volume was also higher in August because of back-to-school shopping.

The risk manager is able to make several decisions driven by this data. The first decision is to provide more waterproof mats for all stores in the Northeast and Florida. Additionally, caution signs are sent to each store to be posted at the entrance during inclement weather. The risk manager reviews parking lot snow and ice removal procedures with store managers and whether salt supplies are adequate. There are also discussions with store managers in Florida about checking parking lot areas for water accumulation during storms and closing off those areas.

This example illustrates how the model for data-driven decision making can be applied in risk management and insurance contexts. The model began with the important first step of clearly defining the problem. Appropriate data was selected and prepared by removing claims with missing or inaccurate data. Relevant variables were selected. There was interaction between the risk manager and the data analytics team to discuss the problem. The data analytics team developed a method to discover patterns and correlations in the data. The risk manager was able to use the results to make a data-driven solution.

Apply Your Knowledge

A claims manager wants to learn which defense attorneys are providing the most effective outcomes. The manager selects these variables: attorney assigned to a claim, litigation expenses, length of time from attorney assignment to claim resolution, whether the claim went to trial or was settled prior to trial, amount of award or settlement, and whether an appeal was filed. Some of the data is missing the date of assignment to defense counsel and whether the claim went to trial.

Which one of the following is the first step the claims manager should take?

a. Analyze the data

b. Improve data quality

c. Select the analytical technique

d. Make a data-driven decision

Feedback b: The first step the claims manager should take is to improve the data quality, as the manager has already defined the problem—finding which defense attorneys are providing the most effective outcomes. There are problems with data quality, because two data fields are missing some of the claims. Therefore, the claims manager will need to have those fields completed or eliminate the claims with missing fields from the dataset. The data analytics team will select the analytical technique. It is not possible to make a data-driven decision at this stage of the process.

SUMMARY

Although insurance has always involved data analytics, technology and big data provide many more sources and a much larger quantity of data. The additional sources and quantity of data now available cannot be organized and analyzed with traditional techniques. Data science is a new field that provides methods to obtain data from new sources such as the Internet and the Internet of Things. It also provides methods to organize and analyze the data to provide relevant knowledge. Organizations can then use that knowledge strategically to improve business decisions.

Big data has various characteristics and sources that distinguish it from traditional data. The characteristics include not only the amount of data, but also its accuracy, whether it is structured or unstructured, its velocity, and the value it adds to an insurer's business decisions. Sources include an insurer's own internal data and external data, both structured and unstructured. By applying data science techniques to big data, insurers can increase their access to useful information to guide their business decisions and strategies.

Data mining is the application of techniques, such as classification, regression analysis, association rule learning, and cluster analysis, to develop models that can be used to analyze big data. CRISP-DM is a standard process for data mining that organizations should use to obtain business solutions from big data.

Although risk managers and insurers have traditionally made decisions based on data, the amount and sources of data have increased exponentially and will continue to do so. Additionally, the methods to gather, process, and analyze data have also increased and become more sophisticated. To gain competitive advantage and operate more effectively, insurers and risk managers must be able to frame business problems and questions and use the techniques of data science to perform analysis that will improve results.

ASSIGNMENT NOTES

1. Foster Provost and Tom Fawcett, "Data Science for Business" (Sebastopol, Calif.: O'Reilly Media, Inc., 2013), p. 26.

2. Economist Intelligence Unit, "The Deciding Factor: Big Data and Decision Making," Business Analytics, www.uk.capgemini.com/resource-file-access/resource/pdf/The_Deciding_Factor__Big_Data___Decision_Making.pdf (accessed March 15, 2016).

3. Ajay Bhargava, "A Dozen Ways Insurers Can Leverage Big Data for Business Value," Tata Consultancy Services White Paper, www.tcs.com/resources/white_papers/Pages/Business-Value-Big-Data-Insurers.aspx (accessed March 15, 2016).

7

Insurance Policy Fundamentals

Educational Objectives

After learning the content of this assignment, you should be able to:

▷ Describe the characteristics of an ideally insurable loss exposure.

▷ Describe the following characteristics of insurance policies, including common exceptions to these characteristics:

- Indemnity
- Utmost good faith
- Fortuitous losses
- Contract of adhesion
- Exchange of unequal amounts
- Conditional
- Nontransferable

▷ Describe these approaches to insurance policy structure and how they can affect policy analysis:

- Self-contained and modular policies
- Preprinted and manuscript policies
- Standard and nonstandard forms
- Endorsements and other related documents

▷ Describe the purpose(s) and characteristics of each of these types of policy provisions in a property-casualty insurance policy:

- Declarations
- Definitions
- Insuring agreements
- Exclusions

7

Educational Objectives, continued

- Conditions
- Miscellaneous provisions
- Describe the primary methods of insurance policy analysis.

Insurance Policy Fundamentals

IDEALLY INSURABLE LOSS EXPOSURES

Although insurers insure many loss exposures, not all loss exposures are ideally insurable. To be insurable, a loss exposure should have certain characteristics.

Most insured loss exposures do not completely embody all of the characteristics of an ideally insurable loss exposure. However, the criteria are useful to an insurer when deciding to offer new coverages or to continue offering existing coverages. See the exhibit "Six Characteristics of an Ideally Insurable Loss Exposure."

Six Characteristics of an Ideally Insurable Loss Exposure

1. Pure risk—involves pure risk, not speculative risk
2. Fortuitous losses—subject to fortuitous loss from the insured's standpoint
3. Definite and measurable—subject to losses that are definite in time, cause, and location and that are measurable
4. Large number of similar exposure units—one of a large number of similar exposure units
5. Independent and not catastrophic—not subject to a loss that would simultaneously affect many other similar loss exposures; not catastrophic
6. Affordable—premiums are economically feasible

[DA02747]

Pure Risk

The first characteristic of an ideally insurable loss exposure is that it should be associated with pure risk, not speculative risk. Pure risk entails a chance of loss or no loss, but no chance of gain. Conversely, a speculative risk presents the possibility of loss, no loss, or gain. Insurance is not designed to finance speculative risks. A purpose of insurance is to indemnify the insured for a loss, not to enable the insured to profit from the loss. Indemnification is the process of restoring the insured to a pre-loss financial condition. Limiting insurance coverage to only pure risks reduces the complexity of the loss exposures insured by the policy to two situations: having a loss or not having a loss.

Fortuitous Losses

The second characteristic of an ideally insurable loss exposure is that the loss associated with the loss exposure should be fortuitous (occurring by chance) from the insured's standpoint.

Some causes of loss may be fortuitous from one point of view only. For example, vandalism and theft are intentional (and therefore not fortuitous) acts from the perspective of the individual or organization committing the acts. However, vandalism and theft are fortuitous (and insurable) from the victim's standpoint because the victim did not intend or expect these acts to occur. Other causes of loss are fortuitous regardless of the perspective from which they are examined. For example, naturally occurring events such as windstorms, hail, or lightning are fortuitous events whether one is the insurer, the insured, or any third party associated with the loss exposure.

For a loss to be fortuitous, the insured cannot have control over whether or when a loss will occur. If the insured has control, the insured might have an incentive to cause a loss. This is known as a moral hazard. For example, arson committed by an insured is not a fortuitous act. Ideally, insurance is suitable for situations in which there is reasonable uncertainty about the probability or timing of a loss without the threat of a moral hazard. If insureds were compensated for losses they cause, they might be encouraged to generate losses for property they no longer wish to own. This practice could undermine the pricing structure for insurance and increase insurance premiums for all policyholders.

Definite and Measurable

The third characteristic of an ideally insurable loss exposure is that it is definite and measurable.

Three components are required for a loss exposure to be definite: time, cause, and location. The insurer must be able to determine the event (or series of events) that led to the loss, when the loss occurred, and where the loss occurred. For example, Cindy parks her car in a public parking lot and upon returning to her vehicle discovers that its driver's side door is badly damaged. She could state that this happened on a certain date and within a certain period of time. It was clear from the damage and transfer of paint chips that another vehicle had hit her car. Therefore, the cause of the damage is known. Because Cindy parked her car in the parking lot, the location was established.

All insurance policies have a policy period that specifies the precise dates and times of coverage. A typical property-casualty policy has a policy period ranging from six months to one year. After receiving notice of a claim, the insurer usually needs to determine that the event occurred during the policy period. For some events, this may be a difficult process; insurers are reluctant to insure such events.

For example, an insurer is considering insuring a gas station against environmental pollution. A definite environmental pollution loss would be a fire that ruptured an underground gas tank and caused gas to leak into the surrounding soil. However, had no fire occurred and had the tank been slowly leaking for an indeterminate number of years, it would be impossible to pinpoint the exact date or the cause of the pollution. Therefore, it may be impossible to determine whether the event occurred during the policy period. Because they are not definite, these types of loss exposures are not ideally insurable.

A loss exposure also needs to be measurable to be ideally insurable. Insurers cannot determine an appropriate premium if they cannot measure the frequency or severity of the potential losses. For example, a house fire is a measurable loss exposure. Underwriters can analyze data from past fire losses to single-dwelling, wood-frame homes within a set geographic area. From the analysis, frequency and severity patterns are used to determine potential fire losses and the premium needed. In addition, the cost to repair or replace a house damaged by fire can be objectively measured before a loss, and coverage can be priced accordingly.

Conversely, contagious diseases are an example of a potential loss exposure that is difficult to measure. Flu viruses mutate constantly. The strength of the virus, as well as the age group susceptible, may vary from one flu season to the next. Also, the geographic territory where the virus strikes can vary from year to year. All these factors make it difficult for an underwriter to measure future losses. Insurers are reluctant to insure losses that are highly uncertain without receiving substantial compensation (high premiums).

Large Number of Similar Exposure Units

The fourth characteristic of an ideally insurable loss exposure is that the loss exposure is one of a large number of similar exposure units. Some common loss exposures that satisfy this requirement include homes, offices, and automobiles. Each exposure unit has a value that can be at risk when exposed to loss.

For example, Steve purchases a single-family home for $300,000. He faces loss exposures of fire, theft, burglary, windstorm, hail, collapse, and so forth. His exposure is the value of his home. If the home were destroyed by fire, he could not afford to replace it. This risk is transferred with the purchase of a homeowners insurance policy. The insurer does not want to insure only Steve's home, but rather thousands of single-family homes that face similar exposures. Based on past losses, the insurer knows that although all homes have a fire exposure, only a small percentage will experience a fire loss. The insurer can therefore spread the risk of fire loss over its entire pool of insured homes and thereby maintain manageable premium levels.

Independent and Not Catastrophic

The fifth characteristic of an ideally insurable loss exposure is that it is independent and not catastrophic. Independent means that a loss suffered by one insured does not affect any other insured or group of insureds. For example, Steve's home is located in a large subdivision of 1,000 homes and is surrounded by a wooded area. Steve's insurer would not want to insure all the homes in the subdivision because the forest fire loss exposure would put all 1,000 homes at risk of fire. The risk would not be independent for each home.

A catastrophic loss is severe; it involves numerous exposure units suffering the same type of loss simultaneously, with significant financial consequences for the insurer. Insurance operates economically because many insureds pay premiums that are small relative to the cost of the potential losses they could each incur. The cost can stay relatively small because insurers project that they will incur far fewer losses than the loss exposures they have. However, if a large number of insureds who are covered for the same type of loss were to incur losses simultaneously, the insurance mechanism would not operate economically and losses to the insurer could be catastrophic.

For example, to avoid a catastrophic hurricane loss, an insurer will diversify the homes and businesses it insures and will not have a large concentration in any one geographic area. Single events or a series of events can also present catastrophic risk to an insurer. Similarly, a small insurer should not insure a multimillion-dollar property, such as an oil refinery. Although the loss exposure may be independent of the other properties the insurer has chosen to insure, a loss at such a single location may cause the insurer severe financial difficulty.

Affordable

The final characteristic of an ideally insurable loss exposure is that the insurer is able to charge an economically feasible premium—one that the insured can afford to pay. Insurers seek to cover only loss exposures that are economically feasible to insure. Because of this constraint, loss exposures involving only small losses, as well as those involving a high probability of loss, are generally considered uninsurable.

Writing insurance to cover small losses may not make sense when the expense of providing the insurance probably exceeds the amount of potential losses. Insurance covering the disappearance of office supplies, for example, could require the insurer to spend more to investigate and to issue claim checks than it would for the insured to simply absorb the cost of replacing the supplies.

It also may not make sense to write insurance to cover losses that are almost certain to occur. The premiums would probably be as high as or higher than the potential amount of the loss. For example, insurers generally do not cover damage because of wear and tear on an automobile because automobiles are certain to incur such damage over time.

Apply Your Knowledge

Jim's summer job is to work as an intern for an insurance agency. When preparing a listing of the agency's homeowners book of business, Jim notes that seventy-five clients' homes are located within one-half mile of the river in a designated flood plain. Jim is concerned because one of the agents told him that flood exposure is not covered under the homeowners policy. Jim proposes to his manager that the agency sell a flood coverage endorsement to each of the homeowners clients. Jim's manager reviews with Jim the six characteristics of an ideally insurable loss exposure. Jim determines that the exposure of flood possesses only three of the six characteristics: pure risk, fortuitous losses, and definite and measurable.

If you were in Jim's position, how would you arrive at this determination?

Feedback: The exposure is a pure loss because a loss that occurs as a result of a flood does not result in financial gain for the insured; thus, there is either a loss or no loss. It is fortuitous because the insured does not have control over whether and when a flood loss will occur. It is definite in time, cause, and location, and flood data are available that can be measured. Conversely, there is not a large number of similar exposure units. Additionally, the loss is not independent because all of the homes in the flood plain will be exposed. Finally, because only those who believe they are at risk for a flood loss would purchase the flood endorsement, the insurer will not be able to offer an economically feasible premium.

DISTINGUISHING CHARACTERISTICS OF INSURANCE POLICIES

An insurance policy is a formal written contract by which an insurer provides protection if an insured suffers specified losses. Insurance policies display certain distinguishing characteristics not often found in other types of contracts. Some of the distinguishing characteristics that apply to insurance policies are also called insurance principles because they adhere to the economic theory behind the business of insurance. Understanding these characteristics assists insurance and risk management professionals in analyzing insurance policies.

The distinguishing characteristics of insurance policies are these:

- Indemnity
- Utmost good faith
- Fortuitous losses

- Contract of adhesion
- Exchange of unequal amounts
- Conditional
- Nontransferable

Although these characteristics are unique to insurance policies, not all insurance policies exhibit every one of these characteristics.

Indemnity

Principle of indemnity

The principle that insurance policies should provide a benefit no greater than the loss suffered by an insured.

Contract of indemnity

A contract in which the insurer agrees, in the event of a covered loss, to pay an amount directly related to the amount of the loss.

The goal of an insurance policy is to indemnify (make whole) the insured who has suffered a covered loss. An insurance policy adheres to the **principle of indemnity**; the policyholder should not profit from insurance. This adherence to the principle of indemnity means that an insurance policy is a **contract of indemnity**.

In practice, an insurance policy does not necessarily pay the full amount necessary to restore an insured who has suffered a covered loss. Most insurance policies contain a dollar limit, a deductible, or other provisions or limitations that result in the insured's being paid less than the entire loss amount. Furthermore, insurance policies do not always indemnify the insured for the inconvenience, time, and other nonfinancial expenses involved in recovering from an insured loss. The valuation method used to value the loss is also a major factor in determining the level of indemnity the insured receives from the insurance policy.

Some insurance policies violate the principle of indemnity. For example, certain insurance policies are valued policies, not contracts of indemnity. Under the terms of a valued policy, the insurer agrees to pay a pre-established dollar amount in the event of an insured total loss. That dollar amount may be more or less than the value of the insured loss. For example, rare objects of art are often insured with a valued policy. If the artwork is destroyed, the policy pays the dollar value specified, regardless of the value of the artwork at the time of the loss.

Despite the fact that some policies do not adhere to the principle of indemnity, in order to reduce or avoid moral hazards, insurance policies should not do either of these:

- Overindemnify the insured
- Indemnify insureds more than once per loss

Insurance Should Not Overindemnify

Insureds should be compensated, but not overcompensated (overindemnified), for a loss. Ideally, the insured should be restored to approximately the same financial position that he or she was in before the loss. The principle of indemnity implies that an insured should not profit from an insured loss.

The potential for overindemnification can constitute a moral hazard. For example, a rundown building that is insured for more than its value might be a tempting arson target for an insured owner who could use the insurance money to build a better building on that site. Insurers can reduce moral hazard (and thereby reduce the potential for overindemnification) by clearly defining the extent of a covered loss in the policy provisions and by carefully setting policy limits.

Insureds Should Not Be Indemnified More Than Once per Loss

Ideally, a loss exposure should be the subject of only one insurance policy and only one portion of that insurance policy. Multiple sources of recovery (payment from many policies or more than one portion of the same policy) could result in the insured's overindemnification. To limit overindemnification, most property and liability insurance policies contain clauses called "other insurance provisions" that limit multiple sources of recovery.

However, sometimes duplicate recovery is both available and justifiable. For example, people can be insureds under more than one policy when they carry multiple policies, such as auto and health insurance. If an insured who has overlapping coverage has been charged an actuarially fair premium for the duplicate portion of coverage, it may be unfair for an insurer to deny coverage simply because the insured has more than one policy. In some instances, prohibiting duplicate recovery for an insured could unfairly absolve the responsible parties from bearing the financial consequences of the loss.

To illustrate, if a person (the plaintiff) sues another (the defendant) for injuries suffered as a result of the defendant's negligence and the court finds in favor of the plaintiff, it is not acceptable for the negligent party to avoid paying some or all of those damages because the plaintiff can also recover money under his or her own insurance policies. This is known as the **collateral source rule**.

Utmost Good Faith

An insurance policy is generally more vulnerable to abuses such as misrepresentation or opportunism than other contracts, for two reasons: information asymmetry and costly verification.

Information asymmetry exists when one party to a contract has information important to the contract that the other party does not. For example, a homeowner may know that an insured home is in a state of disrepair that makes a loss more likely. If the insurer does not know this, then information asymmetry exists.

To reduce information asymmetry, the insurer attempts to gather as much relevant information as possible during the underwriting process. For example, the insurer could conduct an inspection to verify the condition of

Collateral source rule
A legal doctrine that provides that the damages owed to a victim should not be reduced because the victim is entitled to recover money from other sources, such as an insurance policy.

the property. If the property is in disrepair, the insurer may charge a higher premium or require a higher deductible than it would have charged had the house been in good condition. However, verification of information is often time consuming and expensive (costly verification). The more difficult or more costly it is to verify information provided by the insured, the less likely it is that the insurer will expend the resources to verify information, and the information asymmetry will remain.

Information asymmetry can lead to adverse selection; that is, the insurer may improperly price insurance policies by charging a higher-risk insured a lower than actuarially fair premium. Similarly, it may lead to the insurer's issuing a policy on a loss exposure that it may not want to insure at all. Such situations can be prevented if all parties exercise the utmost good faith in the insurance transaction.

Utmost good faith is an obligation to act with complete honesty and to disclose all relevant facts. The characteristic of utmost good faith has its roots in early marine insurance transactions, when underwriters could not verify the condition of ships and their cargoes. Therefore, insurance policies became agreements founded in the utmost good faith that the statements made by both the insured and insurer could be relied upon as accurate fact. Although the principle of utmost good faith has been eroded somewhat by court decisions, the doctrines of misrepresentation, fraud, and concealment in insurance policies are based on utmost good faith.

The most common violations of the concept of utmost good faith in insurance policies involve fraud and/or buildup in insurance claims filed by insureds. Fraud is the misrepresentation of key facts of a claim, and buildup is the intentional inflation of an otherwise legitimate claim. For example, filing a claim for an auto accident that never occurred would be fraud. Overstating the extent of injuries suffered in a legitimate auto accident would be buildup.

Fortuitous Losses

Fortuitous losses are losses that happen accidentally or unexpectedly. For a loss to be fortuitous, reasonable uncertainty must exist about its probability or timing. For insurance purposes, the loss must be fortuitous from the insured's standpoint. For example, although robbery is an intentional act from the perpetrator's standpoint, it is a fortuitous loss from the victim's standpoint.

If an insured knows in advance that a loss will occur and the insurer does not, the insured has an information advantage over the insurer. This information asymmetry, if acted on by the insured (the insured purchases an insurance policy covering the known loss), promotes adverse selection, thereby changing the loss distribution in the pool the insurer insures. Therefore, the premium the insurer charges the pool is no longer actuarially fair, because the loss distribution on which the premium was based has changed. Underwriting is designed to minimize the effect that adverse selection can have on the insurer's loss distribution. One method of avoiding adverse selection is precluding coverage for losses that are not fortuitous.

Fortuitous losses are not necessarily covered by insurance. Many losses happen fortuitously but are not covered. For example, earthquake is a fortuitous cause of loss that is excluded by most property insurance policies.

Many finite risk insurance contracts cover losses that have occurred but have not been settled. In such cases, some uncertainty remains about the final settlement values. For example, an auto manufacturer may have recalled a model because of a faulty part that was responsible for fifty accidents that involved bodily injury and property damage. Although all the accidents have been reported, none of the claims have been settled. Both the auto manufacturer and insurer would have an estimate of the ultimate claims settlement amounts; however, there is still some uncertainty regarding both the timing and the amount of the settlements. The insurer may be willing to provide liability insurance coverage to the auto manufacturer for these fifty accidents after the fact for a very high premium because the insurer believes that it will be able to negotiate settlements that would make the transaction profitable.

Contract of Adhesion

The amount of negotiation required to formulate a contract varies widely. Some contracts are the result of extensive negotiation between parties, in which every clause is discussed before agreement is reached. Other contracts involve little or no negotiation. Between these two extremes are contracts that contain some standard clauses, leaving the remainder of the contract to be negotiated.

Insurance policies typically involve little or no negotiation (except for unique loss exposures that require special underwriting consideration, such as a highly valued property). An insurer generally chooses the exact wording in the policies it offers (or uses the wording developed by an insurance advisory organization), and the insured generally has little choice but to accept it.

A basic insurance policy might be altered by endorsements, but the insurer or advisory organization also typically develops these endorsements. Consequently, a party who wants to purchase an insurance policy usually has to accept and adhere to the standard policy forms the insurer or advisory organization drafts. The typical insurance policy is, therefore, a **contract of adhesion**.

Contract of adhesion
Any contract in which one party must either accept the agreement as written by the other party or reject it.

Courts have ruled that any ambiguities or uncertainties in contracts are to be construed against the party who drafted the agreement because that party had the opportunity to express its intent clearly and unequivocally in the agreement. Therefore, unless the insured drafted the policy (which is rare), ambiguities in an insurance policy are interpreted in the insured's favor. The insurer has a good-faith obligation to draft a policy that clearly expresses what it intends to cover. Any policy provision that can reasonably be interpreted more than one way can be considered ambiguous.

Standard insurance policies are sometimes constructed with acceptable ambiguities. If an insurance policy can be interpreted in two different ways and the insurer is satisfied with either interpretation, no expansion of the policy is necessary to make it more precise.

An important consideration affecting the interpretation of a contract's ambiguity is the level of sophistication of the parties to the contract. In cases concerning insurance policies, the level of sophistication of the insured has had these effects on court decisions:

- Unsophisticated insured—Usually, the insurer has drafted a ready-made policy, and the insured has little or no control over the policy's wording. This is true of most homeowners and personal auto insurance policies. Ambiguities in these cases are typically interpreted against the insurer. This is the case for most personal insurance consumers.

- Sophisticated insured—In a minority of cases, the insured (or its representatives) drafts all or part of the insurance policy. Alternatively, the insurer and a sophisticated insured negotiate the policy wording. In these cases, the contract of adhesion doctrine may not apply. Courts do not necessarily interpret any ambiguity in the insured's favor if the insured had some understanding and ability to alter the policy wording before entering the agreement. Sophisticated insureds include many medium to large organizations with dedicated risk management functions.

The courts consider several factors when determining whether an insured can be considered sophisticated. These factors include the size of the insured organization, the size of the insured organization's risk management department, use of an insurance broker or legal counsel with expertise in insurance policies, and the relative bargaining power of the insured in relation to the insurer.

The most common examples of insurance policies that are not contracts of adhesion are manuscript policies or policies that contain manuscript forms. When the insured contributes to the precise wording of the contract, courts generally do not apply the standards that are common under contracts of adhesion.

Reasonable expectations doctrine

A legal doctrine that provides for an ambiguous insurance policy clause to be interpreted in the way that an insured would reasonably expect.

An extension of the contract of adhesion doctrine is the **reasonable expectations doctrine**, which is a legal doctrine that provides for an ambiguous insurance policy clause to be interpreted in the way that an insured would reasonably expect. For example, the reasonable expectations doctrine is sometimes applied to the renewal of insurance policies that contain a change from the original policy. Unless an oral or a written notification and explanation accompanies the renewal policy, the insured can reasonably expect that the renewal policy is the same as the expiring policy.

The reasonable expectations doctrine is an important extension of the contract of adhesion doctrine because it accounts for the fact that most insureds are not practiced in policy interpretation. However, insureds should not rely on the reasonable expectations doctrine because not all courts recognize it.

Exchange of Unequal Amounts

Consideration is an element of any enforceable contract. For insurance policies, the consideration offered by the insured is the premium; the consideration offered by the insurer is the promise to indemnify the insured in the event of a covered loss. There is no requirement that the amounts exchanged be equal in value. In most insurance policies, the tangible amounts exchanged, the premium from the insured, and any payments made by the insurer, will be unequal.

Consideration

Something of value or bargained for and exchanged by the parties to a contract.

For example, consider an insurer that charges a $1,500 premium to insure a property valued at $500,000. An infinite number of potential losses could occur. However, the potential losses fall into the following four categories:

- The insured does not suffer a loss during the policy period. The insured paid the $1,500 premium, and the insurer pays nothing to the insured.
- The insured suffers losses of less than $1,500 during the policy period. The insured pays the $1,500 premium and the insurer reimburses the insured for the loss amount (ignoring any deductible).
- The insured suffers losses exactly equal to $1,500 during the policy period.
- The insured suffers losses of more than $1,500 during the policy period.

It is impossible to predict which of the four possible situations will occur, but it is highly unlikely that the tangible amounts exchanged between the insurer and insured will be equal. The four situations consider only the exchange of tangible values—the premium paid by the insured and the recovery of losses paid by the insurer (if any)—not the intangible value of the insurance promise.

It is difficult to explicitly value the reduction in volatility of losses and the reduction in the maximum amount at risk that insurance policies provide for an insured because they vary based on the insured's level of risk aversion. However, when both the tangible and intangible values are jointly considered, the values exchanged between the insurer and the insured are closer in value.

Although the tangible values exchanged between an insurer and insured may not be equal, in general they are equitable—that is, the premium the insurer charges the insured is directly proportional to the insured's expected losses on an actuarially sound basis. This is often called the equitable distribution of risk costs. That is, the insured's premium should be commensurate with the risk it presents to the insurer. By charging the appropriate premium, the insurer can ensure that the tangible consideration offered by the insured is equitable compared with the intangible consideration offered by the insurer.

Finite risk insurance policies involve an exchange of amounts closer in value than other types of policies, because their premiums are often close to the present value of the limit stated on the policy. Finite risk insurance involves little or no actual risk transfer and often functions as a loan.

Conditional

Conditional contract

A contract that one or more parties must perform only under certain conditions.

Insurance policies are **conditional contracts** because the insurer is obligated to pay for losses incurred by the insured only if the insured has fulfilled all of the policy conditions. For example, under a property insurance policy, an insured must allow the insurer to inspect the damaged property after a covered cause of loss, such as a fire. The insurer is not obligated to fulfill the insurance policy (pay for any covered losses) unless the insured meets this condition. If the property is not available for inspection, the insurer has the right to deny the claim because the insurer was unable to verify that the loss actually occurred.

The most common exception to "the conditional nature of an insurance policy" occurs when the insurer is willing to waive some of the conditions of the insurance policy. This often occurs in practice. For example, an insurer may be willing to pay a claim without making an inspection, thereby waiving the condition that the insured make damaged property available for inspection.

Nontransferable

Insurance policies are sometimes referred to as "personal contracts" to indicate their nontransferable or nonassignable nature. An insurance policy is a contract between two parties; most property and liability policies contain a condition stating that the insured cannot assign (transfer) the policy to a third party without the insurer's written consent. For example, although property, such as a residence or a business, can be sold to a third party, the insurance policy that covers the property cannot be sold with it unless the insurer approves the transfer in writing.

Insurers sometimes transfer policies to other insurers. Insureds are notified of the transfer or assignment, but their written approval is not required. For example, if an insurer wants to exit from a line of business or geographic area, the insurer can sell its entire portfolio for that business or area to another insurer. Alternatively, an insurer can transfer all of its business if it is acquired by another insurer, or a state regulator can assign insurance policies from an insolvent insurer to other insurers that are licensed in that state.

Insurance policies typically do not contain any condition prohibiting the insurer from transferring or assigning the policy to a third party without the insured's written consent. If insureds are not receptive to the transfer or assignment by the insurer, they essentially have two choices. First, they may cancel their policies and purchase policies from other insurers. Second, they may pursue claims through the courts based on the notion that the consideration offered by the transferee (new insurer) is lower than the consideration offered by the transferor (original insurer).

In essence, the insured would be claiming that the transferee's claim-paying ability is not equal to the transferor's. However, typically the consideration offered by the new insurer is equal to or greater than that of the original insured, improving the insured's position. When a policy is transferred from an insolvent insurer, insureds' coverage is more secure.

Some policies contain exceptions to the usual assignment condition in order to help insureds manage situations that arise in normal commercial operations. For example, ocean marine hull insurance policies typically contain a change of ownership clause, which states that the policy will terminate automatically with a change in the insured vessel's ownership. However, this clause usually has an exception stating that the policy does not terminate if a change in ownership occurs while the insured vessel is at sea.

For example, a vessel is transporting cargo across the Atlantic Ocean when its owner sells the vessel to another company. The hull policy covering the vessel would remain in force for the new owner without the written consent of the insurer. This exception to the change of ownership clause is designed to ensure that coverage remains in force, given that the change in ownership would have little or no effect on the risk of loss to the insured vessel while at sea. Once the vessel reaches the final port of discharge, the hull policy will automatically terminate, and the new owner must obtain its own insurance on the vessel.

STRUCTURE OF INSURANCE POLICIES

Understanding the various ways in which insurance policies can be structured helps insurance and risk management professionals analyze and interpret any particular policy.

The structure of an insurance policy can be either self-contained or modular. The form or forms used to make up a policy can be either preprinted or manuscript, and either standard or nonstandard. In addition to forms, related documents of various types can be incorporated in a policy.

Self-Contained and Modular Policies

The basic structure of every property-casualty insurance policy can be classified as either self-contained or modular.

A **self-contained policy** contains, within one document, all the provisions needed to make up a complete insurance policy. Endorsements can be added to a self-contained policy to provide additional, optional coverages or to exclude unnecessary coverages. An endorsement is a document that amends an insurance policy.

Self-contained policy

A single document that contains all the agreements between the insured and the insurer and that forms a complete insurance policy.

A self-contained policy is appropriate for insuring loss exposures that are similar among many insureds. For example, private passenger auto insurance is typically provided in a self-contained policy (such as the ISO Personal Auto Policy). Such a policy is used for each of an insurer's individual auto policyholders throughout a state—and potentially in several different states. Endorsements, such as the Towing and Labor Costs Coverage endorsement or the Customizing Equipment Coverage endorsement, can be added as needed.

Package policy
Policy that covers two or more lines of business.

Monoline policy
Policy that covers only one line of business.

Modular policy
An insurance policy that consists of several different documents, none of which by itself forms a complete policy.

A self-contained policy can be either a **monoline policy** or a **package policy**. An example of a self-contained monoline policy is an insurance agent's errors and omissions liability policy. An example of a self-contained package policy is a homeowners policy, which provides both property and liability coverages.

A **modular policy** is created by combining a set of individual components, such as one or more coverage forms, one or more causes of loss forms, and one or more conditions forms. The modular approach is often used in commercial insurance because the insured's loss exposures are typically unique and require more customization of the insurance policy than is the case with other lines of insurance.

A modular policy can be either a monoline policy or a package policy. An example of a modular monoline policy is a commercial property policy that consists of a commercial property coverage form, a causes of loss form, a commercial property conditions form, and a common policy conditions form. An example of a modular package policy is a commercial package policy that consists of multiple forms for providing commercial property coverage, commercial general liability coverage, commercial auto coverage, and commercial crime coverage.

The insured has the option of purchasing multiple standalone policies or a single package policy to cover the same loss exposures. However, relative to self-contained policies, modular policies have these advantages:

- Carefully designed and coordinated provisions in the various forms minimize the possibility of gaps and overlaps that might exist when several monoline policies are used.
- Consistent terminology, definitions, and policy language make coverage interpretation easier for the insured.
- Fewer forms are required to meet a wide range of needs.
- Underwriting is simplified because much of the basic information that must be analyzed applies to all lines of insurance.
- Adverse selection problems can be reduced when the same insurer provides several lines of insurance for an individual insured.
- Insurers often give a package discount when several coverages are included in the same policy.

Minimal coverage gaps, consistent terminology, and fewer forms are important advantages to insurance and risk management professionals conducting policy analysis. Analyzing multiple self-contained policies is usually more difficult than analyzing a modular policy.

Multiple self-contained policies will often use inconsistent terminology and have gaps and overlaps in coverage, making policy analysis more difficult. Well-coordinated modular policies typically offer a better framework for policy analysis than multiple self-contained policies.

Preprinted and Manuscript Forms

The forms used to make up insurance policies can be classified as either pre-printed forms or manuscript forms.

Most insurance policies are assembled from one or more preprinted forms and endorsements. Preprinted forms are developed for use with many different insureds. Therefore, they refer to the insured in general terms (such as "the insured" or "you") so that the forms can be used in multiple insurance policies without customization. The declarations page then adds the specific informa-tion about the insured that customizes the insurance policy.

Using preprinted forms significantly reduces the paperwork necessary for an insurance policy. When the policy is issued, insurers send the insured the generic preprinted policy and the customized declarations page. The declara-tions page indicates the form number or numbers and edition dates of the insurer's form or forms that apply to the insurance policy. When insureds update (for example, change deductibles) or renew their policies, the insurer can simply send the insureds new declarations pages without having to resend entire new policies containing copies of the preprinted forms (provided the preprinted forms have not been changed).

Furthermore, if they are using preprinted forms, the insurer and its producer do not have to keep a complete duplicate of each insured's entire policy in their files. All that needs to be filed is the declarations page, either on paper or as an electronic file. Details of specific coverage can be obtained by exam-ining copies of the preprinted forms referenced in the declarations page. See the exhibit "Preprinted Forms as Electronic Forms."

Preprinted Forms as Electronic Forms

Although they are still referred to as preprinted forms in the insurance industry, printing technology has reduced the need for producers and insurers to maintain a supply of actual preprinted forms. Producers and insurers can now quickly print the electronic copies of all the forms and endorsements as needed.

[DA05792]

Preprinted forms typically are interpreted as contracts of adhesion. The word-ing of preprinted forms and endorsements is carefully chosen by the insurer (or developed by an advisory organization and then adopted by the insurer). Courts tend to interpret any ambiguities in policy language in favor of the insured, because the insured did not have an opportunity to choose the policy wording.

Manuscript form

An insurance form that is drafted according to terms negotiated between a specific insured (or group of insureds) and an insurer.

In contrast to preprinted forms, **manuscript forms** are custom forms developed for one specific insured—or for a small group of insureds—with unique coverage needs.

If an insurance policy includes a manuscript form, it is often referred to as a manuscript policy. A manuscript form can be specifically drafted or selected to cover a unique loss exposure or to customize regular coverage to meet an insured's particular specifications.

Because the insurer and the insured develop policy language together, manuscript policies are not generally considered to be contracts of adhesion. Therefore, courts do not automatically interpret ambiguous policy provisions in the insured's favor. Manuscript forms are the most difficult to interpret during policy analysis. These forms, because they often contain unique wording, can vary widely in their interpretation.

Manuscript forms do not have the same history of court interpretations for insurance and risk management professionals to rely on during policy analysis. This fact can lead to differences between how an insurance or a risk management professional interprets a manuscript form and how the insured or courts will interpret the same form. Consequently, substantial delays in claim adjusting or strained relations between the insurer and insured can occur. To reduce the likelihood of such problems, most manuscript forms are not individually composed but are adapted from wording previously developed and used in standard forms or other insurance policies.

Standard and Nonstandard Forms

An insurer may use the standard forms that are also used by other insurers, or it may develop its own nonstandard forms. A nonstandard form drafted or adapted by one insurer is sometimes called a company-specific or proprietary form.

Insurance service and advisory organizations, such as Insurance Services Office, Inc. (ISO) and the American Association of Insurance Services (AAIS), have developed standard insurance forms for use by individual insurers. These standard forms are accompanied by portfolios of coordinated endorsements that apply necessary state variations or customize coverage. Because they are widely used, standard forms provide benchmarks against which nonstandard forms can be evaluated.

Standard forms are typically easier than nonstandard forms for insurance and risk management professionals to evaluate during policy analysis. Standard forms are widely used and usually have been more consistently interpreted by the courts than other forms. Furthermore, most professionals have more experience working with standard forms than with nonstandard forms.

Many insurers have developed their own company-specific preprinted forms, especially for high-volume lines of insurance (such as auto or homeowners) or for coverages in which the insurer specializes (such as recreational vehicle insurance). Other insurers use manuscript forms to provide nonstandard policy wordings for either individual customers or small groups of customers. By their very nature, all manuscript forms are nonstandard forms. Nonstandard forms (whether preprinted or manuscript) include provisions that vary from standard-form provisions and often contain coverage enhancements not found in standard forms.

Similar to preprinted standard forms, preprinted nonstandard forms are typically easier than manuscript forms for insurance or risk management professionals to evaluate during policy analysis. Although these preprinted forms are referred to as nonstandard, many of them are widely used by some of the largest insurers.

Endorsements and Other Related Documents

Documents other than insurance forms can become part of an insurance policy, either by being physically attached to or by being referenced within the policy. Subject to statutory and regulatory constraints, an insurance policy may incorporate a wide range of documents in addition to policy forms. Examples include endorsements, the completed insurance application, and various other documents.

Endorsements, if added to the policy, form part of the policy. An endorsement may be a preprinted, computer-printed, typewritten, or handwritten line, sentence, paragraph, or set of paragraphs on one or more pages attached to the policy. In rare cases, an endorsement may take the form of a handwritten note in the margin of the policy and be dated and initialed by an insured and the insurer's authorized representative.

Because endorsements are usually intended to modify a basic policy form, the endorsement provisions often differ from basic policy provisions. This difference can lead to questions of policy interpretation. These two general rules of policy interpretation apply to endorsements:

- An endorsement takes precedence over any conflicting terms in the policy to which it is attached.
- A handwritten endorsement supersedes a computer-printed or typewritten one. Handwritten alterations tend to reflect true intent more accurately than do preprinted policy terms.

In several lines of business, policies are issued with what many practitioners call "standard" endorsements included in the policy. These are endorsements that are included with most of the policies written in that line. Because they are so common, they essentially become part of the basic policy form. In addition, certain states require state-specific endorsements to be included with every policy sold in that state. This results in most policies' having multiple endorsements attached.

An insurance application is the documented request for coverage, whether given orally, in writing, or electronically (over the Internet). The application contains information about the insured and the loss exposures presented to the insurer. Underwriters use the information provided on the application to decide whether to provide the requested insurance and, if so, to price the policy. Although the declarations page often contains much of the same information as the application, the insurer usually keeps the completed application to preserve the representations made by the insured. The application can be used, if necessary, to provide evidence of misleading or false material information supplied by the insured. In some jurisdictions, statutes explicitly require that any written application be made part of the policy for certain lines of insurance.

In certain circumstances, the insurer's bylaws are incorporated into an insurance policy. For example, the policyholders of mutual and reciprocal insurers typically have some rights and duties associated with managing the insurer's operations, and these rights and duties are specified in the policy.

Insurance policies sometimes incorporate the insurer's rating manual (or the insurer's rules and rates, whether found in the manual or elsewhere) by referring to it in the policy language. Although the rules and rates themselves do not appear in the policy, reference to them makes them part of the policy.

Other documents incorporated in insurance policies include premium notes (promissory notes that are accepted by the insurer in lieu of a cash premium payment), inspection reports, and specification sheets or operating manuals relating to safety equipment or procedures. If, for example, an insurer and an applicant agree that the coverage provided by a particular property or liability insurance policy is conditional on the use of certain procedures or safety equipment, then a set of operating instructions or a manual of specifications can be incorporated into the policy by reference and then used to define the agreed-upon procedures or equipment.

Any of these related documents can alter the forms that are included in a policy. Therefore, related documents make policy analysis more difficult for insurance professionals because they add to the volume and complexity of forms that must be evaluated. As the number of related documents grows, so does the likelihood that one or more of the documents may contradict, exclude, or expand provisions in the basic forms.

POLICY PROVISIONS

Every insurance policy is composed of numerous policy provisions. A policy provision is a contractual term included in an insurance policy that specifies requirements or clarifies intended meaning. Despite wide variation in property-casualty insurance policy provisions, each provision can typically be placed into one of six categories, depending on the purpose it serves. Comprehending the purpose(s) and characteristics of each of these categories of policy provisions assists insurance and risk management professionals in analyzing and interpreting insurance policies.

The exhibit lists the six categories of policy provisions, briefly describes each category, and summarizes the effect that policy provisions in each category may have on coverage. Each of the policy provisions must be examined during policy analysis to determine its exact effect on coverage. See the exhibit "Property-Casualty Insurance Policy Provisions."

Property-Casualty Insurance Policy Provisions

Policy Provision Category	Description	Effect on Coverage
Declarations	Unique information on the insured; list of forms included in policy	Outline who or what is covered, and where and when coverage applies
Definitions	Words with special meanings in policy	May limit or expand coverage based on definitions of terms
Insuring Agreements	Promise to make payment	Outline circumstances under which the insurer agrees to pay
Conditions	Qualifications on promise to make payment	Outline steps insured needs to take to enforce policy
Exclusions	Limitations on promise to make payment	Limit insurer's payments based on excluded persons, places, things, or actions
Miscellaneous Provisions	Wide variety of provisions that may alter policy	Deal with the relationship between the insured and the insurer or establish procedures for implementing the policy

[DA03052]

Declarations

Insurance policy declarations typically contain not only the standard information that has been "declared" by both the insured and the insurer but also information unique to the particular policy. The declarations (commonly referred to as the **declarations page**, or simply dec page) may be only one page or several pages in length and typically appear in the front of an insurance

Declarations page (declarations, or dec.)

An insurance policy information page or pages providing specific details about the insured and the subject of the insurance.

policy. The declarations state important facts about the particular policy, such as these:

- Policy or policy number
- Policy inception and expiration dates (policy period)
- Name of the insurer
- Name of the insurance agent
- Name of the insured(s)
- Names of persons or organizations whose additional interests are covered (for example, a mortgagee, a loss payee, or an additional insured)
- Mailing address of the insured
- Physical address and description of the covered property or operations
- Numbers and edition dates of all attached forms and endorsements
- Dollar amounts of applicable policy limits
- Dollar amounts of applicable deductibles
- Rating information and the policy premium

Sometimes endorsements also contain information similar to that contained in the declarations. For example, an endorsement to a homeowners policy may contain a "schedule" listing descriptions and limits of coverage for valuable pieces of personal property that need special insurance treatment.

Definitions

Most insurance policies or forms include a section that contains definitions of certain terms used throughout the entire policy or form. Boldface type or quotation marks are typically used in the body of the policy to distinguish words and phrases that are defined in the definitions section.

Many of the definitions that appear in insurance policies are there because of real or perceived ambiguity that has arisen regarding the use of those terms in previous policies.

Most insurance policies refer to the insurer as "we" and the named insured as "you." These and other related pronouns, such as "us," "our," and "your," are often defined in an untitled preamble to the policy rather than in a definitions section.

Words and phrases defined within an insurance policy are interpreted according to their definitions in the policy. Undefined words and phrases are interpreted according to these rules of policy interpretation:

- Everyday words are given their ordinary meanings.
- Technical words are given their technical meanings.

- Words with an established legal meaning are given their legal meanings.
- Consideration is also given to the local, cultural, and trade-usage meanings of words, if applicable.

Insuring Agreements

Following the declarations, and possibly preceded by a section containing definitions, the body of most insurance policies begins with an **insuring agreement**.

Policies typically contain an insuring agreement for each coverage they provide. Consequently, package policies contain multiple insuring agreements. For example, the Personal Auto Policy of Insurance Services Office, Inc. (ISO) contains a separate insuring agreement for each of these four parts of the policy:

- Part A—Liability Coverage
- Part B—Medical Payments Coverage
- Part C—Uninsured Motorists Coverage
- Part D—Coverage for Damage to Your Auto

The term "insuring agreement" is usually applied to statements that introduce a policy's coverage section. However, "insuring agreement" can also be used to describe statements introducing coverage extensions, additional coverages, supplementary payments, and so on.

Insuring agreements can be classified into two broad categories: comprehensive and limited. Whether comprehensive or limited, insuring agreements state the insurer's obligations in relatively broad terms. The full scope of coverage cannot be determined without examining the rest of the policy because the insurer's obligations are clarified or modified by other policy provisions.

Comprehensive insuring agreements provide an extremely broad grant of unrestricted coverage that is both clarified and narrowed by exclusions, definitions, and other policy provisions.

In commercial property insurance, a comprehensive insuring agreement is called special-form coverage (or open perils coverage), and a limited insuring agreement is called either basic-form or broad-form coverage (or named perils coverage).

The special-form coverage provides protection against causes of loss that are not specifically excluded. This comprehensive approach covers all the named causes of loss included in the basic- or broad-form coverage, as well as additional causes of loss that are not otherwise excluded.

Limited insuring agreements restrict coverage to certain causes of loss or to certain situations. Exclusions, definitions, and other policy provisions serve to clarify and narrow coverage but may also broaden the coverage.

Insuring agreement
A statement in an insurance policy that the insurer will, under described circumstances, make a loss payment or provide a service.

The limited insuring agreements in commercial property insurance are the named perils, specified perils, or specified causes of loss coverage, referred to as the basic-form or broad-form coverages. The basic-form coverage protects against a list of named causes of loss, and the broad-form coverage protects against the named causes of loss in the basic form plus some additional named causes of loss.

In liability insurance, a limited or single-purpose insuring agreement (which uses specific policy language to define the policy terms) applies to a limited number of incidents. In contrast, comprehensive liability insuring agreements are much broader and do not limit coverage to a particular location, operation, or activity. Additional policy provisions, such as exclusions, limit the coverage of these policies.

Many insurance policies include secondary or supplemental coverages in addition to the main coverage in the insuring agreement. These coverages are described by terms such as "coverage extensions," "additional coverages," or "supplementary payments." The terms "coverage extensions" and "additional coverages" are often used in property coverages. "Supplementary payments" clarify the extent of coverage for certain expenses in liability insurance. The provisions that express these secondary or supplemental coverages are considered insuring agreements.

Exclusions

Exclusion

A policy provision that eliminates coverage for specified exposures.

Exclusions state what the insurer does not intend to cover. The word "intend" here is important; the primary function of exclusions is not only to limit coverage but also to clarify the coverages granted by the insurer. Specifying what the insurer does not intend to cover is a way of clarifying what aspects the insurer does intend to cover. An exclusion can serve one or more of six basic purposes:

- Eliminate coverage for uninsurable loss exposures
- Assist in managing moral and morale hazards
- Reduce likelihood of coverage duplications
- Eliminate coverages not needed by the typical insured
- Eliminate coverages requiring special treatment
- Assist in keeping premiums reasonable

Eliminate Coverage for Uninsurable Loss Exposures

Some loss exposures possess few, if any, of the ideal characteristics of an insurable loss exposure. The first purpose of exclusions is to eliminate coverage for loss exposures that are considered uninsurable by private insurers. For example, most property and liability insurance policies exclude coverage for loss exposures relating to war. (The main exception is the "war risks coverage" often available in ocean marine insurance policies covering vessels or cargoes, even those that might pass through war zones. Insurers charge appropriately higher rates for such coverage.)

In addition to war, examples of loss exposures that most private insurers consider to be uninsurable, and therefore widely exclude, are criminal acts committed by the insured and normal wear and tear of property. Each of these excluded loss exposures is lacking one or more of the characteristics of an ideally insurable loss exposure. For example, war involves an incalculable catastrophe potential, and the other examples involve losses that are not fortuitous from the insured's standpoint.

Assist in Managing Moral and Morale Hazards

The second purpose of exclusions is to assist in managing moral and morale hazards. Both moral and morale hazards can cause individuals and organizations to behave differently when they are insured because they do not have to assume the entire cost of a loss.

Exclusions help insurers minimize these hazards because they ensure that the individual or organization remains responsible for certain types of loss. For example, to manage moral hazards, the property section of the ISO Homeowners 3—Special Form excludes "any loss arising out of any act an 'insured' commits or conspires to commit with the intent to cause a loss."[1] This exclusion reduces moral hazard incentives by eliminating coverage for intentional loss caused by an insured.

Some exclusions assist in managing morale hazards by making insureds themselves bear the losses that result from their own carelessness. For example, the Neglect exclusion in ISO homeowners forms eliminates coverage for property loss caused by "neglect of an 'insured' to use all reasonable means to save and preserve property at and after the time of a loss."[2]

Reduce Likelihood of Coverage Duplications

The third purpose of exclusions is to reduce the likelihood of coverage duplications. Having two insurance policies covering the same loss is usually unnecessary and inefficient. It is unnecessary because coverage under one policy is all that is needed to indemnify the insured (unless policy restrictions or limits of insurance preclude full recovery).

It is inefficient because, at least in theory, each policy providing coverage for certain types of losses includes a related premium charge. Therefore, an insured with duplicated coverage is paying higher premiums than is necessary. Exclusions ensure that multiple policies can work together to provide complementary, not duplicate, coverage and that insureds are not paying duplicate premiums.

For example, assume Karim has both a personal auto policy and a homeowners policy. If Karim leaves his laptop computer in his car and the car is stolen, he can submit a claim for the laptop under his homeowners insurance. Therefore, the loss of the laptop does not need to be covered under his personal auto policy. If it were covered under his auto policy, Karim would likely be paying more than necessary for his auto insurance. Excluding the laptop under the auto insurance avoids duplication of coverage.

Eliminate Coverages Not Needed by the Typical Insured

The fourth purpose of exclusions is to eliminate coverages that are not needed by the typical purchaser of a given line of insurance. Elimination of such coverages avoids the situation of all insureds having to share the costs of covering loss exposures that relatively few insureds have.

For example, the typical auto owner or homeowner does not own or operate private aircraft or rent portions of the family home for storage of others' business property. Therefore, homeowners policies typically exclude coverage for such loss exposures. People who do have these loss exposures may be able to obtain coverage separately through endorsements to their policies (for an additional premium) or by purchasing separate insurance policies.

Insurers are not always permitted to exclude coverage for loss exposures not faced by the typical insurance purchaser. For example, insurers may want to exclude auto liability coverage for drivers who have accidents while driving under the influence of alcohol. However, state insurance regulators are unlikely to approve such an exclusion because it tends to eliminate a source of recovery for the victims of drunken drivers. The effect is that auto policyholders who never drink and drive are required to share the costs of accidents caused by those who do.

Eliminate Coverages Requiring Special Treatment

The fifth purpose of exclusions is to eliminate coverages requiring special treatment. Such special treatment may entail underwriting, risk control, or reinsurance that is substantially different from what is normally required for the policy containing the exclusion. For example, commercial general liability policies issued to professionals are usually endorsed to exclude their professional liability loss exposures. These insureds can purchase separate professional liability insurance to cover claims alleging that they made errors or omissions in providing their professional services.

Assist in Keeping Premiums Reasonable

The sixth purpose of exclusions is to assist in keeping premiums at a level that a sufficiently large number of insurance buyers will consider reasonable. All exclusions serve this purpose to some extent. However, for some exclusions it is the primary or sole purpose, whereas for others it is simply one of the effects.

Excluded losses are not necessarily uninsurable. In many cases, few people are willing to pay the premiums necessary to include coverage for losses that ordinarily are excluded. For example, auto physical damage coverage typically excludes loss due and confined to mechanical breakdown or road damage to tires. These loss exposures are not uninsurable. In fact, many auto dealers, tire shops, and various other organizations offer insurance-like service warranties covering such loss exposures.

An insurance policy could probably be priced to reflect the expected costs of mechanical breakdowns or tire losses, but the insured would be paying the projected costs of maintenance plus the insurer's expenses in administering insurance to cover the maintenance costs. The additional premium might exceed the typical costs associated with these losses.

Conditions

Some **policy conditions** are found in a section of the policy titled "Conditions," while others are found in other sections of the forms, endorsements, or other documents that constitute the policy. For example, a standard homeowners insurance policy has three major sections in which conditions are listed: Section I Conditions, Section II Conditions, and Sections I and II Conditions.

Policy condition
Any provision that qualifies an otherwise enforceable promise made in the policy.

In a policy's insuring agreement, the insurer promises to pay to the insured, to pay on behalf of the insured, to defend the insured, and/or to provide various additional services. However, the insurer's promises are enforceable only if an insured event occurs and only if the insured has fulfilled its contractual duties as specified in the policy conditions.

Examples of policy conditions include the insured's obligation to pay premiums, report losses promptly, provide appropriate documentation for losses, cooperate with the insurer in any legal proceedings, and refrain from jeopardizing an insurer's rights to recover from third parties responsible for causing covered losses. If the insured does not comply with these conditions, then the insurer may be released from any obligation to perform some or all of its otherwise enforceable promises.

Miscellaneous Provisions

In addition to declarations, definitions, insuring agreements, exclusions, and conditions, insurance policies often contain miscellaneous provisions that deal with the relationship between the insured and the insurer or help to establish working procedures for implementing the policy. However, such provisions do not have the force of conditions. Consequently, even if the insured does not follow the procedures specified in the miscellaneous provisions, the insurer may still be required to fulfill its contractual promises.

Miscellaneous provisions often are unique to particular types of insurers, as in these examples:

- A policy issued by a mutual insurer is likely to describe each insured's right to vote in the election of the board of directors.
- A policy issued by a reciprocal insurer is likely to specify the attorney-in-fact's authority to implement its powers on the insured's behalf.

POLICY ANALYSIS

Each pre-loss question posed or post-loss claim filed by an insured is a unique situation that may require a review of policy provisions.

Insurance professionals should conduct pre-loss policy analysis to prepare themselves to answer an insured's coverage questions and to ensure that the policy being sold is appropriate for the insured's loss exposures. Insureds should conduct pre-loss policy analysis to verify that the policy they're purchasing adequately addresses their loss exposures. After a loss, the insurer must analyze the policy to determine whether it covers the loss and, if necessary, the extent of coverage the policy provides.

Pre-Loss Policy Analysis

Pre-loss policy analysis almost exclusively relies on scenario analysis to determine the extent of coverage (if any) the policy provides for the losses generated by a given scenario. For insureds, the primary source of information for generating scenarios for analysis is their past loss experience. Particularly if the insured has never suffered a loss that triggered insurance coverage, friends, neighbors, co-workers, and family members can also provide information about their experiences with losses and the claim process. Such information can help an insured formulate scenarios for pre-loss policy analysis.

Another source of information for the insured's scenario analysis is the insurance producer or customer service representative consulted in the insurance transaction. Such insurance professionals need to be able to accurately interpret coverage questions raised. Producers may have specialized knowledge of the loss exposures covered under the policy. They also understand the alternative ways insurance policies may describe the same coverage and may be aware of any policy provisions that depart from customary wording. For example, homeowners who have read news articles about toxic mold may consult their insurance producers to determine whether their homeowners insurance policy covers mold, fungus, or wet rot.

One of the limitations of scenario analysis is that, because the number of possible loss scenarios is theoretically infinite, it is impossible to account for every possibility. For example, most insurance professionals or insureds would not have envisioned the terrorist attacks of September 11, 2001. Alternatively, the insured or insurance professional may recognize the possibility of an event but underestimate the extent of potential loss. For example, the damage Hurricane Andrew caused in 1992 was unprecedented, as was the extent of flooding New Orleans experienced following Hurricane Katrina in 2005. These events prompted insurers to fundamentally change the methods used to evaluate these types of risks.

Post-Loss Policy Analysis

When an insured reports a loss, the insurer must determine whether the loss triggers coverage and, if so, the extent of that coverage. The primary method of post-loss policy analysis is the DICE (an acronym representing the policy provision categories: declarations, insuring agreements, conditions, and exclusions) method, which is a systematic review of all the categories of property-casualty policy provisions. See the exhibit "DICE Decision Tree."

The DICE method entails following four steps to determine whether a policy provides coverage. The first step is an examination of the declarations page to determine whether the information provided by the insured precludes coverage. For example, an insured may report to the property insurer that a fire occurred at the insured premises on May 5. The declarations page contains both the policy inception and expiration dates (delineating the policy period). If the policy period ended on April 30, then the policy would not provide coverage for this loss.

If nothing in the declarations precludes coverage, the insurance professional would move to the second step in the DICE method, an analysis of the insuring agreement. For example, in the homeowners policy, the insurer agrees to provide coverage in exchange for the insured's payment of the premium. If the premium is not paid, the policy would not cover the claim. The insuring agreement or agreements often contain policy provisions regarding the covered property or events, covered causes of loss, and coverage territories. If these provisions contain specially defined terms, those definitions should be analyzed. If a provision in an insuring agreement precludes coverage, the claim will be denied.

DICE Decision Tree

To determine whether a policy covers a loss, many insurance professionals apply the DICE method. ("DICE" is an acronym for categories of policy provisions: declarations, insuring agreement, conditions, and exclusions.) The DICE method has four steps:

1. Review of the declarations page to determine whether it covers the person or the property at the time of the loss
2. Review of the insuring agreement to determine whether it covers the loss
3. Review of policy conditions to determine compliance
4. Review of policy exclusions to determine whether they preclude coverage of the loss

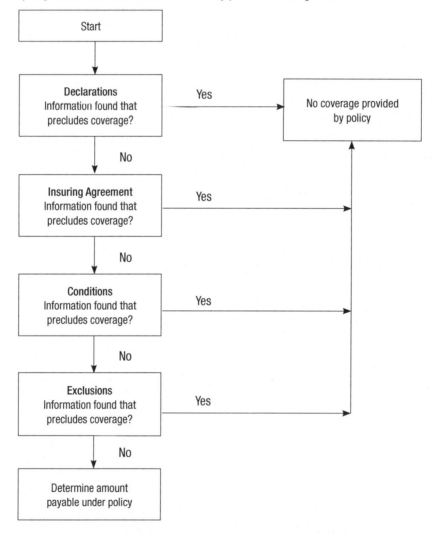

Each of these four steps is used in every case. Other categories of policy provisions should be examined. For example, endorsements and terms defined in the policy should be reviewed in relation to the declarations, insuring agreement, exclusions, and conditions.

If nothing in the insuring agreement precludes coverage, the insurance professional proceeds to the third step of the DICE method, analyzing conditions. Policy conditions specify the duties of the insurer and the insured. Examples of common policy provisions include the insured's obligation to report losses promptly, provide appropriate documentation for losses, and cooperate with the insurer in any legal proceedings. Violating a condition can change the coverage on an otherwise-covered claim. Examining the policy conditions can help the insurance professional clarify these important points:

- Whether fulfillment of certain conditions, such as premium payment conditions, is required for there to be an enforceable policy

- Whether coverage will be denied if an insured party breaches a policy condition

- Whether coverage triggers and coverage territory restrictions affect the loss

- Whether conditions concerning the rights and duties of both parties to maintain the insurance policy apply (for example, the insurer's right to inspect covered premises, the rights of either or both parties to cancel the policy, and the insurer's right to make coverage modifications)

- Whether the post-loss duties of the insured and the insurer affect coverage

- Whether conditions have been or need to be adhered to regarding claim disputes

- Whether subrogation and salvage rights and conditions must be considered

One breach of a condition that can occur under a homeowners policy is the concealment of a material fact. For example, assume an insured has a primary business running a furniture refinishing operation in his home. If he fails to disclose this fact when obtaining his homeowners coverage, in violation of one of the policy's coverage conditions, the policy would not cover a fire caused by flammable rags used to polish furniture.

If the insured has complied with all of the policy's conditions, the insurance professional performs the final step of the DICE method, analyzing policy exclusions and any other policy provisions not already analyzed, including endorsements and miscellaneous provisions. This is the fourth and final step of the DICE method. Exclusions, which can appear anywhere in the policy, state what the insurer does not intend to cover. The primary function of exclusions is not only to limit coverage but also to clarify the coverages granted by the insurer. They also eliminate coverage for uninsurable loss exposures (such as intentional acts) and can be used to reduce the likelihood of coverage duplications, eliminate coverages not needed by the typical insured, eliminate coverages requiring special treatment, or assist in keeping premiums reasonable. For example, an exclusion in a homeowners policy precludes coverage for claims resulting from earth movement caused by an earthquake, landslide, or subsidence that damages a dwelling or its contents.

After using the DICE method to determine whether the claim is covered, the insurer must then determine how much is payable under that insurance policy. The amount payable under a given insurance policy can be affected not only by the value of the loss but also by policy limits and deductibles, or self-insured retentions. For property insurance, the amount payable is affected by several factors. The valuation provision indicates how the property will be valued for claim purposes, which could be on the basis of its replacement cost, its depreciated actual cash value, or some other valuation method. The amount payable is also affected by applicable policy limits and can be limited by a coinsurance provision or other insurance-to-value provisions. Some policies designate a deductible to be subtracted from the amount otherwise payable. For liability insurance, the valuation of a covered loss is established by the courts or, more commonly, by a negotiated settlement. The amounts payable for both property and liability insurance losses can also be affected by other insurance.

SUMMARY

These are the six characteristics of an ideally insurable loss exposure:

- Pure risk—Involves pure risk, not speculative risk.
- Fortuitous losses—Subject to fortuitous loss from the insured's standpoint.
- Definite and measurable—Subject to losses that are definite in time, cause, and location and that are measurable.
- Large number of similar exposure units—One of a large number of similar exposure units.
- Independent and not catastrophic—Not subject to a loss that would simultaneously affect many other similar loss exposures; loss would not be catastrophic.
- Affordable—Premiums are economically feasible.

These are the distinguishing characteristics of insurance policies:

- Indemnity
- Utmost good faith
- Fortuitous losses
- Contract of adhesion
- Exchange of unequal amounts
- Conditional
- Nontransferable

The physical structure of an insurance policy can be that of a self-contained policy or that of a modular policy. The forms of which a policy is composed may be preprinted forms or manuscript forms, and standard forms or nonstandard forms. In addition to forms, endorsements and other related documents may be incorporated in a policy. All of these approaches to policy structure affect policy analysis.

Every insurance policy is composed of numerous policy provisions. Each provision can be placed into one of six categories, depending on the purpose it serves:

- Declarations
- Definitions
- Insuring agreements
- Exclusions
- Conditions
- Miscellaneous provisions

Being able to classify policy provisions into these categories is an important part of analyzing an insurance policy.

Insureds and insurers should analyze an insurance policy before a loss occurs in order to ensure that the policy adequately covers the loss exposures it is intended to address. The primary method of pre-loss policy analysis is scenario analysis. After a loss occurs, an insurer uses the DICE method to determine whether the insurance policy provides coverage.

ASSIGNMENT NOTES

1. Copyrighted material of Insurance Services Office, Inc., with its permission. Copyright, ISO Properties, Inc., 1999.
2. Copyrighted material of Insurance Services Office, Inc., with its permission. Copyright, ISO Properties, Inc., 1999.

8

Common Features of Insurance Policies

Educational Objectives

After learning the content of this assignment, you should be able to:

▷ Given a case, evaluate one or more entities' insurable interests.

▷ Explain why insurance to value is important to property insurers, how insurers encourage insurance to value, and what insureds can do to address the problems associated with maintaining insurance to value.

▷ Explain how property is valued under each of the following valuation methods in property insurance policies:

- Actual cash value

- Replacement cost

- Agreed value

- Functional valuation

▷ Explain how the amount payable for a claim covered under a liability insurance policy is determined.

▷ Explain how deductibles in property insurance benefit the insured.

▷ Explain why deductibles are not commonly used in some liability policies but are commonly used in other liability policies, and how a self-insured retention differs from a deductible.

▷ Describe the multiple sources of recovery that may be available to an insurance policyholder for a covered loss.

Common Features of Insurance Policies

8

INSURABLE INTEREST

When determining whether a loss is covered under a property insurance policy, a professional must determine whether the insured, who is claiming a financial loss, has an insurable interest in the property that was damaged or destroyed. The analysis must determine two things: whether the claimant is an insured under the policy and, if so, whether the insured has an insurable interest in the property.

An insured under a property policy must have an insurable interest in property that is damaged or destroyed in order to have a legitimate claim. Several legal bases can be established for an insurable interest. In some situations, multiple parties can have an insurable interest in the same property; for example, spouses who have tenancy in the same property both have an insurable interest in it. An examination of when and why insurable interest is required, along with the descriptions of the legal bases for insurable interest and the multiple parties that can have an insurable interest, will help insurance and risk management professionals determine whether the insurable interest requirement is met when an insured submits a property claim.

When and Why Insurable Interest Is Required

An **insurable interest** arises as the result of a relationship with a person or a right with respect to property. Whether an insurable interest exists depends on the relationship between the claiming party and the property, person, or event that is the subject of the insurance policy. For example, to make a claim under a property insurance policy, the claimant must stand to suffer a financial loss if the insured property is damaged or destroyed.

The requirement for an insurable interest is a matter of law and exists even in the absence of policy provisions specifically addressing insurable interest. However, policies often include provisions that limit insureds' right of recovery to no more than their interest in the covered property at the time of the loss.

The requirement for insurable interest is different in property-casualty insurance than in life insurance. In life insurance, the beneficiary must have an insurable interest in the life of the insured when the policy is purchased, but not necessarily at the time of the insured's death. For example, Mary is the beneficiary on her husband's life insurance policy. If the couple divorces, Mary may no longer have an insurable interest in her ex-husband's life, but she

Insurable interest
An interest in the subject of an insurance policy that is not unduly remote and that would cause the interested party to suffer financial loss if an insured event occurred.

would not be prevented from collecting under the policy in the event of his death.

In contrast, insurable interest in property-casualty insurance must be present at the time of the loss. For example, if Jacob sold his home but did not cancel his homeowners insurance, he could not present a valid claim under that policy if the property were subsequently damaged because he would have no insurable interest in the home at the time of the loss.

Insurance policies have an insurable interest requirement for these three reasons:

- It supports the principle of indemnity.
- It prevents the use of insurance as a wagering mechanism.
- It reduces the moral hazard incentive that insurance may create for the insured.

Insurable interest supports the principle of indemnity by ensuring that only those parties who suffer financial loss are indemnified, and then only to the extent of their loss. Requiring an insurable interest prevents individuals or organizations from wagering (gambling) by insuring an event from which they would not suffer a loss and then profiting when that event occurs. In addition, because the insurable interest requirement limits insureds' ability to profit from insurance, the incentive to cause losses intentionally (moral hazard incentive) is reduced.

Legal Bases for Insurable Interest

Insurable interest can arise from a legal relationship between the party filing the claim and the subject of insurance. The legal bases for insurable interest include these:

- Ownership interest in property
- Contractual obligations
- Exposure to legal liability
- Factual expectancy
- Representation of another party

Ownership Interest in Property

Ownership of property creates an insurable interest in that property, and ownership rights are legally protected. For example, property owners have a legal right to sell, give away, and use their property. The extent of legal ownership determines the extent of insurable interest in the property.

Although the term "property" is commonly used to refer to tangible objects such as buildings and their contents, it also includes intangible items, such as copyrights, patents, trademarks, intellectual property, and stock certificates.

Ownership rights to both tangible and intangible property have economic value and are guaranteed and protected by law.

Contractual Obligations

Insurable interest can arise out of some contractual obligations. Generally, contractual rights and related insurable interests fall into two major categories:

- Contractual rights regarding people—A contract may give one party the right to bring a claim against a second party without entitling the first party to any specific property that belongs to the second party. For example, if Anthony does not pay his credit card debt, the credit card company can bring a claim against Anthony for the outstanding balance on the card. However, the credit card company does not have the right to repossess any of Anthony's property as payment for the debt. In this case, the credit card company is an unsecured creditor. Unsecured creditors do not have an insurable interest in debtors' property.
- Contractual rights regarding property—Some contracts allow one party to bring a claim against specific property held by a second party. For example, if Anthony obtains a mortgage loan in order to buy a house, the mortgage holder can repossess the house if Anthony fails to make his mortgage payments. This type of contract typically creates an insurable interest in the secured property equal to the debt's remaining balance.

Exposure to Legal Liability

Sometimes one party can have legal responsibility for property owned by others. Having this type of legal responsibility creates an insurable interest in that property because the responsible party can suffer a financial loss if the owner's property is damaged. These examples illustrate insurable interests based on exposure to legal liability:

- A hotelier has an insurable interest in guests' property.
- A tenant has an insurable interest in the portion of the premises the tenant occupies.
- A contractor typically has an insurable interest in a building under construction.

In these cases, the responsible party has an insurable interest based on potential legal liability for damage to the owner's property. The extent of that insurable interest is the property's full value, including the owner's use value.

Factual Expectancy

A majority of states have accepted **factual expectancy** as a valid basis for an insurable interest. In these states, a party does not have to establish a specific property right, contractual right, or potential legal liability to prove insurable interest. The party need only demonstrate potential financial harm resulting

Factual expectancy
A situation in which a party experiences an economic advantage if an insured event does not occur or, conversely, economic harm if the event does occur.

from the event to be insured. The focus is on the insured's financial position rather than on a legal interest.

For example, Tina's fiancé gives her a diamond engagement ring that he had stolen from a relative. When Tina's apartment is subsequently burglarized, the ring is one of the items taken. During the investigation of Tina's claim, the origin of the ring is discovered. Because a person cannot legally own property that rightfully belongs to another, Tina was never the legal owner of the ring. Nonetheless, courts would probably find that she would be entitled to recover for the ring under her tenant's policy based on her factual expectancy of loss.

Representation of Another Party

Insurable interest can be based on one party's acting as a representative of another party. In this case, the representative can obtain insurance on property for the benefit of the property's owner. These examples illustrate insurable interests based on representation of another party:

Agent

In the agency relationship, the party that is authorized by the principal to act on the principal's behalf.

Trustee

Someone who has the legal title to a property but is responsible that it be used, handled, and transferred solely for the benefit of the beneficiary.

Bailor

The owner of the personal property in a bailment.

- Agents—An **agent** may insure property in the agent's name for the principal's benefit. Although the insurance proceeds are ultimately payable to the principal, the agent has an insurable interest.
- Trustees—A **trustee** may insure property in the trustee's name for the trust's benefit. The trustee has an insurable interest but must give the insurance proceeds to the trust.
- Bailees—A bailee may insure property in the bailee's name for the bailor's benefit. The bailee has an insurable interest, but if the bailor's property becomes damaged or destroyed, the bailee pays any insurance proceeds to the **bailor**.

In these situations, the party obtaining the insurance is not required to have an independent insurable interest in the property. The party derives its interest from its relationship with the party it represents. See the exhibit "Practice Exercise."

Multiple Parties With Insurable Interests

Under some circumstances, more than one party has an insurable interest in the same property and, as a result, the sum of all insurable interests exceeds the property's value. For example, a property owner and the lender holding a mortgage on the property both have an insurable interest in that property. The mortgage holder's interest is the amount of the unpaid loan, and the owner's interest is the property's full value. Combined, the amount of these two interests could greatly exceed the property's value.

For example, Nina purchased a $500,000 home using $100,000 of her savings and a $400,000 mortgage loan. The mortgage holder's interest is $400,000 and Nina's interest is the full $500,000, because she has full use of the property. Their combined interest is $900,000, well above the total value of the

Practice Exercise

Canston Holdings, Inc. is a property management firm that owns a number of commercial properties. Canston recently sold one of its buildings to Sisterdale & Worthley, an accounting firm. The local Blazek Bank holds Sisterdale & Worthley's mortgage on the building. The two-story building is located at 123 Malvern Street. Sisterdale & Worthley have their offices on the ground floor and lease the second floor to Janasok Communications, a call center. Next door to the building is Courton Eats, a small diner that is popular with staff at both the accounting firm and the call center. Approximately 75 percent of the diner's traffic comes from these two neighboring businesses. Complete the table to show which of the following organizations has an insurable interest in the building at 123 Malvern Street and to describe the basis for that interest.

Organization	Insurable Interest? (Y/N)	Basis of Interest
Canston Holdings		
Sisterdale & Worthley		
Blazek Bank		
Janasok Communications		
Courton Eats		

Answer

The table should be completed as shown here:

Organization	Insurable Interest? (Y/N)	Basis of Interest
Canston Holdings	No	Not applicable
Sisterdale & Worthley	Yes	Ownership
Blazek Bank	Yes	Contractual (secured creditor)
Janasok Communications	Yes	Exposure to liability
Courton Eats	No	Not applicable

[DA06038]

property. However, if the home were completely destroyed, neither Nina nor the mortgage holder could claim more than their actual loss under the homeowners policy. Assuming the dwelling was insured for its full value, the insurer would pay no more than $100,000 to Nina and $400,000 to the mortgage holder.

When more than one person owns the same property, the nature of the ownership affects the extent of each party's insurable interest. Property may be jointly owned according to these interests:

- Joint tenancy
- Tenancy by the entirety

- Tenancy in common
- Tenancy in partnership

Joint Tenancy

In joint tenancy, each owner, referred to as a "tenant," owns the entire property and has a right of survivorship. This is an automatic right of one tenant to the share of the other tenant when that other tenant dies. For example, if Manuel and Gerard are joint tenants of a restaurant building, each owns the entire building. If Manuel died, Gerard would automatically become the sole owner of the building and vice versa.

Because any one joint tenant could become the property's sole owner, each tenant has an insurable interest in the property's full value. If the restaurant were insured for its full value of $1 million, Manuel and Gerard would each have a $1 million interest. Therefore, their combined interest would be $2 million, or twice the value of the property. Nonetheless, if the restaurant were destroyed by fire, their insurance policy would pay no more than the property's value, subject to the $1 million policy limit and any other policy provisions. That payment would probably be made to the first named insured in the declarations.

Tenancy by the Entirety

Tenancy by entirety is a joint tenancy between a husband and wife. As with a joint tenancy, if spouses jointly own a property, each of them owns the entire property. If one of them dies, the other becomes the sole owner; consequently, each spouse has an insurable interest equal to the full value of the property. As a result, the combined interests of both spouses would be twice the property value. However, as with a joint tenancy, in the event of a loss, an insurance policy would pay no more than the property's value.

Tenancy in Common

Tenancy in common is a concurrent ownership of property, in equal or unequal shares, by two or more owners. Unlike joint tenants or tenants in the entirety, tenants in common do not have survivorship rights. For example, Andrew, Colin, and Rita are tenants in common of a factory, each holding a one-third interest. If Andrew died, Colin and Rita would still each own only one-third of the factory. Andrew's third would pass to his heirs.

With tenants in common, each party's insurable interest is limited to that owner's share of the property. In this example, each has an interest worth one-third of the value of the property; therefore, their combined interests are equal to the property value. Any insurance payouts would probably be made to the first named insured, who would then be responsible for distributing the appropriate share of the money to the other tenants in common.

Tenancy in Partnership

Tenancy in partnership is a concurrent ownership by a partnership and its individual partners of personal property used by the partnership. This type of tenancy is similar to a joint tenancy in that the partnership and all partners have rights of survivorship. Therefore, with a tenancy in partnership, both the partnership entity and the individual partners have an insurable interest in property used by the partnership.

Depending on the size of the partnership, the combined interests could be many times the actual property value because each partner, and the partnership, would have an interest worth the entire insurable amount. If a loss occurred, the claim settlement would be paid to the first named insured, which could be the partnership entity or one of the partners. See the exhibit "Practice Exercise."

Practice Exercise

Stone, Rajdev, Lee & Partners is a civil engineering consulting firm. The three original founders, Stone, Rajdev, and Lee, were all major partners in the company, which had several minor partners as well. The company rents space in an office tower, and the insurable value of the office contents is $750,000. The three principal partners chartered a small airplane to attend a meeting with a potential client. The plane crashed, and Stone, Rajdev, and Lee were killed. Who has an insurable interest in the contents of the office, and what is the value of those interests?

Answer

The partnership entity and each of the remaining minor partners has an insurable interest in the office contents. The value of each of those interests is the full $750,000.

[DA06039]

INSURANCE TO VALUE

An important goal of insurers selling property insurance is to motivate each insured to buy a limit of insurance that approximates the full value of the covered property, commonly called "insurance to value."

Insurance to value is beneficial for both the insurer and the insured. Insurers benefit from insurance to value because it ensures that premiums are adequate to cover potential losses and it simplifies underwriting. The insured benefits because sufficient funds are available in the event of a loss. Insurers use a variety of policy provisions to encourage insureds to purchase adequate limits of insurance. Although maintaining insurance to value over time can be challenging, various measures are available to assist insureds and insurance professionals with maintaining insurance to value.

Insurance to value

Insurance written for an amount approximating the full value of the asset(s) insured.

Why Insurers Seek Insurance to Value

Insurers seek to achieve insurance to value in the property insurance policies they write. The need for insurance to value can be understood by first examining **loss frequency** and **loss severity**.

Loss frequency

The number of losses that occur within a specified period.

Loss severity

The amount of loss, typically measured in dollars, for a loss that has occurred.

During the risk management process, loss exposures are assessed to determine potential loss frequency and loss severity. For property loss exposures, the severity loss distribution is often skewed. That is, most of the losses that occur to property, especially real property, are small losses, with a total loss being a rare occurrence. This point can be illustrated through a hypothetical severity distribution of a house valued at $150,000. See the exhibit "Probability Distribution of Severity of Residential Property Losses."

Probability Distribution of Severity of Residential Property Losses

Size Category of Losses (bins)	Probability of Loss	Cumulative Probability of Loss	Average Bin Value	Expected Value of Loss	Expected Value Truncated	
$0–$1,000	.700	.700	$ 500	$ 350	$ 350	Probability of Loss × Average Bin Value
$1,001–$5,000	.200	.900	3,000	600	600	
$5,001–$10,000	.050	.950	7,500	375	375	
$10,001–$15,000	.020	.970	12,500	250	250	
$15,001–$25,000	.015	.985	20,000	300	300	
$25,001–$50,000	.0075	.993	37,500	281	187.5*	
$50,001–$100,000	.005	.998	75,000	375	125*	Expected Value of Insured Losses: $25,000 Policy Limit
$100,001–$150,000	.0025	1.000	125,000	313	62.5*	
Total	1.000			$2,844	$2,250	Expected Value of Insured Losses: Insured to Value

*For each of these expected values of insured losses, the probability of loss is multiplied by $25,000 (the maximum amount payable) instead of the average bin values.

[DA06036]

The Probability Distribution table shows that if a loss occurs, 90 percent of the time, that loss is less than $5,000 (because the cumulative probability is 90 percent). Because the cumulative probability of a loss less than $25,000 is 98.5 percent, then only 1.5 percent of the time is the loss greater than $25,000. The maximum possible loss for the property is $150,000, which would occur only if the property were totally destroyed.

Using a very simplified method, the insurer could calculate the insurance rate and premium to insure the property by combining the severity distribution shown in the Probability Distribution table with a frequency distribution. For example, the severity distribution in the exhibit has an expected value of approximately $2,844. If the insurer were to assume a simple frequency distribution that has only two possibilities—80 percent of the time no loss would occur, and 20 percent of the time one loss would occur—then the insurer would be able to calculate an expected loss of approximately $569 [(0.8 × $0) + (0.2 × $2,844) = $569]. If the insurer had a 40 percent expense ratio, the premium it would charge would be $948 [$569 ÷ (1 − 0.40) = $948].

The importance to the insurer of insurance to value can be illustrated by showing how the lack of insurance to value affects premium adequacy. For example, suppose that the insurer provides a property insurance policy with a policy limit of $150,000 and that the premium is based on an insurance rate per $100 of coverage. Dividing $150,000 by $100 yields 1,500 units of coverage that the insurer is providing.

The insurer, charging a premium of $948 for a policy with a limit of $150,000 (the value of the property), is using an insurance rate of approximately $0.63 per unit of coverage ($948 ÷ 1,500 = $0.63). Further, suppose that the insured evaluated the severity distribution and chose to retain the 1.5 percent probability that losses would be above $25,000 by buying a policy with a limit of only $25,000.

The insurer would lose money on the $25,000-limit policy (250 units of coverage) if it charged the same rate ($0.63 per unit of coverage) as for the policy with the $150,000 limit; this would result in a premium of only $158 (250 units × $0.63 = $158), and the lower premium would not be sufficient to cover the expected losses under the policy.

If the severity distribution that the insurer faces stops at $25,000, the expected value of that distribution is now $2,250. With the same frequency distribution as used previously, the expected loss is now $450 [(0.8 × $0) + (0.2 × $2,250) = $450], and, assuming the same expense loading, the premium would be $750 [$450 ÷ (1 − 0.4) = $750]. For a policy limit of $25,000, the insurer is offering 250 units of coverage with a rate of $3.00 per unit of coverage. This is substantially higher than the $0.63 per unit rate that was calculated when the property insurance limit was equal to the property's total value.

The insurer is then faced with a decision to either charge a higher rate for property insurance when the policy limit is less than the property's value or require insureds to choose policy limits that are close to the full value of the property. Insurers generally prefer the second choice, referred to as insurance to value.

Insuring to value is typically beneficial for both the insurer and the insured. The insurer benefits in two ways. First, the premium is adequate to cover potential losses. Second, it simplifies the underwriting process by reducing the need to determine exact values during underwriting. The determination of underinsurance (not insuring to value) is made at the time of loss; therefore, the underwriter does not need to determine whether the property is being underinsured.

The insured benefits from insurance to value because sufficient funds are available in the event of a total loss, and the uncertainty associated with large retained losses is reduced. See the exhibit "Insurance to Value Liability Policies."

Insurance to Value Liability Policies

Determining the maximum possible loss for most liability loss exposures is impossible because the severity of such exposures, in theory, is limitless. That is, the law generally does not limit the dollar amount of damages that a court can award to an injured party as damages payable by the responsible party. Therefore, insurers do not seek insurance to value for liability policies.

However, liability insurers use insurance rates that are adequate for whatever "layer" of coverage they are insuring. For example, the rate charged for a primary liability policy (which covers the highest frequency of covered claims) is normally higher than the rate charged for an excess liability policy covering claims that exceed the primary policy's limit of insurance.

Although insurance to value does not apply to liability policies, it is still important for insureds to estimate the potential severity of their liability loss exposures and buy appropriate limits of liability insurance to cover those exposures.

[DA06037]

How Insurers Encourage Insurance to Value

Insurance-to-value provision

A provision in property insurance policies that encourages insureds to purchase an amount of insurance that is equal to, or close to, the value of the covered property.

Coinsurance clause

A clause that requires the insured to carry insurance equal to at least a specified percentage of the insured property's value.

As an incentive for insuring to value, many policies include **insurance-to-value provisions** that reduce the amount payable for both partial and total losses if the insured has not purchased adequate limits of coverage. These provisions, which include **coinsurance clauses** and similar provisions, serve a dual purpose: rewarding those who have insured to value and penalizing those who have not.

Many commercial property insurance policies contain coinsurance clauses, which make the insured responsible for retaining part of any loss if the property is underinsured below some specified percentage of the property's insurable value. The most common coinsurance percentages for buildings and business personal property are 80, 90, and 100 percent. The insurable value is the actual cash value (ACV), the replacement cost value, or whatever other valuation basis applies, according to the policy's valuation clause.

The coinsurance formula explains how the amount payable is determined if the coinsurance requirement has not been met, and can be expressed in this manner:

$$\text{Amount payable} = \frac{\text{Limit of insurance}}{\text{Value of covered property (at time of loss)} \times \text{Coinsurance percentage}} \times \text{Total amount of covered loss}$$

Insurance students often remember this formula as "did over should times loss," which can be written as shown:

$$\text{Amount payable} = \frac{\text{Did}}{\text{Should}} \times \text{Loss,}$$

where

"Did" = The amount of insurance carried (the policy limit), and

"Should" = The minimum amount that should have been carried to meet the coinsurance requirement based on the insurable value at the time of the loss.

For example, a business owns a building with a replacement cost value of $10 million. It insures the building for $9 million with a property insurance policy providing replacement cost coverage subject to a 100 percent coinsurance clause. If a covered peril causes $5 million of damage to the building, the insured would not receive the full $5 million from its insurer, because the building is underinsured. Instead, the claim settlement would be $4.5 million, calculated by dividing the policy limit by the amount of insurance required and then multiplying that percentage by the amount of the loss ($9,000,000 ÷ $10,000,000 × $5,000,000 = $4,500,000).

Business income and extra expense policies also commonly include coinsurance requirements, but the requirements are based on projected net income and operating expenses for the one-year policy period rather than on property values. The coinsurance percentages available for business income and extra expense insurance are 50, 60, 70, 80, 90, 100, and 125 percent, reflecting the fact that some businesses may be able to resume operations in six months or less (roughly corresponding to 50 percent coinsurance), while others may require a year or more to resume operations (roughly corresponding to 100 percent or 125 percent coinsurance).

Insurance-to-value provisions in homeowners (HO) and businessowners (BOP) policies also encourage insureds to purchase adequate limits, but they do so in a different way than the commercial property coinsurance provision does. With the HO and BOP insurance-to-value provisions, the amount payable by the insurer will never be less than the ACV of the damaged property, subject to policy limits. With coinsurance, the amount payable (depending on the degree of underinsurance) can be less than the property's ACV. Under the HO and BOP insurance-to-value provisions, the amount payable by the insurer will be one of these amounts:

- The replacement cost value of the property—effectively, a reward for those insured to at least 80 percent of the replacement cost value of the property

- The actual cash value of the property—effectively, a penalty for those not insured to at least 80 percent of replacement cost value of the property

- An amount between the replacement cost value and the ACV of the property, determined by the same "did over should times loss" formula used in the coinsurance penalty, with which the loss amount is on a replacement cost basis

Addressing Insurance-to-Value Problems

Maintaining insurance to value avoids coinsurance penalties and other insurance-to-value provision penalties that might reduce the amount payable in the event of a loss. Underinsurance penalties are not a concern for insureds who maintain property insurance limits that meet or exceed coinsurance requirements or the insurance-to-value requirement. However, maintaining such limits is difficult, for at least these reasons:

- The amount of insurance necessary to meet coinsurance requirements is based on the insured property's value at the time of the loss, but the policy limit is selected when the policy is purchased.

- When selecting insurance limits, an insurance buyer typically estimates property values based on an informed guess.

- The insurable value at the time of the loss often cannot be precisely measured until the property is actually rebuilt or replaced.

- Values change over time.

Insurance professionals can help property insurance buyers minimize problems associated with valuation by recommending that they take these steps:

- Hire a qualified appraiser to establish the property's current replacement cost value and set policy limits accordingly. The property owner should adjust the appraisal using indexes and/or a record of additions and deletions each year and should reappraise the property every few years.

- Review and revise policy limits periodically to ensure that they are adequate to cover potential losses.

- Consider appropriate coverage options—for example, **agreed value optional coverage**, **inflation guard protection**, and the **peak season endorsement**.

Agreed Value optional coverage

Optional coverage that suspends the Coinsurance condition if the insured carries the amount of insurance agreed to by the insurer and insured.

Inflation guard protection

A method of protecting against inflation by increasing the applicable limit for covered property by a specified percentage over the policy period.

Peak season endorsement

Endorsement that covers the fluctuating values of business personal property by providing differing amounts of insurance for certain time periods during the policy period.

PROPERTY VALUATION METHODS

When covered property is lost or damaged, the amount payable under a property insurance policy depends on the property's value. Every property policy states how the insurer and the insured determine that value. The policy's valuation method is contained in its valuation provision.

For some policies, **actual cash value (ACV)** is the standard valuation method, with **replacement cost** available as an option. For other policies, replacement cost is the standard valuation method, with ACV available as an option. Although ACV and replacement cost are the most common valuation methods, property insurance policies may also use other methods.

Actual cash value (ACV)

Cost to replace property with new property of like kind and quality less depreciation.

Replacement cost

The cost to repair or replace property using new materials of like kind and quality with no deduction for depreciation.

Actual Cash Value

Actual cash value is one of the most prevalent methods used with property insurance policies to determine the amount payable for a property loss because it supports the principle of indemnity by restoring the insured to its pre-loss condition. ACV is typically calculated as the property's replacement cost at the time of loss minus depreciation.

The term "actual cash value" is rarely defined in insurance policies, and the definition adopted by courts often varies by jurisdiction and the type of property insured. Although the traditional definition of ACV has been limited to replacement cost minus depreciation, other methods of determining ACV have evolved, including the use of market value and the broad evidence rule.

When a property insurance policy specifies that property will be valued on an ACV basis, the insured must choose a policy limit to fully insure the property on that basis. The following is the actual cash value policy provision from the Insurance Services Office (ISO) Building and Personal Property (BPP) Coverage Form (subsections b.–e. change the valuation methods for special items such as glass, outdoor equipment, and tenant's improvements and betterments):[1]

> 7. **Valuation**
>
>   We will determine the value of Covered Property in the event of loss or damage as follows:
>
>   **a.** At actual cash value as of the time of loss or damage, except as provided in **b., c., d.** and **e.** below.

Replacement Cost Minus Depreciation

Most property has its highest value when new and depreciates at a fairly steady rate as a result of age and use. Depreciation reflects the value of the use that the insured has already received from the property. Although depreciation can be based on physical wear and tear, which usually increases with age, it can be based on age alone. It can also be based on obsolescence caused by fashion, technological changes, or other factors that occur rapidly and suddenly. Disagreements regularly develop about how to determine the appropriate amount of depreciation to deduct.

The important distinction about depreciation in calculating ACV is that the ACV calculation is based on economic depreciation, not accounting depreciation. See the exhibit "Accounting Depreciation and Economic Depreciation."

Accounting Depreciation and Economic Depreciation

In accounting, if property is expected to have a useful life greater than one year, organizations can depreciate the property over its useful life rather than expensing it in the year of the purchase. This accounting depreciation expense is the allocation of the property's value, as reflected in an organization's accounting and tax records, over the property's useful life (usually a schedule set by tax codes).

Accounting depreciation is distinct from the economic depreciation of property. Economic depreciation is the difference between the replacement cost of the property and its current market value. Economic depreciation is typically the result of physical or functional depreciation. Physical depreciation is the wear and tear on the property and is usually reflected in a reduction in the property's ability to perform its intended function, regardless of use.

Functional depreciation is usually the result of technological advances because the function performed by the capital expenditure is no longer needed or can be performed better by other methods. For example, personal computers that an organization purchased three years ago would have a greatly reduced current value even if they had never been taken out of their original cartons.

[DA03232]

Market Value

Market value

The price at which a particular piece of property could be sold on the open market by an unrelated buyer and seller.

Many courts have ruled that ACV means **market value** (also referred to as fair market value). Market value is easily established for autos, personal computers, and other property that has many buyers and sellers and for which information is available about recent sales. However, it can be difficult to establish market value if there have been few recent transactions involving comparable property. For example, it may be difficult to determine a market value using recent sales of unique manufacturing machinery and equipment.

Market valuation is also useful when property of like kind and quality is unavailable for purchase, such as with antiques, works of art, and other collectibles. These types of property may be irreplaceable, making replacement cost calculations impossible. Although these types of property may not fit the standard of having many comparable sales, examining the sales history of a piece of art and recent transactions involving other pieces of similar quality may be the only method of determining its value. Market valuation can also be the most accurate way to determine the value of some older or historic buildings built with obsolete construction methods and materials.

The market value of real property reflects the value of the land and its location, as well as the value of any buildings or structures on the land. Because most insurance policies cover buildings and structures but not land, the land's value must be eliminated in establishing insurable values of property.

Broad Evidence Rule

The **broad evidence rule** arose when courts stipulated that insurers had to consider more than just depreciation or market value when determining ACV. The exhibit contains a sample of some of the elements that various courts have used in applying the broad evidence rule to determine a building's ACV. See the exhibit "Factors Considered in Determining a Building's ACV."

Broad evidence rule
A court ruling explicitly requiring that all relevant factors be considered in determining actual cash value.

Factors Considered in Determining a Building's ACV

- Obsolescence
- Building's present use and profitability
- Alternate building uses
- Present neighborhood characteristics
- Long-term community plans for the area where the building is located, including urban renewal prospects and new roadway plans
- Inflationary or deflationary trends
- Any other relevant factors

[DA03234]

Replacement Cost

The second valuation method in property insurance policies is replacement cost. Replacement cost is commonly used in insurance policies covering buildings and in many policies covering personal property. The exhibit contains the replacement cost valuation provision from the ISO HO-3 policy. See the exhibit "Replacement Cost Valuation Provision in the ISO HO-3 Policy."

According to the terms set out in the exhibit, if property covered on a replacement cost basis is damaged or destroyed, the insured is entitled to the current cost of repairing damaged property or of buying or building new property of like kind and quality, even if the destroyed property is several years old, and even if its replacement cost exceeds the original purchase price. If the cost of new property has decreased, as often happens with computers or other electronic equipment, replacement cost coverage pays the current lower cost.

Often, a particular model or style of electronic equipment is no longer made. Although the equipment is technically irreplaceable, the replacement cost

Replacement Cost Valuation Provision in the ISO HO-3 Policy

C.   Loss Settlement

2.   Buildings covered under Coverage **A** or **B** at replacement cost without deduction for depreciation, subject to the following:

a.   If, at the time of loss, the amount of insurance in this policy on the damaged building is 80% or more of the full replacement cost of the building immediately before the loss, we will pay the cost to repair or replace, after application of any deductible and without deduction for depreciation, but not more than the least of the following amounts:

(1) The limit of liability under this policy that applies to the building;

(2) The replacement cost of that part of the building damaged with material of like kind and quality and for like use; or

(3) The necessary amount actually spent to repair or replace the damaged building.

If the building is rebuilt at a new premises, the cost described in (2) above is limited to the cost which would have been incurred if the building had been built at the original premises.

b.   If, at the time of loss, the amount of insurance in this policy on the damaged building is less than 80% of the full replacement cost of the building immediately before the loss, we will pay the greater of the following amounts, but not more than the limit of liability under this policy that applies to the building:

(1) The actual cash value of that part of the building damaged; or

(2) That proportion of the cost to repair or replace, after application of any deductible and without deduction for depreciation, that part of the building damaged, which the total amount of insurance in this policy on the damaged building bears to 80% of the replacement cost of the building.

d.   We will pay no more than the actual cash value of the damage until actual repair or replacement is complete. Once actual repair or replacement is complete, we will settle the loss as noted in **2.a.** and **b.** above.

However, if the cost to repair or replace the damage is both:

(1) Less than 5% of the amount of insurance in this policy on the building; and

(2) Less than $2,500;

we will settle the loss as noted in 2.a. and b. above whether or not actual repair or replacement is complete.

e.   You may disregard the replacement cost loss settlement provisions and make claim under this policy for loss to buildings on an actual cash value basis. You may then make claim for any additional liability according to the provisions of this Condition C. Loss Settlement, provided you notify us of your intent to do so within 180 days after the date of loss.

for property of comparable material and quality can still be determined. For example, a manufacturer might have discontinued a particular television model. However, a comparable television can be purchased, often from the same manufacturer. The insured is usually willing to settle a claim based on the existing model's cost, provided the replacement item is not inferior.

Even when the replacement cost method of valuation is specified by the property insurance policy, certain types of property are not valued using that method. For example, replacement cost coverage often does not apply to property such as antiques or artwork, primarily because there is no adequate replacement for such property. These types of property are typically valued at their ACV as determined by market value.

Technically, replacement cost coverage violates the principle of indemnity. An insured who sustains a loss to old, used property and receives insurance payment for new property has profited from the loss. To reduce the moral hazard, most replacement cost policies pay out only after the insured has actually replaced the damaged or destroyed property or, in some cases, only if the loss is a relatively low value.

In many policies with replacement cost provisions, the insured has the option of settling the claim based on ACV and then has 180 days to refile the claim on the replacement cost basis. This gives the insured the opportunity to obtain funds from the insurer at the time of loss, use those funds to help pay for the rebuilding, and then collect the full replacement cost value on completion.

If the policy specifies that property is covered on a replacement cost basis, the insured must select a policy limit to fully insure the replacement cost property value. For buildings, the replacement cost value is usually higher than the property's depreciated ACV. Property insurance rates per $100 of insurance are usually the same whether the property is insured for replacement cost or ACV. However, replacement cost insurance is more costly because higher limits are required to insure to value because replacement cost is generally higher than ACV.

Other Valuation Methods

Although insurers usually settle losses by paying the replacement cost or ACV of lost or damaged property, many other valuation provisions are used for special classes of property, sometimes within policies that value most property on a replacement cost or ACV basis.

These are two of the more common other valuation methods:

- Agreed value method
- Functional valuation method

Agreed Value Method

Agreed value method

A method of valuing property in which the insurer and the insured agree, at the time the policy is written, on the maximum amount that will be paid in the event of a total loss.

Some property insurance policies are valued policies, not contracts of indemnity. These policies typically cover commercial watercraft, antiques, paintings, and other objects whose value can be difficult to determine. The valuation provision in such policies uses the **agreed value method**. If a total loss occurs, the insurer will pay the agreed value specified in the policy. Partial losses are paid based on actual cash value, repair cost, replacement cost, or whatever other valuation method the policy specifies. Although the agreed value method is not a specific formula as are some of the other valuation methods, it is nonetheless useful when it would otherwise be difficult to calculate a precise value. The agreed value method does not stipulate what the agreed value has to be relative to the true value of the property. The only stipulation is that both parties have to agree to the value in the policy.

The agreed value method should not be confused with the agreed value optional coverage, which is an arrangement for suspending the coinsurance clause in commercial property insurance coverages such as the Building and Personal Property Coverage Form or the Business Income Coverage Form.

Functional Valuation Method

Functional valuation method

A valuation method in which the insurer is required to pay no more than the cost to repair or replace the damaged or destroyed property with property that is its functional equivalent.

The **functional valuation method** is sometimes used when replacing buildings or personal property with property of like kind and quality is not practical and when the ACV method does not match insurance needs.

For example, suppose an organization that has been using a former schoolhouse as an office suffered a fire that destroyed the building. The functional valuation method would value the building at the cost to rebuild an office, not a schoolhouse. In the functional valuation method, the insurer is required to pay no more than the cost to repair or to replace the damaged or destroyed property with property that is its functional equivalent. This method is available by an endorsement to a commercial property policy. It is also used for residential buildings covered by the ISO Homeowners Modified Coverage Form, sometimes called Form HO-8.

When applied to personal property, the functional valuation method requires the insurer to pay no more than the cost to replace with equivalent but less expensive property. This method is commonly used with electronics and computers—for example, when new computers may be more functional but less expensive than the models that have to be replaced. The insurer might also pay the actual repair cost or the applicable policy limit, if either is less than the cost of functionally equivalent property.

When applied to real property, the functional valuation method permits the insurer to use common construction methods and materials. For example, a three-coat plaster wall might be replaced with wallboard, restoring its function but not using the same material.

VALUATION OF LIABILITY CLAIMS

A crucially important issue in post-loss analysis of liability insurance policies is the valuation of covered claims.

Unlike property insurance policies, liability insurance policies (or the liability coverage provisions within a multiline policy) usually do not specify how the amount of a covered claim is determined. Under most circumstances, the maximum amount the insurer pays is the lesser of two amounts:

- The compensable amount of the claim
- The applicable policy limit(s)

Compensable Amount of the Claim

The compensable amount of the claim depends mainly on the variables involved in how the claim is settled and the extent of **damages** ultimately awarded to the claimant.

Damages

Money claimed by, or a monetary award to, a party who has suffered bodily injury or property damage for which another party is legally responsible.

Settlement of the Claim

Most liability claims do not go to a formal trial, and the compensable amount of the claim is determined by negotiations between the liability insurer (or its attorney) and the claimant (or the claimant's attorney). During these negotiations, the parties try to anticipate what a court or jury would do if presented with the same facts. Both parties have an incentive to reach an out-of-court settlement because of the uncertainty, time, and expense involved in a formal trial.

Most liability insurance policies give the insured/defendant no right to prohibit the insurer and the claimant from reaching a settlement within policy limits. Often, an insured wants its insurer to mount a vigorous defense and vindicate the insured. However, the insurer's goal is usually to minimize its total costs for defense or damages. Sometimes the insurer pays a claim that might successfully have been defended because defending the claim would cost more than paying damages. In other cases, the insurer does not want to risk losing a lawsuit that would set a dangerous precedent for other, similar claims.

If a settlement cannot be reached by the parties involved, the liability claim will go to trial, and the extent of the insured's liability to the claimant is then based on legal principles. The compensable amount of the claim is the amount the jurors decide to award to the plaintiff as damages. Subject to policy conditions and limits, the insurer pays that amount on the insured's behalf. In some situations, the judge exercises the power to reduce or set aside an award or reduce or overturn an award on appeal. This may be done if the judge believes the jury award was excessive or not based on legal principles. Although policy limits restrict the insurer's liability, neither the jury nor the judge is bound to confine an award to policy limits. If the court awards a judgment that exceeds policy limits, the insured/defendant is responsible for paying the excess award.

For claims exceeding policy limits, the insured has a right to legal counsel, usually at the insured's expense, to protect the insured's interests. Otherwise, the liability insurer usually has control over defense costs and the amount it wants to offer as a settlement.

Extent of Damages

When the insured is liable for damages, the key issue affecting the valuation of a liability claim is the amount of monetary compensation that will reasonably indemnify the party who incurred the loss. Although a judge or jury may ultimately determine this amount, the insurer, the insured, and the claimant try to estimate this amount during any settlement negotiations.

The United States common-law system requires the amount of damages awarded to compensate the claimant for loss incurred as of the trial date. This presents a problem if not all damage has been repaired by the trial date or settlement date. In some cases, such as those involving permanent disability, damages must be partly based on an estimate of future expenses.

The claimant usually has the burden of proof regarding bodily injury and property damage. The claimant must establish what losses were proximately caused by the insured. However, even though the insured caused the loss, the claimant has a duty to mitigate loss. Consequently, the claimant may not recover for damages that result from the claimant's lack of care after the accident.

When property is damaged, the owner may recover the reasonable cost to repair the property or to replace it if it cannot economically be repaired. When property must be replaced, the owner is entitled to its reasonable market value before damage or destruction. Generally, the owner may also recover damages to compensate for the loss of use of the property for a reasonable period. For example, a claimant could recover the cost of renting a substitute car while a damaged car is being repaired.

Under certain circumstances, a claimant may also recover for profits lost from the inability to use the damaged or destroyed property. For example, the owner of a damaged truck or tractor-trailer might lose revenue while the vehicle is being repaired, especially if the owner cannot rent a substitute vehicle. Similarly, the owner of a damaged building might lose rent from tenants or sales from customers while a building is out of use. A few jurisdictions also permit third-party damages for the reduction in value of property that has been damaged and repaired.

Unlike property damage claims, evaluation of bodily injury claims considers a much broader range of damage elements for the claimant, such as these:

- Reasonable and necessary medical expenses incurred and those expected to be incurred in the future
- Type of bodily injury
- Wage loss or loss of earning capacity because of the bodily injury
- Other out-of-pocket expenses, such as household assistance
- Current and future pain and suffering resulting from the bodily injury
- Extent and permanency of disability and impairment
- Disfigurement resulting from the bodily injury
- Preexisting conditions that could have contributed to the bodily injury

When bodily injury results in a claimant's death, the claim is generally categorized as either a survival action (how much would have been recovered if the claimant had lived) or a wrongful death action (monetary loss to the survivors). The category into which the claim falls affects its valuation.

Policy Limits

The insurer's payment of the claimant's compensable damages for which the insured is liable is capped by the policy's applicable limit(s).

A liability policy (or the liability provisions within a multiline policy) may be subject to only one policy limit or to several. For example, the only limit applicable to liability coverage in many commercial auto policies is a dollar amount, such as $1 million, which is the most the insurer will pay for all damages because of bodily injury or property damage in any one auto accident. In contrast, commercial general liability (CGL) policies typically contain multiple policy limits, such as those shown in the exhibit. See the exhibit "Examples of Multiple Policy Limits in a CGL Policy."

Examples of Multiple Policy Limits in a CGL Policy

EACH OCCURRENCE LIMIT	$1,000,000	
DAMAGE TO PREMISES		
RENTED TO YOU LIMIT	$ 100,000	Any one premises
MEDICAL EXPENSE LIMIT	$ 5,000	Any one person
PERSONAL & ADVERTISING INJURY LIMIT	$1,000,000	Any one person or organization
GENERAL AGGREGATE LIMIT		$2,000,000
PRODUCTS/COMPLETED OPERATIONS AGGREGATE LIMIT		$2,000,000

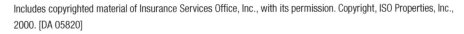

When a liability policy contains multiple limits, the maximum amount payable for a covered claim depends on a complete analysis of the interactions among the various limits. For example, a covered CGL claim for $600,000 in damages may be within the $1 million each occurrence limit, but if prior claims paid during the same policy period have reduced the applicable aggregate limit (the most the insurer will pay during the policy period) to $200,000, the insurer's payment will not exceed $200,000. If the same claim is subject to the policy's $100,000 Damage to Premises Rented to You limit, then the insurer's payment will not exceed $100,000.

In addition to covering the claimant's damages, insurers also agree to pay defense costs and various supplementary payments, such as the cost of surety bonds required in connection with claims, court costs taxed against the insured, and interest on judgments. In many common policies (such as homeowners policies, personal and commercial auto policies, businessowners policies, and CGL policies), defense costs and supplementary payments typically do not reduce the policy limits. However, once the insurer has paid out the applicable limit(s) for a claim, the insurer's duty to defend and pay supplementary payments ends.

In other policies (such as directors and officers liability policies, pollution liability policies, and other specialty liability policies), the insurer's payments for defense costs and supplementary payments are typically applied to reduce the policy limits. In such policies, defense costs can consume a significant part of the applicable limit(s).For example, if an insured with a $1 million policy limit were held liable for a $950,000 judgment and defense costs were $100,000, the insurer would pay only $900,000 of the judgment after having paid the defense costs. If instead the insured had a liability policy that covered defense costs in addition to the limit, the insurer would pay both the $100,000 in defense costs and the $950,000 judgment in full.

REASONS FOR PROPERTY INSURANCE DEDUCTIBLES

Deductibles are a risk financing technique that requires the insured to retain a portion of the loss that is being transferred to an insurer. Knowing how deductibles in property insurance can benefit insureds assists insurance and risk management professionals in selecting or recommending deductibles.

By requiring the insured to retain some part of each loss covered by property insurance, deductibles reduce the premium cost to the insured through these effects:

- Encourage risk control by the insured
- Eliminate the need for the insurer to process small losses, thereby reducing the insurer's loss costs and loss adjustment expenses

Encourage Risk Control

Having some of the insured's own funds at stake theoretically gives the insured the risk control incentive to prevent or reduce losses. A deductible serves this purpose most effectively when it is large enough to have a noticeable financial effect on the insured. Deductibles that are too small do not offer enough financial incentive, and deductibles that are too large defeat the purpose of transferring the loss exposure to the insurer.

Deductibles are not particularly effective when used with large property exposures, especially those that are not likely to incur a partial loss. For example, consider the costs involved in launching a satellite. With hundreds of millions of dollars at stake, even a $100,000 deductible on satellite launch insurance would neither encourage additional risk control nor substantially reduce the insurer's costs.

Reduce Insurer's Costs

A typical property deductible eliminates the insurer's involvement in low-value losses. It is not cost-efficient for an insurer to deal with low-value losses because the insurer's loss adjustment expenses often exceed the amount of indemnity payable to the insured.

The expensive and inefficient process of insuring small claims is sometimes called **dollar trading** (or trading dollars).

Risk transfer mechanisms in general—and insurance in particular—are not designed to cope with these types of low-severity losses. Sizable property insurance deductibles help to eliminate dollar trading. The insured retains small losses as normal, out-of-pocket expenses and uses insurance to protect against major, unpredictable losses. Deductibles are most effective in reducing insurers' expenses for coverages such as auto collision, in which small, partial losses are common.

Deductibles reduce the premiums insurers must charge and ultimately benefit the insured because they (1) reduce insurers' overall loss costs and loss adjustment expenses, (2) provide insureds with risk control incentives, and (3) reduce the morale and moral hazard incentives. For most property insurance policies, insureds can choose from a variety of deductible levels. In making this choice, the insured must balance the benefits of the premium reduction with the need for insurance protection for large losses.

For most property insurance policies, the premium reduction is not directly proportional to the size of the deductible. Because small losses are more frequent than large losses, the premium reduction is on a sliding scale—that is, the premium credit increases much more slowly than the size of the deductible, as illustrated in the exhibit. See the exhibit "Hypothetical Premium Credits for Various Deductibles."

Dollar trading

An insurance premium and loss exchange in which the insured pays the insurer premiums for low value losses, and the insurer pays the same dollars back to the insured, after subtracting expenses.

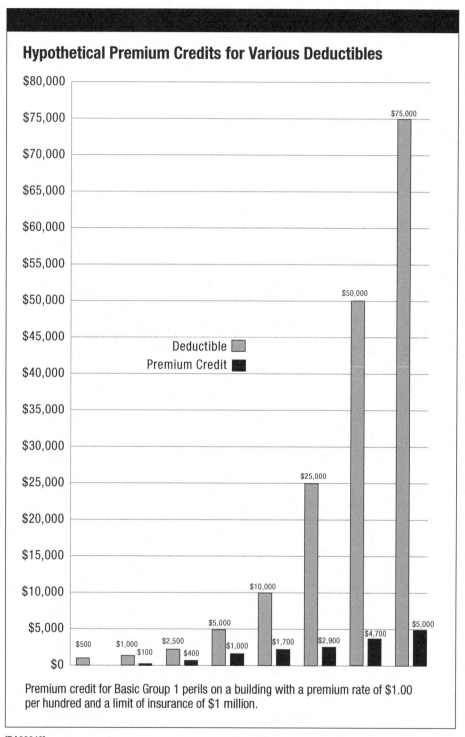

Hypothetical Premium Credits for Various Deductibles

Premium credit for Basic Group 1 perils on a building with a premium rate of $1.00 per hundred and a limit of insurance of $1 million.

[DA03248]

As shown in the exhibit, shifting from a $500 deductible to a $2,500 deductible reduces the policy premium by $400 while increasing retained loss exposures by $2,000. The premium reduction for shifting from a $50,000 deductible to a $75,000 deductible is only $300, and retained losses are increased by $25,000. Given these figures, shifting from a $500 deductible to a $2,500 deductible would be attractive in many cases.

However, shifting from a $50,000 deductible to a $75,000 deductible is not as attractive. Even if the pricing is actuarially sound and the organization could absorb the extra $25,000 loss, few organizations would choose to retain an extra $25,000 in property losses to save $300 in premium unless other factors were involved, such as the insurer offering much broader coverage when the high deductible applies.

When premium costs are considered, premium credits tend to encourage the use of medium-sized deductibles that eliminate dollar trading for small losses but that provide a reliable source of recovery for large losses. What constitutes "medium-sized" varies substantially among both families and organizations that purchase property insurance.

LIABILITY DEDUCTIBLES AND SELF-INSURED RETENTIONS

Knowing when and why a deductible or a self-insured retention (SIR) is appropriate for a particular liability policy helps insurance and risk management professionals to arrange coverage competently.

Although deductibles are commonly used with most types of property insurance policies, deductibles are seldom used for some types of liability insurance but are commonly used for other types. In some cases, a **self-insured retention (SIR)** is used instead of a deductible in liability policies.

Reasons for Limited Use

Insurers have multiple reasons for restricting the use of deductibles in liability policies.

If a liability insurance policy has a deductible, the insured may not report seemingly minor incidents until the situation has escalated. However, because insurers want to control liability claims from the outset, they want to be involved in even small liability claims. Liability claim investigation involves determining not only the nature and extent of damages, but also who is legally responsible for paying those damages.

In addition, for most liability insurance policies, deductibles would not noticeably reduce premiums. One reason for this is that relatively few liability claims involve small amounts. Although most property losses are small enough for the insurer to avoid them by using a moderate deductible, liability losses tend to be larger. More important, as mentioned, the liability insurer wants to be involved in all claims, including small ones. Even with a deductible, the liability insurer usually pays all costs without contribution from the insured,

Self-insured retention (SIR)
A dollar amount specified in an insurance policy that the insured must pay before the insurer will make any payment for a claim.

for investigation and defense coverage, just as it does for policies without deductibles. Usually the deductible applies only to the damages paid to the claimant, not to defense costs.

With property insurance, the insurer simply subtracts the deductible from the covered loss amount to determine the amount payable to the insured. However, in liability insurance, the insurer must recover the deductible from the insured. The insurer usually must pay the third-party claimant the agreed-upon settlement in full, without reduction for any deductible. The insurer then has the right to recover the amount of the deductible from the insured. Sometimes, the insured may be financially unable or unwilling to pay the deductible. So, the insurer may ultimately have to bear the deductible cost.

Consequently, insurers are selective in choosing the insureds for which they will consider a liability deductible because the deductible, while providing a premium discount to the insured, can present problems for the insurer.

Deductibles are not usually included in commercial general liability, personal liability, or auto liability policies. However, significant deductibles are common with some specialty liability policies, such as those covering professional liability or directors and officers liability. By involving the insured in each loss, these deductibles are used primarily to encourage risk control. Deductibles are also common in bailee legal liability coverages, such as those for warehouses and auto service businesses. These coverages protect the insured against loss to a specified category of property, and the deductibles function similarly to those used with property insurance.

Self-Insured Retentions

Some liability insurance policies include an SIR. The differences between a deductible and an SIR are these:

- With a liability insurance deductible, the insurer defends on a first-dollar basis, pays all covered losses, and then bills the insured for the amount of losses up to the deductible.

- With an SIR, the insurer pays only losses that exceed the SIR amount. The insurer does not defend claims below the SIR amount. Consequently, the organization is responsible for adjusting and paying its own losses up to the SIR amount.

- With an SIR, the full policy limit is payable on top of the SIR, while a liability policy deductible may reduce the policy limit. (Individual policies can vary on this point of comparison.)

To compensate for the insurer's lack of control over self-insured claims, a policy with an SIR usually requires strict reporting to the insurer of any claims that have the potential of exceeding the SIR amount.

SIRs are common in professional liability insurance policies and some other specialty policies. SIRs are also commonly found in the "drop-down" coverage of umbrella liability policies. The drop-down coverage of an umbrella policy provides primary coverage, subject to the SIR, on claims that are not covered by an underlying primary insurance policy and not excluded by the umbrella policy.

OTHER SOURCES OF RECOVERY

In many cases, an insured will have one or more other sources of recovery for a loss covered by the insured's policy. In post-loss coverage analysis, insurance and risk management professionals seek to ascertain all other sources of recovery so that the appropriate policy provisions can be applied.

Additional sources of recovery may violate the principle of indemnity because the insured could be indemnified more than once for the amount of loss. Various insurance policy provisions, such as other-insurance provisions and subrogation provisions, have been developed to manage situations in which multiple recoveries may be possible. Before applying these policy provisions, one must identify the other sources of recovery, which can include these:

*   Noninsurance agreements
*   Negligent third parties
*   Other insurance in the same policy
*   Other insurance in a similar policy
*   Other insurance in dissimilar policies

Noninsurance Agreements

Individuals and organizations often have a contractually enforceable source of recovery that does not involve insurance. Examples of noninsurance agreements that may overlap with insurance coverage of the loss include these:

*   A lease agreement might make a tenant responsible for damage to leased property that is also covered by insurance.
*   A credit card protection plan might protect the cardholder against claims for damage to a rented car, partially duplicating auto physical damage coverage in the renter's personal auto policy.
*   A credit card protection plan might protect property purchased with the card against theft or accidental damage. The same property could be covered under a homeowners policy.
*   An extended auto warranty, home warranty, appliance service agreement, or other plan can provide a contractually enforceable source of recovery that may overlap with an auto or a homeowners policy, depending on the cause of loss.

Although credit card benefits are often underwritten by an insurer, the benefit itself is provided through a contract between the credit card company and the cardholder. The cardholder is contractually entitled to the benefits promised by the credit card company, which often duplicate insurance benefits. Even if the property is also insured, a cardholder might find it desirable to claim benefits from the credit card company. Unlike property insurance, the credit card benefit generally is on a first-dollar basis with no deductible.

To respond to the overlap in coverage provided by noninsurance agreements, many homeowners policies include a provision addressing noninsurance (service) agreements. This provision indicates that the coverage provided by the homeowners policy is excess over any recovery that the insured may be able to get from a service agreement provider.

Negligent Third Parties

As a matter of law, a party who is injured or whose property is damaged by a negligent third party generally has a right to recover damages from the third party—regardless of whether the third party has liability insurance. The recovery from a third party (or the third party's liability insurance) could overlap with any first-party property insurance coverage (the insured's own property insurance policy). Most first-party insurance policies have policy provisions that address these situations. Although two types of policies might be involved (the third party's liability insurer and the insured's property insurer), the relevant policy language is captioned "subrogation" rather than "other insurance."

For example, Tara and David are both drivers in a state that does not have no-fault insurance (the example may not apply in no-fault states). Tara's car is struck and damaged by David, a negligent driver. David has liability insurance; that is, an insurer has agreed to pay liability claims on his behalf. Tara has a right under tort law to seek recovery from David, who will file a claim with his insurer. Tara also has a contractual right to recover under her own insurer's collision coverage. Tara's first-party right of recovery from her insurer does not reduce or eliminate David's obligation to pay damages to Tara. Nor can Tara's insurer deny her claim because David has liability insurance.

Regardless of whether a careless driver like David has liability insurance, his legal obligation to pay damages does not affect the contractual obligations of the insurer providing first-party property coverage—unless the insurance contract specifies otherwise. David is legally obligated, and Tara's insurer is contractually obligated, to pay for the damage to her car. However, that does not mean Tara will recover twice the amount of loss she incurred. According to the subrogation provision in Tara's personal auto policy, if she recovers from her own insurer, that insurer can attempt to recover from David or his insurer. If David's insurer pays Tara directly, she is required to reimburse her insurer.

Other Insurance in the Same Policy

A third other source of recovery is other insurance in the same policy. Property and/or liability insurance policies may provide two or more coverages under the same policy. When these package policies are used, a given loss may be covered by more than one of the coverages offered. Therefore, an insurance professional needs to analyze the policy to determine whether it contains a policy provision that limits the number of coverages that apply.

These are examples of losses for which insurance is provided by more than one coverage:

- A scheduled personal property endorsement attached to a homeowners policy provides coverage for scheduled (specifically listed) items, many of which are also covered under the unscheduled personal property coverage of the homeowners policy.

- Personal property used to maintain or service a building—such as fire extinguishing equipment, outdoor furniture, or refrigerators—is specifically covered under the building coverage of many commercial property insurance forms. The same items may also qualify for coverage as personal property under another insuring agreement of the same form.

- A passenger injured while riding in a car may have medical payments coverage for medical expenses regardless of who was at fault. The passenger may also bring a bodily injury liability claim against the driver of the car (if the driver was partly at fault for the accident) and may have a right of action against any other drivers involved. Coverage might apply under the liability, medical payments, and uninsured motorists coverages of the car owner's personal auto policy, depending on the facts of the case.

Because the insured's loss is covered, it might not seem important to know which coverage applies. However, although each of these examples may appear to involve a distinction that does not have a material effect on the claim, the distinction may be material to the amounts payable. Consequently, it is important to be aware of the applicability of more than one coverage in an insurance policy and to be able to determine which coverage applies in a given situation.

If the multiple coverages involved have different valuation provisions or deductibles, the insured may be able to recover more by filing under one coverage instead of another. The second example shows that under certain commercial property insurance policies, personal property used to maintain the building may be considered part of the building as well as personal property. For example, if the insured suffers a fire that destroys a storage shed and all the landscaping equipment that was stored in it, the insured may claim the equipment as a personal property loss or a building loss. If the building is insured on a replacement cost basis and personal property is insured on an actual cash value basis, the insured may be better off claiming the loss as a building loss.

Alternatively, the insured may have the option of combining (stacking) the limits of coverage of all the coverages that apply. That is, the insured can combine the various limits to cover losses that are larger than any one individual limit.

To illustrate, suppose Rick and Ann have two cars insured under their personal auto policy, and each vehicle has $50,000 in uninsured motorists coverage. Rick suffers a $75,000 loss resulting from bodily injury caused by an auto accident with an uninsured motorist. Based on the statutory regulations of the state in which they live, if the uninsured motorists limits are stackable, Rick and Ann have a total of $100,000 in uninsured motorists coverage that will pay for the entire $75,000 in bodily injury losses.

Other Insurance in a Similar Policy

A fourth other source of recovery is other insurance in a similar policy. In some cases, coverage overlaps because the same party is protected by two or more policies usually issued by different insurers.

For example, suppose Fred moves to a new home and buys a homeowners policy to cover it, but does not cancel the homeowners policy on his old home, which is still for sale. Both policies simultaneously cover some of Fred's loss exposures, such as personal property at other locations. Other-insurance situations like this usually involve more than one insurer as well as more than one policy. The question is therefore not simply which coverage applies to a loss, but which insurer will pay and how much. These situations are often resolved with each insurer sharing some portion of the loss, in accordance with the policies' other-insurance provisions.

Other Insurance in Dissimilar Policies

A fifth other source of recovery that affects amounts payable in liability insurance is other insurance in dissimilar policies. A loss is sometimes covered by more than one type of insurance, often from two or more insurers. Some examples of losses that may be covered by dissimilar policies include these:

- Bill owns a utility trailer. Under some circumstances, liability claims involving the trailer might be covered by both Bill's homeowners policy and his personal auto policy.

- A restaurant offers valet parking on its premises. The valet parking activity might be covered under both the restaurant's commercial general liability policy and its commercial auto policy.

- Janice is injured in an auto accident while performing work-related activities. Janice may be able to recover under her personal auto insurance, her individual or group medical expense or disability insurance, or her employer's workers compensation insurance.

Dissimilar insurance policies do not necessarily include provisions that clearly coordinate coverage with other types of policies. Because of the typical lack of provisions governing coordination of coverage for dissimilar policies, these types of overlaps in coverage are often the most difficult to resolve. In some cases, the relationship between policies when more than one policy is in place is governed by the policies' other-insurance provisions.

SUMMARY

Legal bases for insurable interest include an ownership interest, contractual obligations, exposure to legal liability, factual expectancy, and representation of another party. In some situations, multiple parties can have an insurable interest in the same property. In joint tenancy, tenancy by the entirety, and tenancy in partnership, all owners have survivorship rights. In tenancy in common, when an owner dies, that owner's share passes to his or her heirs.

Insurance to value benefits insurers because it ensures that premiums are adequate to cover potential losses and it simplifies underwriting. The insured benefits by having sufficient coverage in the event of a loss. Insurers use coinsurance clauses and other insurance-to-value provisions to encourage insureds to purchase adequate coverage limits. Determining and maintaining insurance to value may involve having a qualified appraiser value the property, revising policy limits periodically, and exploring coverage options such as the agreed value optional coverage.

Insurance policies that provide property coverage use various methods for valuing covered property. The two most common property valuation methods are actual cash value and replacement cost. Examples of other valuation methods include agreed value and functional valuation.

The valuation of liability claims is based on the amount of damages for which the insured is legally liable, not to exceed the applicable limit(s) in the policy. Liability claims can also include defense costs and other supplementary payments, which, depending on the particular policy, may be payable in addition to limits or included within limits.

Reasonable deductibles can reduce property insurance premiums by encouraging the insured to practice risk control and by reducing insurer costs.

When arranging liability coverage, an insurance or a risk management professional needs to know when and why deductibles and SIRs are appropriate and how an SIR differs from a deductible.

Five other sources of recovery that can affect amounts payable under an insurance policy are noninsurance agreements, negligent third parties, other insurance in the same policy, other insurance in a similar policy, and other insurance in dissimilar policies. After other sources of recovery have been identified, the insured's policy or policies can be reviewed to find any provisions addressing the other sources.

ASSIGNMENT NOTE

1. Copyrighted material of Insurance Services Office, Inc., with its permission. Copyright, ISO Properties, 2007.

Index

Page numbers in boldface refer to pages where the word or phrase is defined.